THE
ALL-AMERICANS
AT WAR

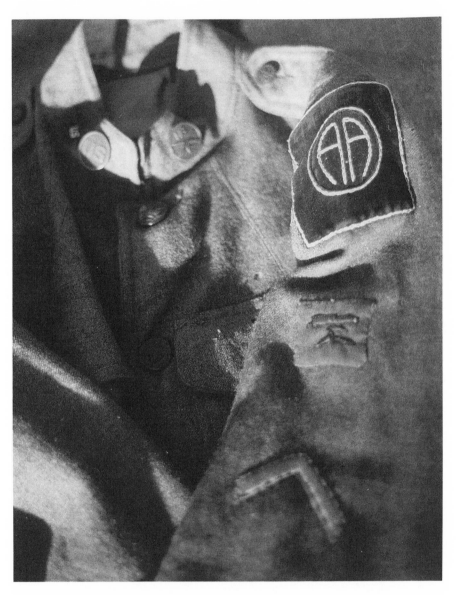

The 82nd Division Patch, 1918. Courtesy David M. McCoy. Used with permission.

THE
ALL-AMERICANS
AT WAR

The 82nd Division in the Great War, 1917–1918

JAMES J. COOKE

Westport, Connecticut
London

Library of Congress Cataloging-in-Publication Data

Cooke, James J.
  The All-Americans at War : the 82nd Division in the Great War,
  1917–1918 / James J. Cooke.
      p.   cm.
  Includes bibliographical references and index.
  ISBN 0–275–95740–3 (alk. paper)
  1. United States. Army. Airborne Division, 82nd—History.
  2. World War, 1914–1918—Campaigns—Western Front.   3. World War,
  1914–1918—Regimental histories—United States.   I. Title.
  D570.3 82nd.C66   1999
  940.4′1273—dc21   98–21782

British Library Cataloguing in Publication Data is available.

Library of Congress Catalog Card Number: 98–21782
ISBN: 0–275–95740–3

First published in 1999

Praeger Publishers, 88 Post Road West, Westport, CT 06881
An imprint of Greenwood Publishing Group, Inc.
www.praeger.com

Printed in the United States of America

The paper used in this book complies with the
Permanent Paper Standard issued by the National
Information Standards Organization (Z39.48–1984).

10 9 8 7 6 5 4 3 2 1

Contents

Introduction

When I became interested in America's role in the Great War I began with a study of the 42nd Infantry Division, a unique National Guard Division that went to France in the fall of 1917 and returned from Germany in the spring of 1919. The "Rainbow Division," as it was called, is still one of the best known of all divisions which America sent to World War One. Drawn from twenty-six states and the District of Columbia, that unit saw major action all through 1918. While a visiting professor at the Air War College at Maxwell Air Force Base, Alabama, I began research on the U.S. Air Service; I was not satisfied that the story of the U.S. air effort had been fully or adequately told. Researching the Rainbow Division, I became aware that air observation had been of primary importance to the AEF's combat units. The pursuit, or fighter, aircraft had been the focus of writers, but the observer plane and the balloon had been considered more important on the Western Front. Also, having been through the rigors of the U.S. Army Command and General Staff College and having served at the divisional level in combat, I had an interest in how General of the Armies John J. Pershing had put together his command and his staff for service in France. That was the third of my book-length studies.

Since the awakening of my interest in World War One, I have also had a desire to know more about the mass of men who were conscripted into the army and went to France to fight. My focusing on the 82nd Division was no accident. I had seen the movie Sergeant York, starring Gary Cooper, and the 82nd Division of World War Two fame was well known. I had served myself alongside men of the 82nd Airborne Division in the Persian Gulf War. At the time, I believed that the 82nd of the Great War had been a division of Southern conscripts who did their Confederate ancestors proud, just as the 167th Infantry Regiment, or old "Bloody 4th Alabama," had in the Rainbow division. I could not have been more wrong.

In fact, Major General William P. Burnham gave to the 82nd Division the nickname the "All-Americans" in August 1918 because they came from all sections of the United States; a large number, almost half, were fairly fresh from Ellis Island, New York. For them the Statue of Liberty was not just a symbol. There were Italians, Russian Jews, Irish, Anglo-Saxon farm boys, all thrown together in one division. This was the melting-pot division, a division difficult to train and command, but one that would take part in the hardset battle the American Expeditionary Forces fought in France. Many were buried as American soldiers before they became American citizens.

This division can tell us a great deal about the America of the early twentieth century, about immigrants, and about the abilities of the American army in combat. Those who look for striking new interpretations will look in vain: what one will find here is an American story. Also interesting is the chaos and confusion that beset the National Army in 1917 as America tried to put a conscript army in the field to fight. The 82nd Division, while perhaps more afflicted with difficulties than other divisions of the National Army, gives the reader insights into just how unprepared the U.S. Army was to enter the Great War. Policies set in the War Department often worked against the formation and training of fighting divisions. The consequences would be tragic on the battlefields of France.

No historian can function without good archivists and their intimate knowledge of the collections' holdings. Over the years I have come to appreciate Mitchell Yockelson of the National Archives; his command of his holdings is first-rate, and his eagerness to help the researcher is deeply gratifying. Timothy K. Nenninger, also of the National Archives, was always willing to be helpful, and his suggestions were always on the mark. These archivists are fine custodians of our nation's documents.

It would be impossible to write military history without visiting the Military History Institute's archives and manuscripts at Carlisle Barracks, Pennsylvania. Dr. Richard J. Sommers, head of the Archives Branch, David A. Keough, Chief of the Manuscript Archives, and Randy Hackenberg of the photographic branch make research a pleasure. They are first-class professionals and cannot be praised enough.

I would like to thank the editors and staff at Praeger Publishing, especially heather Ruland, history editor. The Dean of the College of Liberal Arts of the University of Mississippi gave a small, but still useful, grant. My chairperson, Dr. Robert Haws, must be thanked first for encouragement, then for advice, then for juggling teaching schedules for me. I must also thank Joanna Williams of the History Department for working with me on manuscripts. Professor T. J. Ray always went beyond friendship to help me with my maps of the Western Front; his contribution was great. Dr. David M. McCoy of Brentwood, Tennessee, must be thanked for his great efforts in securing photographs of the 82nd Division; his efforts are appreciated greatly. Last, but never least, I thank my wife, Josephine, the "Editorial Queen," who struggled with my commas and the like and who was ready to say that this or that sentence made no sense.

Prologue: Tokyo Bay, 1945

The day promised to be sunny and warm, almost too nice for the serious business about to be conducted. Ships of the U.S. Navy were anchored in the choppy waters of Tokyo Bay, clustered around the gigantic bulk of the battleship *Missouri*. Sailors scrubbed the decks until they were bright, while officers and petty officers arranged tables and chairs and tested loudspeaker systems. There were masses of movie cameras and hookups for radio. The General, Douglas A. MacArthur, wanted every word heard, every sight recorded. It was the day the war with Japan would end in victory for the United States and the Allies. The table upon which the surrender document was to be signed was simple. Anything more elaborate would have been lost in the great importance of the day. Here was MacArthur, finally arriving, followed by an American and a British general—gaunt and drawn, their faces unreadable masks.

Five Japanese military officers and three diplomats boarded the USS *Missouri* and began the process of surrendering Japan unconditionally to the Allies. Standing beside MacArthur was General Jonathon Mayhew Wainwright, symbol of America's early defeats at the hands of the Japanese. Held as a prisoner of war since 6 May 1942, subjected to humiliations, he had watched the brave survivors of the battle for Corregidor begin the infamous Bataan Death March.

"Jim" Wainwright looked much older than his sixty-two years, but he remained ramrod straight as the representatives of a defeated Japan signed the instrument of surrender. Only a few days before, Wainwright had been released by the Allies from a Japanese prison camp in Manchuria and had been whisked to Tokyo Bay to be present when Japan was humbled before Allied might. How many *banzais* had Jim Wainwright heard in three years? Today there were no victorious shouts from the Japanese, or from the Allies. There were only the calm, stentorian words of Douglas A. MacArthur, the officer Wainwright had succeeded in command in the Philippines.

Wainwright was a professional soldier, graduating from West Point in 1906.

Known as a steady officer with a good grasp of operations and tactics, he was sent to France in 1918. The Great War was kinder to Wainwright than would be the second great global conflict. Did Jim Wainwright in 1945 think back to that first war, to his successes as the G3, or operations officer, of the 82nd Division? This surrender was so very different from the heady days of the armistice of 11 November 1918, when he had been a major assured of a good place in the postwar army. He had been noticed by John J. Pershing, and certainly there were general's stars in Wainwright's future. There had been different emotions in 1918, very different from those he experienced on that second day of September 1945. The battleship *Missouri* was a long way from the hills and the thickets of the Argonne Forest, and Wainwright had come a long way from the staff of the All-Americans of the 82nd Division.

Chapter 1

Do You Speak English?

On 6 April 1917, the Congress of the United States, after several days of rancorous debate, declared war on the German empire. During the presidential campaign of 1916 Woodrow Wilson had campaigned on the slogan "He kept us out of war." The most popular song then was "I Didn't Raise My Boy to Be a Soldier," but that had been a year ago. After provocations by Germany, President Wilson asked the Congress to do its constitutional duty, which the majority did. An unprepared United States was now going "Over There" to fight in this war to make the world safe for democracy, and it was going to do it from a base of almost complete ignorance. The armed might of the United States was small, about a half-million men divided between the regular Army and the state National Guards. The regulars were scattered over army posts in the west, in the possessions, and elsewhere. The National Guard, disliked by the regulars, had a spotty record as far as leadership and training was concerned. However, there was a mechanism for raising a so-called National Army for emergencies, and that was what the new belligerent would have to do if it was going to fight on the Western Front.

On 18 May 1917 the Selective Service Law was passed, and young men began to register for the draft. It had been no easy matter to get from a declaration of war to a draft law. Wilson's secretary of war, Newton B. Baker of Cincinnati, Ohio, had replaced a more activist secretary; Baker himself had been known as a pacifist and an opponent of conscription. At some date after 6 April 1917, Baker had his own road-to-Damascus revelation and became a first-rate secretary in time of war. Even with Baker's conversion to the draft, however, the noise level in Congress became deafening. The memories of the severe inequities of, and the bloody resistance to, the Civil War draft were vivid. There were questions over the drafting of the foreign-born, blacks, industrial workers, and so on. Nevertheless, despite serious opposition the law went into effect, and men registered for the drawings by local boards, which had quotas fixed by population.[1] In the first registration, in June 1917, over 9.5 million registered.[2]

The conscripted men would go into the National Army, which would be until August 1918 separate and distinct from the regular Army and the National Guard. They would fill divisions for service in France, but in the summer of 1917 there were no camps for training, no weapons, no uniforms, no shoes, no knapsacks, little of anything for that willing mass of manpower.

On the other hand, the regular Army officers welcomed the National Army, because they would command it. Soldiers who had been colonels one day would find themselves brigadier and major generals the next. Though such promotions were temporary, for the duration of the crisis, an intelligent officer could reason that success as a division commander would certainly mean permanent promotion later on. The pace of National Army promotions was dizzying, and officers eagerly sought out those commands. It did not go unnoticed that the National Army was perhaps an alternative to the National Guard, whose divisions were also in training to go to France. These new National Army units would not be militia, with political ties to the states; they would be under the wing of the regulars. Even their collar disks would carry a special designation—USNA, the United States National Army.

For every colonel or general there had to be a mass of lieutenants and captains to command platoons and companies. Young men with any promise went off to the officer training schools, usually associated with a division. The idea was a sound one: train an officer for ninety days and return him to his division to assume command; these officers would then train the men they would lead into combat on the Western Front. Officer schools turned out thousands of "ninety-day wonders," but that meant that the National Army units would have a three-month period before they saw their officers. In the long run this meant that units like the 82nd Division spent a lot of time just waiting for officers. General Pershing, the Commanding General of the American Expeditionary Forces in France, wanted troops. The British and the French wanted to see long lines of doughboys marching to the front. It seemed at times, however, that the AEF would never arrive in France. By Christmas 1917 Pershing had only the 1st, 2nd, 26th, and 42nd divisions in France. The first two were regular Army, and the second two were National Guard. Where was the much-heralded National Army?

No one was quite sure how America would take to the idea of being in a war in Europe. From all appearances, the nation was experiencing an outburst of patriotism and outright enthusiasm for the martial experience. However, Wilson and Baker were practical politicians and were very much aware that a voting public could be fickle. Newton Baker had good advice from generals Hugh Scott and Tasker Bliss, but certain decisions had to be made with the voting booth in mind. These decisions would greatly impact on the 82nd Division and all other National Army divisions.

Baker and General Scott discussed how troops would be sent to the AEF. In modern armies, soldiers go into the service, undergo basic training, learn a skill, and then are sent to units needing those skills. Early in the Great War the decision was made to form entire divisions and train them together. Those divisions would then go to France. There were no training camps for replacements who would be sent to divisions. The decision was based on political concerns. Baker later explained, "If we had set up camps containing say one hundred thousand men for the training of replacement troops as such, the country at the outset would have been shocked to discover how large we thought the losses were likely to be."[3]

The result of this decision was severe for the National Army units. As divisions were formed to be shipped overseas, shortages in manpower were filled from other divisions in training. Units like the 82nd Division were constantly supplying soldiers for other divisions, a situation that was especially galling to Major General William P. Burnham, the division's commander. Major General Henry T. Allen, commanding the 90th Division of the National Army, wrote to a friend, "Under the existing policy we find our divisions still being depleted. . . . It is simply heart-breaking to continually take away trained men from company, battalion, regiment-al, and brigade commander."[4] By early 1918, Burnham, like Allen, had had enough and complained continually to the War Department about a policy that constantly kept the 82nd Division in a very uneven state of training.

To build unit cohesion and esprit de corps, drafted men were sent to divisional training camps by region. This was a wise decision, but as time went on the units of the National Army lost their local identification. The 82nd Division was des-ignated as a Southern National Army division, with its enlisted manpower coming from the drafts in Tennessee, Georgia, and Alabama. Construction began on Camp Gordon near Atlanta, Georgia, to house the incoming draftees;[5] on 25 August 1917 the division was formed, with a cadre of noncommissioned officer-trainers from the regular Army's 6th and 17th infantry regiments. There were 783 experienced sergeants to begin the task of turning conscripts into combat infantrymen. A number of educated, motivated soldiers were selected for the ninety-day commis-sioning course that had been set up at Fort McPherson, also near Atlanta.[6]

To command the 82nd Division the War Department first selected Eben Swift, a solid regular, a soldier respected by everyone, including John J. Pershing. Swift had been born at Fort Chadborne, Texas, in 1854; during the Civil War his family had migrated north. As a youth he had attended Racine College in Wisconsin and Dickensen College at Carlisle, Pennsylvania. In 1872 he had entered West Point, graduating with the class of 1876; he had been assigned to the cavalry, seeing action on the frontier. Like most regulars, he fought in the Spanish-American War. In 1916, after forty years of service, Swift was promoted to the rank of brigadier general.

Though an officer with marked eccentricities, Swift was a natural selection for divisional command in 1917, and in the late summer he was sent to Camp Gordon to organize the troops being assembled there. Swift, now a newly minted major general, brought with him Lieutenant Colonel Preston Brown, a respected, experi-enced regular, as chief of staff.[7] There was a problem, however, with General Swift: he was sixty-three years old, considerably older than most of newly commissioned major generals commanding National Army divisions.

Eben Swift had a chief of staff, but no staff. He had a camp, but no soldiers, and he had a few empty warehouses next to an untested railhead. There were a few hundred regular Army NCO's, who had little to do but stand around because there was no one to train. In short, the 82nd Division existed in name only. On 5 September 1917, however, the first group of Southern draftees began to arrive at Camp Gordon, and by the end of September the division numbered 830 officers and 12,650 enlisted men.[8] This was far short of the twenty-eight thousand soldiers required for a World War One infantry division, but the arrival of any more would have been a disaster, because Camp Gordon was not complete. Buildings to house officers, enlisted men, and NCO's, as well as mess halls, supply rooms, latrines, and the like were not finished. Many of the men had no uniforms, and there were no weapons available for training. All Swift could do was to march the troops and drill them.[9]

One of the first tasks required for turning civilians into soldiers is to toughen them by physical activity. While America of 1917 lacked the labor-saving machines so common in the last decade of the twentieth century, those who arrived at the various camps were in no condition to march many miles with heavy shoes, huge knapsacks, and weapons. Also, a raw recruit must be turned into a functioning member of a military organization by drilling as part of a platoon or company. This begins the remaking process that all armies go through. It was not lost on Swift and his Regular Army cadre that all of this could be done without the weapons that were unavailable anyway. As Swift told the War Department at the end of September, "Marches have been held every week, average distance being about nine miles. The men who fell out on marches have been examined by surgeons with a view to eliminating the unfit."[10]

Early in September the division's 319th Field Artillery Regiment was organized, although it had no artillery pieces with which to train. There were over a hundred officers, most of them fresh from officers' school at Fort McPherson, Georgia, and one private, "he being the one on exhibition at headquarters." The officers drilled each other and waited for the trains to bring in comrades for the lonely and often-inspected private. Once the regiment was filled with earnest cannon firers, General Swift announced he would review the unit. Swift, accompanied by his ugly mongrel terrier, led the so-called "review" for miles on horseback. One soldier remembered, "We maintained the feeling of having been honored for the first five miles. After that we began to fear. . . that the General had become lost. . . . Towards the end of the march he would fall out of the column and 'review' us—to see how many of the column had fainted or died away."[11]

The officers of the 319th soon discovered something about a National Army division. The draft laws prohibited men from volunteering for a particular division. Volunteering could be done for the regular Army and the National Guard, and many educated men elected to rush to their local National Guard armories to enlist so as to serve with their friends and relatives.[12] In the 82nd Division, the first cohort of conscripts was from the rural South, and this was a shock for the newly commissioned officers. "A more motley crew never whittled a pine stick or spit tobacco juice on the doorstep. To them, every person who wore leather legging was a sergeant, the captain was invariably called boss, reverence for rank and authority was a thing unknown and illiteracy was appalling. . . . But they could sing, and they worked as hard as any of the officers, trying to learn what was expected of them."[13]

By the end of October the division had 16,023 soldiers, but it had lost 267 officers.[14] While organization and individual training was taking place a number of officers were transferred to other divisions or to central training centers, such as the artillery school at Fort Sill, Oklahoma. This, of course, caused serious disruption for the division at a time when the conscripts were adapting to their officers and NCO's. To complicate matters, the 82nd had just received a number of expert British and French trainers, but they had no weapons or equipment with which to train.

In November the 82nd Division underwent a major transformation. Almost every draftee left the division to fill up the 30th and 31st divisions, which were Southern National Guard units scheduled to leave for France. Many young officers, who had trained their men and were seeing results, were also transferred to the two divisions. It all seemed to have been a waste of time. Company commanders now had no one to command, and some companies had disappeared entirely. An officer in the 319th Field Artillery Regiment lamented, "The regiment was reduced to about six men per battery, these being the non-commissioned officers and the cooks."[15] To compound the problem, on 24 November Major General Eben Swift was called to the War Department, and Lieutenant Colonel Preston Brown received orders to join the AEF in France. Brigadier General James B. Erwin, an officer unknown to the 82nd, took command of the division. To replace Preston Brown, Major—soon to be Lieutenant Colonel—Royden E. Beebe was sent to Camp Gordon.[16] There were rumors, which proved to be true, that Erwin was scheduled to take a regular Army division to France and that his tenure with the 82nd Division would be short.

The month of November was a depressing time for the skeleton crew that remained at Camp Gordon. At least the men who were in the Officer Training School were left alone by the War Department; soon there would be a number of fresh second lieutenants in the division. By the end of the month another group of Southern draftees would arrive at Camp Gordon, but they would be as green as grass, just as the first group had been.

Then word reached the division that the War Department had tasked several camps in the north to send men to fill out the division. The regulars shook their heads; this would be a golden opportunity for camp commanders to rid themselves of misfits, undesirables, and troublemakers, who would all pour into Camp Gordon. By the end of the month 4,428 men had arrived from Camp Upton, New York; 4,970 from Camp Dix, New Jersey; and 4,484 from Camp Devens, Massachusetts. More were on the way from other camps in the Midwest, and from Camp Lee, Virginia, and Camp Meade, Maryland.[17] When the officers and NCO's formed their companies, their worst fears were realized. A large number of these troops could not speak English, and many were not yet citizens of the United States. To add to the misery, the recent immigrants, with limited language skills, had not yet received even the rudiments of a soldier's skills. Congress had amended the draft laws in the late summer of 1917; non-enemy aliens had become subject for the draft, and over a half-million had registered.[18] It seemed that every one of them had descended on Camp Gordon. Nonetheless, by the end of November the 82nd Division was back up to 26,920 officers and men.

Not only were the infantry and artillery units in a state of confusion, the divisional staff was incomplete. Neither General Swift nor Erwin had a staff prepared to train the 82nd Division for eventual combat. When Swift organized his staff in early September he had no one to serve as operations, intelligence, or training officers. It was unclear in 1917 even what a divisional staff should look like. Pershing and the AEF in early 1918 would define the G system, comprising G1 (personnel), G2 (intelligence), G3 (operations), G4 (logistics), and G5 (training).

However, in the fall of 1917 the need for a G2, G3, and G5 section was obvious, even though the officers who held those positions would not have been designated as a G staff. Where the divisional staff had strength was in the logistical area, but that could have been expected in that logistics played a vital role at Camp Gordon. The fact remained that at no level were there officers to conduct training for the division or for members of the staff who would prepare and write orders in actual combat. There were no brigade or regimental staffs in place; eventually someone would have to be trained to receive, rewrite, and distribute combat orders to subordinate commands.[19] The 82nd had a divisional command that was not progressing well. Although few of the National Army units were faring any better, given the system which was in place in 1917, the 82nd seemed to have more than its share of internal problems.

Typical of the continual confusion was the assignment of Brigadier General Charles T. Menoher to command the 157th Field Artillery Brigade of the division. His orders were dated 2 September 1917, but when that day came there was no Menoher. The brigade commander-designate had been in France for several months, where Pershing was busy trying to find a suitable division command for him. Colonel Earl D'A. Pearce, commanding the 319th Field Artillery Regiment, was made acting brigade commander. The 157th did not get a permanent commander until Brigadier General Charles D. Rhodes was assigned in February 1918. In the interim, the regiment was without the services of the officer designated to lead them into combat.[20]

There were more problems on the horizon for the 82nd, and for other National Army divisions as well. The War Department was learning from Pershing and his fledgling AEF what was required for modern combat. This was not the warfare of 1861 or 1898. The Great War battlefield was three-dimensional, with the air playing a vital role. The telephone gave commanders instant communications with subordinates (if all worked well), and the day of the gallant, mounted general in the thick of the fight was over. There was gas, and there were mines, electronic intercept devices, motorcars, tanks, etc. War had always been bravery, musketry, cannonade, fog, and friction, but now it was also technological, and the way the War Department planned to raise troops for the AEF would cause the National Army divisions to suffer.

In mid-September the War Department required all divisions to take an occupational census of their troops. This census had the objective of identifying men with critical skills in telephonics, auto mechanics, and the like. While not stating the ultimate disposition of such men, Washington clearly intended to separate them from their divisions for service elsewhere. The War Department appointed a "Committee on Classification of Personnel in the Army," and the National Army division commanders were required to appoint a captain from the reserves with a background in business personnel to compile the census.[21]

A week later the War Department sent out a follow-up memorandum stating directly that men with critical skills would be taken from their divisions and that the divisions would have to adjust their training schedules accordingly. The next day an additional memorandum specified areas where skilled soldiers were needed: engineers, ordnance, signal corps, aviation, and field artillery.[22] The lack of a technologically competent army was becoming apparent, quickly. In the rush to get troops to France able to do all the tasks required of a modern force in combat, the War Department had selected perhaps the only course open to it.

As far as the 82nd Division was concerned, in September 1917 the levy of skilled soldiers was not a real problem, given the low skill and educational level of its Southern recruits. A massive turnover in November would bring an influx of soldiers from the industrialized areas of the United States, however, and the skill question would become important. The War Department then became more insistent that the National Army divisions comply with its directives: "[The divisions] must yield to the interests of the army as a whole."[23] The army was now robbing Peter to pay Paul, and it was paying a price for years of neglect.

Another aggravation for the division was the constant demands by the War Department for extra tasks and details away from Camp Gordon. A firmly established modern division takes in stride a certain amount of temporary duty away from the unit; the 82nd was not established, and in late October it was receiving the first arrivals from the various camps. On 4 October the War Department ordered the 82nd Division to provide a detail of officers and NCO's to take 1,300 soldiers of the 1st Provisional Regiment (Colored), attached to the division, from Camp Gordon to Newport News, Virginia, where it would perform labor duties on the docks.[24] No one was sure what to do with a black provisional regiment, because the conscripting of black soldiers had begun only in late September.[25] Given the War Department's less-than-friendly view of black troops, it was not surprising that it directed the 82nd to provide white officers and NCO's to oversee the movement to Virginia. One colonel, six captains, two first lieutenants, and seventeen second lieutenants received orders to escort the regiment to Newport News.[26] The colonel was Amos H. Martin, commanding Camp Gordon's 157th Depot Brigade, a unit which provided critical services to the 82nd Division, and which would be without a commander for several weeks. This type of detail was fairly typical of the many disruptions that beset the National Army divisions and that especially troubled the 82nd, given its recent history of manpower turnover.

Despite what appeared to be a conspiracy against training in the 82nd Division, the month of November saw an influx of new troops. General Erwin and his cadre began the process of turning civilians into combat soldiers, and Erwin actually made more progress than Swift had. On 7 November a divisional grenade school was opened. Each unit was required to conduct a road march with packs, lasting no less than one and three-quarters hours, five days a week.[27] The 307th Field Signal Battalion, which had been stripped of all enlisted men in early October, was reconstituted in November and began training on radio and telephone operations under Major John E. Hemphill.[28] The 307th Engineer Regiment had also lost almost every soldier on 15 October, but the new troops had filled the regiment by the first week of November. They were, however, so ignorant of basic military skills that the engineers had to train as infantry for several weeks; schools were then begun in the construction of trenches, revetments, and roads. Due to the low state of training of the troops, mornings were devoted to infantry subjects and the afternoons were set aside for engineer work. Colonel Julien L. Schley of the regular Army engineers felt that the regiment, which would be critical for the division in combat, was finally making some progress.[29]

If the infantry, signaleers, and engineers could finally see progress, there were other components of the division that were still in the slough of despond. Nowhere was this more evident than in the 157th Field Artillery Brigade, where no training was taking place, due to a lack of guns. To make matters worse there was no clear doctrinal material to study, and officers and noncommissioned officers were unsure of their basic combat duties. In a division composed of two infantry brigades of two regiments each and an artillery brigade of three regiments, this inability to train nearly one-third of its combat power was troubling.[30]

The trench mortars were receiving no training at all, due to the fact that there were no up-to-date mortars available for the 82nd Division. The division was promised two Stokes mortars for training sometime in January 1918. Sniping, a skill in combat constantly stressed by British and French advisors, was simply not taught, because there were no modern sniping rifles available for the division. Bayonet training moved slowly, due to a lack of equipment, but at least small groups were being trained. Gas training also languished because of equipment shortfalls, and by December divisional inspectors conceded that this vital training would take much longer than anyone had thought.[31]

Equally frustrated by the slow pace of progress were the French and British advisors and trainers assigned to the division. On 3 October 1917 the War Department informed each National Army division commander that ten French and ten British soldiers were to be assigned to work in the areas of artillery, automatic rifles, hand grenades, liaison, engineers, machine guns, mortars, bayonet drill, anti-gas and flame defense, and sniping. These men were to be housed with the division, and the War department directed that their expertise be used.[32] After a number of questions from division commanders, the War Department clarified the role of the allied instructors: stating "These officers are to be under your direct authority and control for the purposes specified, and it is requested that you accord to them every courtesy." But the War Department added that to ensure uniformity of training and progress, a senior French officer would be in charge of inspecting the American units. As with all inspectors and inspections, the divisions were assured that these senior officers were there to help.[33]

About the time the 82nd Division experienced such a massive turnover in manpower, Major Jean M. Dereviers of the French Army, with a captain, two lieutenants, and four sergeants, arrived at Camp Gordon. They were followed by a British team under the command of Major E. E. Godfrey. Godfrey's group consisted of another major, three captains, a sergeant-major, four sergeants, and three privates. The officers were housed in what became known as the Foreign Officers Quarters, and the enlisted men were housed with the headquarters detachment of the camp.[34] They had little to do, as many of the new recruits could not yet do a proper right-face or left-face. Every allied soldier sent to the United States was a combat veteran of the trenches of the Western Front and elsewhere, and they had much to offer the doughboys of the division, when the time was right to offer it.

November brought some progress. A typical training schedule for the 163rd Infantry Brigade showed that thirty minutes a day was devoted to physical conditioning, another thirty minutes to group singing, then the rest of the day was given over to the manual of arms, in the school of the squad and the company. The training day began at 7 A.M. and ended with a march, concluding about 5 P.M. At night, company officers and noncommissioned officers rehearsed their training for the next day, while the troops did various details and cleaned their weapons and equipment. Every day had at least a half-hour of instruction in target practice and preparation for firing at the range which had been set up at Norcross, Georgia.[35]

For the trains (logistical services), military police, and other non-infantry units the schedules were virtually identical, concentrating on the rudiments of soldiering. From physical exercise to group singing on the march, there were no differences.[36] This reflects the state of the division going into the winter months of 1917–1918. Actual skill-specific training in supply operations for the trains, and in military police techniques, did not begin until well into the new year.

There were some slight alterations in the schedule for units with horses, mainly the artillery units. Their training contained a tremendous amount of simulated training, usually conducted with the help of the French advisors, but without actual guns they could do little but pretend. When the weather dictated that the troops be indoors there were classes on such equine subjects as care and handling of horses, common diseases of horses, and "castrametation." Time and care was also taken to teach map-reading skills for those who would direct the guns in combat.[37]

Very noticeable progress was being made in morale and discipline. Despite the conscript of the 82nd, the severe language problems, and the constant manpower turnover, it appeared that there was little resistance to being in the army. There were lapses, of course. Private George Loukides, who had been born in Greece and migrated to the United States in 1914, could speak no English and did not understand that there was a difference in the dates for Christmas celebration between the Orthodox and Western calendars. He simply went absent without leave (AWOL), found a good supply of wine, and got drunk. For that he got ten days in the guardhouse without pay. Loukides went on to fight, and immediately after the war he received his American citizenship.[38] Court-martial records reflect little major crime in the division.

There still remained the language problem, which hindered training and unit cohesion. The division instituted English-language courses by establishing a Committee of Education.[39] If certain basic words and terms were not comprehended by all, the results in combat could be deadly indeed. Certainly it was hoped that military service and the learning of a common language would go far to "Americanize" the immigrants, and the army finally did address this problem, which impacted on the total force.[40] There were indications that at least in the 82nd Division, the acclimation of the foreign-born was going along with few major problems.

Before Christmas, rumors began to circulate that General Erwin would be leaving the division for a new assignment. The rumors were confirmed: Erwin would leave the 82nd and help form and take command of the regular Army 6th Division. While Erwin never inspired great enthusiasm among the troops, he was a competent officer who had come to the division at a time of great confusion. Under his guidance training had begun, albeit slowly, and unit morale and esprit de corps was high. His replacement was Brigadier General William P. Burnham, a non-West Pointer.

On 26 December Burnham officially took command. Like Erwin, Burnham was very competent and not particularly flamboyant. He was the same age as John J. Pershing, having been born in Pennsylvania in January 1860. In 1877 he had entered West Point, but he had failed to finish the required four years. In 1881 Burnham joined Company E, 4th U.S. Infantry, and by 1883 he had risen to the rank of sergeant. Offered a commission in 1883, he had accepted and served until the outbreak of the war with Spain in 1898. During the war Burnham saw service with the 4th Missouri Infantry Regiment, and after it he was promoted to the rank of captain. In 1906 he was elevated to major and served from 1907 to 1911 on the General Staff in Washington. At the end of this tour he was given the silver oak leaves of a lieutenant colonel, and by 1914 Colonel Burnham was Director, Army School of the Line, at Fort Leavenworth, Kansas. A 1914 graduate of the Army War College, Burnham had risen steadily up the commissioned ladder. He was a solid infantry officer who could be counted on to train the 82nd Division for combat on the Western Front.

There were still severe training problems in the 82nd Division that could be traced to a lack of equipment. There were only six French-made Chauchot automatic rifles in the entire division, and they belonged to the French instructors. Grenades were in such short supply that one infantry regiment had witnessed the firing of only four rifle grenades. Not one soldier in that four-thousand-man regiment fired or threw one grenade, a critical weapon on the Western Front.[41]

Burnham would learn quickly that one of the worst problems for the 82nd Division was manpower turbulence. Soldiers were constantly being pulled from the division for duty with other units. In one week after Burnham's assumption of command, for example, the 307th Engineers lost 1,042 men, and a few days later it received 2,470 replacements. This did not mean that the divisional engineer regiment had a major increase in strength; the shifting over two thousand new soldiers would have to begin training to replace those who had been in training for several months.[42] It is little wonder that General Pershing constantly complained about the uneven training of the arriving combat divisions.

On the other hand, the division was building a base of discipline, morale, and esprit de corps. Officers and NCO's were learning roles they would have in combat. The 82nd Division was a unit made up of immigrants, many of whom could hardly speak English, some not at all. An influx of new Southern conscripts from Alabama, Georgia, and Tennessee would add another ingredient to the distinctly multicultural stew that was the division.

General Burnham and the division looked forward to the new year of 1918. There were good prospects that the 82nd Division would be departing to join Pershing and the AEF in the spring. The unit had in fact come a long way from the hot summer days when Eben Swift and his ugly dog led unending marches across the Georgia countryside. No one doubted that the 82nd still had a long way to go to become a good combat unit, but the raw material was there. It remained now to prepare for that day when their marching orders would send them "Over There."

NOTES

1. David M. Kennedy, *Over Here: The First World War and American Society* (New York: Oxford University Press, 1980), See Chapter 3 for a full discussion.

2. *Second Report of the Provost Marshall General to the Secretary of War on the Operations of the Selective Service System to December 20, 1918* (Washington, DC: Government Printing Office, 1919), 22.

3. Baker to Peyton Conway March, Cleveland, 3 October 1932, in the Peyton C. March Papers, Library of Congress, Washington, DC. [The Library of Congress hereafter cited as LOC with specific collections named.]

4. Allen to Colonel Daniel W. Ketchum, Camp Travis, TX, 10 March 1918, LOC, Henry T. Allen Papers.

5. American Battle Monuments Commission, *82nd Division: Summary of Operations in the World War* (Washington, DC: Government Printing Office, 1944), 1.

6. *Official History of the 82nd Division, American Expeditionary Forces* (Indianapolis, Bobbs-Merrill, 1919), 1–2.

7. War Department, Historical Branch, Personnel Notes, 31 January 1919, in Records Group 120, Records of the AEF, 82nd Division, National Archives, Washington, DC, carton 14 [Hereafter cited as RG 120 with appropriate carton].

8. War Department, Historical Branch, Numerical Strength, 82nd Division, from Monthly Returns, 31 January 1919, RG 120, carton 1.

9. HQ, 82nd Division, Report to War Department, 30 September 1917, ibid.

10. Ibid.

11. Typed copy, "Regimental History of the 319th Field Artillery," 21 December 1918, RG 120, carton 25.

12. See my *The Rainbow Division in the Great War, 1917–1919* (Westport, CT: Praeger, 1994).

13. "Regimental History of the 319th Field Artillery."

14. Numerical Strength, 82nd Division, from Monthly Returns, 31 January 1919, RG 120, carton 1.

15. "Regimental History of the 319th Field Artillery Regiment"; and *Official History of the 82nd Division*, 1–2.

16. Personnel Notes, RG 120, carton 14.

17. HQ, 82nd Division, Report to War Department, ibid.

18. *Second Report of the Provost Marshall General*, 89.

19. HQ, 82nd Division, General Orders No. 2, 2 September 1917, RG 120, carton 69; and HQ, 82nd Division, Memorandum, 14 December 1917, ibid.

20. Typed copy, "History of the Brigade Headquarters, 157th Field Artillery Brigade," c. March 1919, ibid., carton 22.

21. War Department to Corps, Bureaus, and Divisions, 15 September 1917, ibid., carton 85.

22. War Department to Division Commander, National Army, Atlanta, Georgia, 18 September and 22 September 1917, ibid.

23. War Department to Division Commander, Camp Gordon, 24 October 1917, ibid.

24. War Department, Adjutant General's Office to 82nd Division, 4 October 1917, ibid., carton 91.

25. Kennedy, *Over Here*, 158–63.

26. HQ, 1st Provisional Regiment (Colored), Memorandum for Adjutant, 82nd Division, 22 October 1917, RG 120, carton 91.

27. HQ, 82nd Division, Report to War Department, November 1917, ibid., carton 1.

28. Report from Major J. E. Hemphill to Adjutant General's Office, 15 January 1918, ibid.

29. HQ, 307th Engineer Regiment, "Chronological History—307th Engineer Regiment," 28 February 1919, ibid., carton 28.

30. Typed copy, "History of the Brigade Headquarters, 157th Field Artillery Brigade," c. March, 1919, ibid., carton 22.

31. 82nd Division, Progress Report for December 1917, 30 December 1917, ibid., carton 11.

32. War Department to National Army Divisional Commanders, 3 October 1917, ibid., carton 86.

33. War Department to National Army Divisional Commanders, 16 October 1917, ibid.

34. 82nd Division, Statistical Section, Report to War Department, 8 March 1918, ibid.

35. HQ, 82nd Division, Training Memorandum No. 6, 31 October 1917, ibid., carton 89.

36. HQ, Trains and Military Police, Training Memorandum No. 12, 4 November 1917, ibid.

37. HQ, 157th Artillery Brigade, Schedule, 31 October 1917, ibid.

38. Questionnaire, George Loukides, Company H, 326th Infantry, in the U.S. Army Military History Institute's World War One Survey, Carlisle Barracks, Pennsylvania.

39. *Official History of the 82nd Division*, 2–3.

40. Kennedy, *Over Here*, 158.

41. *Official History of the 82nd Division*, 4.

42. Inspector's Report for the 307th Engineer Regiment, 17 March 1918, RG 120, carton 85.

Chapter 2

One U.S. Government Moth Killer

Brigadier General William P. Burnham had been in command of the 82nd Division for three weeks, and he had had enough. Training was going slowly because of a serious lack of equipment, but the main problem was the continual loss of manpower. What had infuriated Burnham was a letter from the Adjutant General's office in Washington warning that there would be another round of removals from the division based on civilian skills. In a blistering letter to Washington Burnham said, "It is far too easy for the special services to pick men of the civilian skill desired by them. It is extremely difficult for the personnel officers to pick the men that are needed as sergeants of infantry and to be leaders of the men that are to hold the front line and send it across no-man's land." Then Burnham saw no reason continually to give up trained soldiers for organizations which would spend their time in France well behind the front lines. Which was more important to the war effort, argued the general: to be behind the lines or in contact with the enemy in battle?[1]

It appeared that the 82nd Division was capable of taking six steps forward but that it would then be forced to take six steps back. Burnham was very pleased with the numbers in the Officers Training School at Camp Gordon; he informed the Adjutant General that there were 609 candidates in training—565 from the National Army and 44 from civilian life. The lion's share of these "ninety-day wonders" would go to the 82nd Division. The course had opened on 5 January and would end on 5 April 1918; those who graduated would be appointed temporary second lieutenants in the National Army.[2] It was a major source of commissioned officers for National Army divisions, and Burnham had every reason to be pleased with the prospect of so many new officers to become leaders in the 82nd. But the problems of transferring trained enlisted men because of civilian skills remained and would surface again.

It was also clear that at some point the National Army divisions would be sent into France. General Pershing continually urged Washington to get troops to France by division. Pershing had two major problems. First by the new year he had only four complete divisions in France, and they were in intensive training. Second his orders from Secretary Baker were to form an American army, fighting under American commanders, in an American sector of the Western Front. The general constantly had to joust with his allies over manpower; the British and French wanted American soldiers, individuals, companies, and battalions to be rmalgam-ated into the depleted and tired allied ranks. The more complete divisions Pershing had, or so he reasoned, the less would be the demands that American combat power be sent to British or French divisions.[3] While the allies complained that Pershing was intractable and difficult to deal with, he could have not done otherwise. His orders from Newton Baker, speaking for President Woodrow Wilson, were clear and not subject to interpretation.

Pershing believed that the allies had lost offensive spirit, sapped by three miserable years in the trenches. The war could only be won, he reasoned, if the troops got out of the trenches and went on the offensive. The general was too good a soldier, however, to overlook the results of such attacks as those by the British on the Somme in 1916, or the French Neville offensive of 1917. Those assaults, frontal attacks against German positions, had resulted in little ground gained and very high casualties. It was not enough just to get out of the trenches: the German army would have to be defeated by maneuver warfare. Exactly what Pershing in-tended was unclear, and how maneuver warfare could be applied was not certain but Pershing did insist that troops training in the United States not be trained in trench warfare. Tactical problems were to focus on maneuver training: physical development and weapons expertise were also expected.

General Pershing and his AEF staff at Chaumont knew what difficulties the National Army divisions labored under in the United States. He was openly critical of the constant shifting of men from their divisions to other units or to specialized units.[4] The longer that practice continued the more difficult it would be for the AEF to field an effective combat force. While Pershing was the supreme military authority in France, there was little he could do to alter the course of army activities in the United States. Consequently, National Army divisions like the 82nd remain-ed in a state of flux as far as meaningful training and manpower stability was con-cerned.

There was a constant scramble for manpower for the 82nd. In late January 1918 the personnel officer of the division wrote to Washington to complain. On 15 December, 1917, three captains, eleven first lieutenants, and six second lieutenants attending the Officer's Training Course at Fort Oglethorpe, Georgia had been assigned by special orders to the 82nd; over six weeks had passed, and the twenty needed officers had not reported. In frustration the division's personnel officer asked the Adjutant General's office whether or not those officers were going to report. It appears that they had been diverted, en route, to another division or specialty unit.[5] The initial correspondence from the Adjutant General's office had specifically stated that over two hundred officers from Fort Oglethorpe would be available for service with the division, and Washington even went so far as to

advise temporarily housing junior officers in designated barracks until more suitable quarters were available. That would have been useful advice if any officers
had reported to Camp Gordon. To add insult to injury, the initial communication
from the Adjutant General's office was addressed to "Commanding General, 82nd
Division, Chillicothe, Ohio."[6] The War Department did not inspire confidence in
the men in the field.

There were some bright spots, however. Several stokes mortars arrived at
Camp Gordon, and the allied instructors were busy designing instruction for
various weapons. The 82nd's Bakery Company 330 was finally at full strength and
could begin instruction in field baking.[7] This was not a trivial matter at all: the
combat division of World War One had to supply its own bread in the field when
practical. Often breakfast was bread, bacon, molasses and coffee; bread was served
whenever possible, along with the constant diet of corned beef stew known as
"slum," the Irish slumgullion. If no bread was available the troops ate hardtack, a
hard army cracker. Getting bread to the troops, especially in combat, was an
important morale factor.

Burnham had reason to be confident that the 82nd Division would make
progress in training in January, 1918. The Chief of Staff of the Army ordered that
all National Army divisions be inspected in early January. While no military organization liked inspections by higher headquarters, this one, under Brigadier
General J. B. McDonald, promised to be fair. The usual comment "I am here to
help" in McDonald's case was true; the inspector recognized the handicaps under
which the 82nd operated in training.

When McDonald left Camp Gordon he wrote a full report which was basically
complimentary of the division's training. His report showed that the training program for infantry, lasting sixteen weeks, was being followed but that "instruction
is somewhat handicapped by the large proportion of men who cannot understand
English." Close-order drill was good, and attack training was progressing, but the
machine gun units of the division were floundering because, it seemed to McDonald, they had a very high number of non–English speakers. The 157th Field Artillery Brigade had no equipment, save for one battery of antiquated three-inch guns.[8]

Much of McDonald's inspection focused on target practice at the Norcross
firing range, about eight miles from Camp Gordon. The actual operation and utilization of the facility meet with McDonald's enthusiastic approval, and weapons
training there was the best in the division. But as the inspector pointed out, there
were problems that no one could do anything about. The Norcross range was the
best site within twenty-five miles, but the heavy winter rains in Georgia often
flooded roads between Camp Gordon and Norcross. When the facility had first
been set up, before Camp Gordon was activated, the War Department had failed to
notice that civilians were in danger zones near the range. Both General Erwin and
Burnham saw the problem and had set up a committee to lease more land near the
range. McDonald urged the War Department to grant a sum of money for this. As
the inspector pointed out, the request had been in Washington for some time but the
division had received no word about any appropriation of funds.[9]

His first recommendation was simply to arm and equip the 82nd Division fully so it could train and get to France. McDonald asked that no further transfers be made from the division, because personnel turbulence disrupted the training for which the unit was at Camp Gordon in the first place. Last but not least, McDonald criticized the War Department for requiring vast quantities of paperwork, reports, surveys, and the like from the division. "This paper work befuddles the mind of every division commander I have seen."[10]

The inspection report gave a good picture of the 82nd Division two and a half months after the influx of new soldiers from the various camps and from the Southern draft levy of December. There had indeed been progress made in training. The great question, however, was the War Department's willingness to keep transfers to specialty units and other divisions at an absolute minimum.

The division was required to do its occupational survey, after the big changes in November and it gives a remarkable view of this National Army division preparing for combat.

To accomplish the survey with any degree of accuracy over eighty-five officers and thirty enlisted men had to be employed on the project, which was completed in February. Men identified as having special skills were known as "flagged" men, because their personnel files got colored tags to denote a special aptitude. In the division there were only 5,056 day laborers; 5,291 reported experience with horses, with 576 claiming to be expert horsehandlers. Over three thousand stated that they had experience with motor cars, and of that number 548 told the personnel officers that they were expert drivers. These men were "green flagged"; this was a highly desirable area of expertise. Over 230 soldiers reported themselves proficient in automotive repair, and they too were green flagged.[11]

There were 719 tailors in the division, mainly from the Russian Jewish community in New York. The variety seemed endless: 622 cooks, 84 bakers, 563 butchers, 128 pigeon raisers, 163 drugstore workers, 82 policemen, 80 firemen, 327 locomotive firemen, 132 motion picture operators, 766 musicians (including composers and pipe organist) 1274 plumbers and pipe fitters, 353 seamen, 83 expert watch repairmen, and on and on. In a special category were the "rare birds" with exotic occupations. There was an expert dog handler from the Italian army, a bird store keeper, an aviator from the Greek army, a diamond setter. In a special category all his own was the official "U.S. Government Moth Killer."[12] No one in the personnel office knew that the United States even had such a job.

This lengthy survey gives a remarkable view of the division, with its cross-section of American life and occupations. Among the 25,500 enlisted men in the 82nd education levels were fairly low, with only 266 men listed as college graduates and 1,659 as high school graduates. The language skills were diverse, with Italian, Russian, and German being among the most numerous. The survey enumerated 472 shoe-machine operators in the division, the vast majority being French-speaking Canadians who had migrated into Massachusetts to work in the large shoe factories. There were Greeks, Norwegians, Danes, Irish, and almost two thousand German speakers. The 82nd Division was truly a melting-pot division, representing the great migration patterns of the early twentieth century. Almost everyone professed a willingness to fight for the United States and become citizens. While the lack of a common language hurt training, it did nothing to lessen morale and esprit de corps.

There were dangers in compiling such a list of occupational specialties, however. The War Department was looking for men to fill service units supporting the AEF in combat. By March, 1918 another three thousand men had been transferred out of the 82nd to other units.[13] To make up for the loss there was another transfer of soldiers from other camps to Camp Gordon. In fact, the division benefitted in that it received two thousand more than had been transferred out, but these were new men, many with minimal training in the basic soldiering skills. Precious time would have to be taken once again to bring those new soldiers up to the same standard as the rest of the men in their companies.

Someone in the War Department or the Office of the Chief of Staff could not do math very well. In February, the division's strength report indicated that there were 23,640 soldiers present for duty. Three months later the strength report stood at 23,831, an increase of about two hundred soldiers in the 82nd Division. The constant transfers of officers and men were causing alarm, because the division was scheduled to leave for France in the spring and was still about five thousand men short of the twenty-eight thousand required. In April some officer in the Office of the Chief of Staff wrote on a report, "The 82nd Division were give about 7000 men and they were short 4000 when we began filling them up."[14]

A good example of the constant failure to stabilize manpower is the case of the 157th Field Artillery Brigade. In January, Colonel Clarence Deems, commanding the 321st Field Artillery Regiment, wrote to Burnham to point out that he was the only field-grade officer in his regiment and that he had several times requested a lieutenant colonel to be his second in command. If he became unfit for duty, the regiment would be commanded by a captain. None of the battalions had field-grade commanders, and in fact, the two battalions had just lost their battalion adjutants, who were detailed to work at the Officers Training School. Of the six battery commanders, three had just been ordered to the artillery firing school at Fort Sill, Oklahoma.[15] When Brigadier General McDonald inspected the 82nd Division in January he noted that the 157th Field Artillery Brigade's commander was Colonel Earl D'A. Pearce, who was also listed as the commanding officer of the 319th Field Artillery Regiment.[16] The brigade still did not have a permanent brigade commander, and one regiment had no command leadership.

Not all was bleak, however. The artillery received a few antiquated three-inch guns at least for practice, and a range was constructed near Marietta, Georgia. Batteries took turns firing the old pieces, and they got some training in the duties of firing batteries, battery supply, and fire direction. The range, named Camp Blackjack, and the troops were adopted by the people of the city. When not firing on the range, the troops were fed by the townspeople, and the officers received numerous social invitations. The people of Marietta were kept awake by the sound of the old guns, and the officers of the various regiments found the young ladies of the town to be most charming.[17]

Finally the 157th got a full-time commander, and Colonel Pearce returned to his regiment. Charles Dudley Rhodes arrived in February 1918; his officers noticed with dismay that he was a cavalry officer. Rhodes felt the pressure immediately and confided to his diary, "A colonel of some twenty-nine years service in the cavalry arm is suddenly appointed by the President a brigadier-general of field artillery, and with but superficial artillery experience, is directed to forthwith prepare his three regiment brigade for active service in France."[18]

Charles "Teddy" Rhodes had been born in Ohio on 10 February 1865. In Washington, he attended Columbian University, now George Washington University, and after earning an A.B. degree in 1885, he entered West Point where he knew upperclassman John J. Pershing. Graduating in 1899, he had served in the 6th Cavalry Regiment campaigning against the Sioux. Rhodes had commanded a cavalry troop during the China Relief Expedition and served in the Philippines, where he had been cited for gallantry under fire in 1901. Known as a solid, steady officer, Rhodes had been detailed to the General Staff from 1903 to 1906. In 1908 he attended the General Staff College at Fort Leavenworth, Kansas, and when the war broke out he had been stationed at Fort Logan, Utah.[19]

It was not unusual in the hectic world of the Army in 1917–1918 to have officers from one branch command units in another. Charles T. Menoher, a career artillery officer, was appointed by Pershing to command the 42nd Infantry Division, and later General Pershing assigned another artillery officer, Charles P. Summerall, to command the 1st Infantry Division. The main factor in these appointments was that these were regular Army officers with a chance at a National Army assignment with a promotion in rank, albeit temporary. Also, Rhodes had been through the course at Leavenworth and was prepared for staff assignments. Since he was not going to be involved in actually placing or firing the guns, intimate knowledge of artillery was not an absolute necessity. Given the paucity of training in the United States, it was evident that the 157th Brigade would have to receive in-depth training in France. Rhodes could learn along with his officers and men. At any rate, Teddy Rhodes was an experienced soldier and a good disciplinarian, with an ability to inspire confidence in his troops, regardless of his background. The 157th Field Artillery Brigade would grow under the firm command of Rhodes and would develop into a good unit on the Western Front.

February was a good month for the 82nd Division as far as training was concerned. The physical conditioning of the troops continued with good results, and the time devoted to "organizational singing" reinforced the already good morale and unit cohesion. The British team set up a divisional machine gun school for junior officers, which went very well despite the fact that requests for more Vickers machine guns were not filled. Bayonet training was also judged to be a success by unit officers and NCOs completing the course. Once the men had completed the course they were expected to return to their units and become trainers. This was sound training doctrine, but the uneven stages in the development of the division due to continual manpower turbulence meant that training at the unit level, while enthusiastic, was slow.[20]

These observations made by American observers were echoed by the British instructional team. In a detailed report by Major H. D. Matson, the enthusiasm of the troops was noted, but several problems were pointed out, especially on the bayonet course, that were beyond the control of the division. Not all men had bayonets. There was a shortage of the weapon, and some men who had them were told not to damage them by charging hay-filled dummies. Citing War Department policies, Matson wrote that "there seems to be an impression at present that this [charging dummies] will damage the bayonet." Matson was very upset over the slow pace of instruction in the Trench Mortar School due to the lack of equipment. It had no shells, fuses, or compasses to work with; he ended his report, "shells and fuzes diverted at Washington."[21]

A very critical area where things did not go well was antigas training. Matson complained that there was not enough equipment to train thoroughly the men who would be the unit instructors. He pointed out that there was a critical shortage of gas masks at the school and that other pieces of equipment were also unavailable. He blamed the quartermaster system in the United States for not sending enough material to conduct training and for requiring the Division Gas Officer to requisition each single item as supplies were used up.[22] The division training officers also reported that there were very high failure rates among the NCOs attending the school because of poor comprehension of the English language.[23] Major Matson concurred with that evaluation, stating that too many men appointed as NCOs had little facility with the language and simply could not understand the instruction. This festering problem for the 82nd Division was noted by the War Department, which suggested that illiterates and non-English speakers "be transferred to Depot Brigades for separate instruction and replaced as soon as possible by English speaking recruits."[24] That sounded well enough in the rarified atmosphere of the War Department in Washington, but for the 82nd Division it meant the loss, again, of a sizeable number of now partially trained soldiers. The division would simply have to cope with the situation as best it could.

Captain André Rostand of France made similar observations about artillery training, where there were no modern guns to fire. In the area of instruction on the French automatic rifle almost nothing had been accomplished by the 82nd Division. The rifle range at Norcross was continually occupied by the infantry and other troops and was impossible to schedule. To compensate for the problems a French lieutenant lectured and conducted simulated drills, but little of practical value had been done. While Rostand rated the personnel of the 157th Field Artillery Brigade as "hardworking men, very desirous to acquire a through knowledge of their specialty," he had little good to say about those attending the automatic rifle school. His report is not as specific as Major Matson's, but it is clear that there were language problems. In the area of artillery Rostand was very clear in his criticisms: three-inch guns "are absolutely inadequate to any serious instruction."[25]

There were rumors that in the spring the 82nd Division would be ordered to France. However, the requirement for a division was twenty-eight thousand officers and men, and Pershing continually demanded that only complete divisions be sent to the AEF. He was fighting battles with the allies over manpower, especially after the first German offensive in March 1918, but throughout February, March, and April the 82nd remained at a constant level of 23,500 men, about 4,500 enlisted men short.[26]

There was another problem looming on the horizon for the division: the War Department had identified about two thousand possible enemy aliens in the ranks of the division. Whether those men would be loyal to the United States was a major question, and no one wanted to send potential troublemakers to France. On the other hand, if the division lost two thousand men at a critical time, would its departure for France be held up until the division was filled? If so, filled with what?

Despite training problems, the division was making progress. It was by and large a healthy group of men made stronger by physical activity, and adjustment to military life did not appear to be causing problems for people who had been civilians a few months before. During a detailed inspection the health of the 82nd was noted as very good, with the exception of the usual camp diseases—mainly measles and mumps. The division surgeon noted over seven hundred cases of venereal disease, but he ascertained that only 5 percent had been contracted by men after reporting for military duty. Intestinal diseases, the scourge of any army camp, was at a minimum due to the command emphasis on cleanliness in the kitchen areas and the mess halls.[27] This was a very good sign for the division, in that it showed attention to detail on the part of mess sergeants, and oversight of kitchen police by mess personnel. NCOs were taking their duties seriously, and that was very encouraging, since many of the corporals and sergeants had themselves just been drafted into the Army.

There were fifty-four kitchens and mess halls in operation in the 82nd Division, feeding about twenty-five thousand soldiers three meals per day. Supervising this massive operation was the divisional cooking school, which had only seven officers and forty-two NCOs. In keeping with training philosophy, these men, drawn mainly from the regular Army, trained about three hundred division cooks in a two-month course. The graduates would then train other unit cooks. What the course did not do, however, was to prepare the division mess personnel for the trying conditions of trench warfare on the Western Front. The assumption was that this training would take place once the 82nd was in France.

During the month of March the cold winter weather ended, and training picked up in intensity as rumors continued to circulate about a May or June departure for France. The arrival of new American-made Vickers machine guns marked a new phase in training. With time at the range, the machine gunners were able to fire barrages to simulate the suppressive fires that would support infantry in the advance. Inspectors noted a new enthusiasm for training among the enlisted men once the new weapons arrived. Bayonet training was combined with live-fire exercises, taking advantage of trenches dug by the 307th Engineers. This offered the soldiers realistic training, which according to the training officers from the division staff, worked well. Although the need for infantry range firing often interrupted training, it was far better than what the division had offered in January.[28]

While some areas were showing marked improvement, gas warfare training remained a grave disappointment due to a critical shortage of gas masks. There were only 4,009 masks in the entire division, and most of those were retained by the gas school to train by battalion and regiment. The gas chamber not only served the needs of the 82nd Division; it was also used by two depot brigades, white and black and also by other troops. There was almost no individual or corrective instruction, due to the large number of students using the fairly small gas chamber; after numerous complaints two American officers were attached to the school as instructors. The number of soldiers to receive gas training and the existence of only one gas chamber mitigated against good training.[29]

There were concrete indications that the 82nd Division would soon depart for France. It was announced that an inspection team from the Office of the Chief of Staff, under Brigadier General Eli Helmick, would spend from 4 to 13 April with the division. The objective of the inspection was to evaluate the division for overseas service. Helmick, who was scheduled to take command of the regular Army 8th Division and take it to France, was known as a hard inspector, a no-nonsense officer. His recommendations would carry a great deal of weight in the War Department.

The inspection was as demanding as everyone thought it would be, and Helmick's team seemed to be able to observe every error the 82nd Division made. Helmick exploded when he saw several young lieutenants walking through the camp eating ice cream cones, which was "unbecoming of an officer and detrimental to discipline." Nothing seemed to go right while Helmick and his team was at Camp Gordon. Infantry drill was a shambles, no one saluted properly, the firing range training was defective; on and on the list of deficiencies went. Helmick would not hear any complaint about the high percentage of men who could not speak English—proper attention to drill would solve that problem.[30]

However, when Helmick returned to Washington, presumably still fuming over the regrettable ice cream cone incident, his recommendations were somewhat different from his litany of official deficiencies at Camp Gordon. Certainly there were problems with the division's discipline and training; as Helmick wrote, "The division as a whole is far from an effective fighting machine." However, "with strenuous training, under competent instructors in Europe, it can be prepared for field service within a reasonable period of time."[31] Unless a calamity occurred the 82nd Division was now slated to go to the AEF in a short period of time.

The tempo of two important and interrelated activities increased dramatically in March. Training, though the inspectors found deficiencies and shortages in equipment, had a stronger emphasis, and logistical activities relating to overseas movement intensified. To move from Camp Gordon to France, a National Army division had to have as close to 100 percent manpower as possible, and it had to have 100 percent of individual and unit combat equipment on hand. Inspections and inventories by divisional logistical personnel in late February and March noted some critical shortages. There were no Model 1910 Bacon Tins in the division, and every soldier was required to have one to carry rations. The famed .45-caliber pistol was unavailable, but 100 percent of the necessary rifles and 99 percent of the required bayonets had finally been issued. There were no haversacks, holsters, or ration bags on hand. Only 55 percent of the important first aid pouches were available.[32] Obviously, the logistics officers had much work to do to bring the 82nd up to deployment standards in equipment.

By the end of March the inventory of required equipment showed a marked improvement, except in the area of the .45-caliber pistol, where only 10 percent of the requisite number were in the division.[33] However, the division was still about four thousand men short, and if the division was filled up for overseas deployment, would the incoming soldiers have the right equipment? Would there be incoming soldiers? The personnel sections were deeply concerned about another round of shifts, changes, and transfers. Could the 82nd Division go to France with so many illiterates, non-English speakers, and, worse, potential enemy aliens in its ranks?

Actually, the problem could be divided into three separate groups of soldiers: aliens, illiterates, and non-English speakers with no hope of learning even the rudiments of the language before combat. The enemy-alien issue would have to be decided by the War Department. Also, it was clear that an American-born illiterate was deemed good enough to carry a rifle and stand in the ranks; not being able to read or write did not bar a soldier from killing the enemy in battle. The thorny question focused on the those soldiers who simply could not speak English at all. General Burnham wanted to get them out of the ranks if at all possible, but first he needed to know from his subordinate commanders and from the education committee how many men there were in that category. Enemy aliens were going to be separated, that became certain. If too many soldiers who had just undergone the required sixteen weeks of training were lost, might it not put the division's move to France in jeopardy?

Burnham had spent a good deal of time monitoring the language problem in the 82nd Division. The Committee on Education, chaired by Major G. Edward Buxton, had on its staff the famous historian Ulrich B. Phillips of Georgia. The committee identified over two thousand troops who in its opinion were unfit for combat. They also urged Burnham to require all subordinate commanders to test their units for language skills. Buxton then suggested to Burnham,

> It has occured to the Committee that since a proportion of the non-English speaking soldiers in the Division are of Italian birth, the military training given these men might be utilized in the near future by sending them as a special American unit with similiar units from other Divisions to the Italian Army. Their presence might help counteract German propaganda in Italian ranks.[34]

Burnham duly required his subordinate commanders to evaluate their troops and report how many men would be unfit for overseas deployment. The results were surprising. Colonel Frank D. Ely, commanding the 327th Infantry Regiment, informed Burnham that he considered 142 soldiers unfit. There were 124 who could speak no English, twelve who were classified as "mental defectives," one coward, one suspected enemy alien, and one who was considered to be simply "malicious."[35] Every one of the soldiers came from the combat infantry companies of the regiment. Captain Bernard A. Percell, commanding the 307th Supply Train, reported that the train was already short twenty-eight soldiers but then requested that 109 men be separated from the train as unfit, the vast majority because they could speak no English.[36] Communications from other subordinate commands indicated similiar numbers of soldiers to be unfit. If all of those soldiers were separated from the division the loss in manpower could very well be over two thousand and this with the 82nd already under deployment strength.

In a classic case of bad timing, Burnham wrote to the Adjutant General's office asking that over two thousand soldiers who either could not speak English or were "mental defectives" be assigned to noncombatant duties in the United States. The majority of the non-English speakers were recent Italian immigrants.[37] This letter arrived in Washington at a time when John J. Pershing was struggling with the allies over the future use of American combat troops and was bombarding the War department with urgent requests that full strength National Army divisions be sent to France as quickly as possible. The Germans had just launched the first of their massive offensives on the Western Front, and infantrymen were needed to stem the tide of their advance.

In uncharacteristically blunt words the Adjutant General informed Burnham that "You will not eliminate from your organization non-English speaking men unless they are enemy aliens. . . . It is not understood why at this late date one thousand [sic] men in your Division should be reported as disqualified on account of lack of knowledge of the English language."[38] The rebuke was clear, and the intent of the War Department was not subject to interpretation: those soldiers were going to go to France with the 82nd Division. There simply was not time to find replacements. The only exception to the ruling was enemy aliens. Burnham was stung by the sharp tone of the response and tried to defend the efforts of the division, but to no avail.[39] The situation was complicated because the War Department had earlier indicated a willingness to separate non-English speakers from the ranks. Now it had changed its mind in no uncertain terms. Also, because Italy had been in the war on the side of the allies since 1915, enemy alien status could not be used to separate Italian-Americans from the 82nd.

The process of removing enemy aliens from the division and transferring them to the depot brigade at Camp Gordon began. Since the enactment of the conscription law it had been clear that Americans wanted immigrants to be drafted in the army.[40] Since local draft boards were under a mandate to bring these recent arrivals into the army to fight, there were attempts to conscript every able-bodied man. It would have been foolish to believe that recent immigrants from Germany and Austria would not receive their notices to report for military training and for overseas deployment to the AEF. When the 82nd Division did its survey of occupations it found that there were over two thousand German speakers in the division. Other National Army divisions had similar language and alien problems, but what set the 82nd apart was the constant stripping of the unit of all enlisted men in the fall of 1917 and then the filling of it with men selected from other divisional training camps. From the records it seems clear that the 82nd Division had special problems.

The problem of identifying enemy aliens was compounded by the fact that many had fled enemy lands for political, social, and economic reasons and had no reason to owe any allegiance to either Germany or Austria. The Provost Marshall General of the Army estimated that there were over 430,000 such men available for the draft.[41] To discharge or transfer everyone was not only impractical, it would have been unfair in the extreme. Consequently, each case would have to be examined by a board to determine loyalty. Some aliens would be firm in their commitment was to the United States. For example, Private Julius Olsen Knud of the 82nd's 163rd Infantry Brigade had been born in Denmark; the land of his birth was neutral in the war. His company commander wanted him transferred to the depot brigade, but Knud, protesting his loyalty, fought the action. His argument was that he had declared his intention to become an American citizen. Knud convinced the board, was promoted for bravery at St. Mihiel, and became an American citizen at the end of the war.[42] The whole question of enemy aliens and disloyalty had to be handled slowly and with care, especially in a division with such a high percentage of immigrants.

While the thorny questions of manpower were being settled between Burnham and the War Department, training of the division for combat showed great improvement during the month of April. British Major Matson was transferred to El Paso to train troops there. The machine gun course slowed down, as the new American instructors became familiar with their duties. Gas training remained a problem in the division, but bayonet and grenade training moved along with little complaint. Rifle ranges operated well, and the division became proficient with basic weapons. The trench mortars increased in number, and inspectors found that that area of training, which once had languished, now appeared to be progressing satisfactorily.[43] Artillery training was still a sore point and would have to be quickly addressed once the 82nd Division got to Europe. Any further infantry training would also have to be done behind the lines of the Western Front. There was no more time.

On 10 April, 1918, elements of the division headquarters left Camp Gordon for Camp Upton, New York, to act as an advance party of the 82nd. Within a few days the 163rd Infantry Brigade ended training and packed its gear for the two-day trip from Georgia to New York. Once that brigade was in place, the 164th Infantry Brigade departed for New York, followed quickly by the 319th Machine Gun Battalion.[44] General Rhodes's 157th Field Artillery Brigade would be next to make the trip, and other divisional units would follow. By the end of April the entire 82nd would be at Camp Upton waiting for ships to take it to Europe.

As the Camp Gordon period came to an end the division's Chief of Staff, Major R. A. Beebe, filed one last training report, which he sent to General Helmick in Washington. The report reviewed the familiar manpower and training shortfalls. Beebe added, "The Division is, however, prepared for a strenuous training behind the lines in Europe. It will make much more rapid progress under serious conditions there than longer in the United States."[45] That had been Helmick's judgment some time before.

The 82nd Division, full of non-English speakers and one official U.S. government moth killer, was ready to begin the next phase of its adventure. Exactly where the men would go and under whom they would train was not clear. But at least the move to Camp Upton brought them closer to the docks from whence the

All-Americans would sail for Europe. How many of them would return to those docks was another matter.

NOTES

1. Burnham to Adjutant General of the Army, 11 January 1918, in Records Group 120, Records of the AEF, 82nd Division, National Archives, Washington, DC, carton 91 [Hereafter cited as RG 120 with appropriate carton].

2. Burnham to Adjutant General's Office, 12 January 1918, ibid., carton 90.

3. See James J. Cooke, *Pershing and His Generals: Command and Staff in the AEF* (Westport, Conn.: Praeger, 1997) for information on AEF activities at this time.

4. John J. Pershing, *My Experiences in the World War*, vol. II (Blue Summit Ridge, PA: Tab Books Reprints, 1989), 3.

5. Personnel Officer, 82nd Division, to Adjutant General's Office, 24 January 1918, RG 120, carton 69.

6. Adjutant General's Office to 82nd Division, 5 December 1917, ibid.

7. Memorandum from Commanding Officer, Bakery Company 330 to Commanding General, 82nd Division, 16 December 1917, ibid., carton 70.

8. Inspection Report to Chief of Staff, 6 February 1918, ibid., carton 11.

9. Ibid.

10. Ibid.

11. 82nd Division, Report from the Personnel Office, c. March 1918, ibid., carton 63.

12. Ibid.

13. *Official History of the 82nd Division, American Expeditionary Forces, 1917-1919* (Indianapolis, IN: Bobbs-Merrill, 1919), 2-3.

14. Office of the Chief of Staff, Memorandum in Regard to Strength of 82nd Division, 28 April 1918, RG 120, carton 1.

15. Deems to Burnham, 10 January 1918, ibid., carton 64.

16. Inspection Report to the Chief of Staff, 5 February 1918, ibid., carton 14. This report is different from the one cited in endnote 8; it is more detailed and contains more facts and figures. McDonald's conclusions and recommendations are the same, however.

17. Typed copy, "Regimental History of the 319th Field Artillery Regiment," 21 December 1918, ibid., carton 25.

18. Introduction to the Rhodes Diary, "1918, Diary of the World War," in the Charles D. Rhodes Papers, U.S. Army Military History Archives, Carlisle Barracks, PA, [Hereafter cite as MHI with appropriate collections].

19. Biographical data from the Rhodes Papers, MHI.

20. Training Report, 82nd Division, 27 February 1918, RG 120, carton 11.

21. Report by Major H. D. Matson, 1 February 1918, ibid., carton 13. The American Training Report for February also reports grave problems in the trench mortar training. Training Report, 82nd Division, 27 February 1918, RG 120, carton 11.

22. Ibid (citing both reports). *Official History of the 82nd Division*, 4, also reports the shortfalls in training equipment.

23. Ibid.

24. War Department, Memorandum for the Chief of Staff, 20 February 1918, RG 120, carton 11.

25. Report by Captain André Rostand, 1 February 1918, ibid., carton 13. Also see typed copy, "History of the Headquarters, 157th Field Artillery Brigade," c. March 1919, ibid., carton 22.

26. Office of the Chief of Staff, Memorandum in Regard to the Strength of 82nd Division, 18 April 1918, ibid., carton 1.

27. Inspection Report to Chief of Staff, 5 February 1918.

28. Training Report, 82nd Division, 27 March 1918, ibid., carton 11.

29. Ibid.

30. War Department, Office of the Chief of Staff to the Adjutant General's Office, Memorandum: Training in 82nd Division, 22 April 1918, ibid., carton 11.

31. War Department, Office of the Chief of Staff, Abstract of Inspection Report, c. 23 April 1918, ibid.

32. Consolidated Report of Percentages of Ordnance Equipment Based on Maximum Strength for Overseas Service, 28 February 1918, ibid., carton 9.

33. Consolidated Report of Percentages of Ordnance Equipment Based on Maximum Strength for Overseas Service, 31 March 1918, ibid.

34. Buxton to Burnham, 26 March 1918, ibid., carton 73.

35. Ely to Burnham, 22 July 1918, ibid. This report is a follow-up to an earlier, less well typed one.

36. Captain Bernard A. Purcell to Burnham, 27 March 1918, ibid., carton 72.

37. Burnham to Adjutant General's Office, 1 April 1918, ibid., carton 73.

38. Adjutant General to Burnham, 3 April 1918, ibid.

39. Burnham to Adjutant General, 5 April 1918, ibid.

40. David M. Kennedy, *Over Here: The First World War and American Society* (Oxford: Oxford University Press, 1980), 157–58.

41. *Second Report of the Provost Marshall General to the Secretary of War on the Operations of the Selective Service System to December 20, 1918* (Washington, DC: Government Printing Office, 1919), 92-107. These pages contain very critical and informative data.

42. Julius Olsen Knud Questionnaire, MHI.

43. Training Report, 82nd Division, 25 April 1918, RG 120, carton 11.

44. Typed copy, "Brief History of the 82nd Division From Its Organization to June 16th 1918," c. December 1918, ibid., carton 1.

45. Memorandum for Brigadier General Helmick, Inspector General, 6 April 1918, ibid., carton 85.

Chapter 3

The All-American Division

Before the division began its trek to New York, Major General John Burnham reconciled himself to having a division with language problems. The time had come to do the best he could do now that the unit would soon be in France training for the Western Front. While at Camp Gordon the 82nd had done an excellent job building morale, esprit de corps, and unit cohesion. Despite all of the problems of language, constant turnover in personnel, and shortages of equipment for training, the 82nd was a disciplined unit, with a good deal of promise. Burnham thought it necessary to give to the division a symbol that would strengthen morale and esprit de corps. In a General Order to the troops Burnham wrote:

> The Eighty-second Division represents the best men from every state in the union. In view of this fact, the commanding general designates this division and orders that it be known as the "All-American Division."[1]

For such a diverse group, and especially for the immigrants, the 100 percent American name was a source of pride.

When the 82nd Division arrived at Camp Upton there were a number of things Burnham had to accomplish. There was the nagging question of enemy aliens to be sorted out, and there were men, several hundred perhaps, who needed to be separated from the division for reasons ranging from mental incompetence to chronic venereal disease. The division was still almost two thousand soldiers short of the authorized strength of twenty-eight thousand men. There were units, such as ambulance companies, that had not yet been formed. General Pershing wanted American combat divisions in France, and there was no time to quibble over strength. Burnham had been assured that his manpower and training needs, especially for the artillery, would be addressed once the 82nd arrived behind the Western Front.

One of the great strengths of the 82nd was in the subordinate commanders.

Burnham had an excellent team, and it would serve him well. Commanding the 163rd Infantry Brigade was Brigadier General Marcus D. Cronin, a West Point graduate, class of 1887. The 164th Infantry Brigade was under Brigadier General Julian R. Lindsey, West Point class of 1892. Charles D. Rhodes, the cavalryman, commanded the 157th Field Artillery Brigade, which was arguably the best led, if the weakest in training.[2] Regimental and other subordinate commands appeared to be well served by first-rate commanders, all of them from the regular Army.

Part of the division was in cantonments at Camp Mills, New York, not far from the majority of the division, encamped at Camp Upton. The advance party was to leave in early April for France, while the remainder of the division would arrive in May and early June.[3] It all depended on the availability of shipping, much of it provided by the British. There was not much time for the units at either Upton or Mills to deal with the pressing personnel problems, but work went on at a hectic pace on screening enemy aliens and others for overseas service.

The 82nd Division had received strict instructions from the Ports of Embarkation to file a certificate that there were no enemy aliens in the ranks. This was of particular concern to port and naval authorities, who feared an enemy alien might signal German submarines in the Atlantic. The fear of German submarine attack haunted the crossing of every American unit, and extra caution had to be taken. There was a final clarification of who was to be considered "enemy." On 17 April the War Department issued guidance "an enemy alien is a subject born on Austrian, German, Turkish, or Bulgarian territory and who has not completed his naturalization, and no exceptions to this rule will be made."[4] A special barracks area at Camp Upton was set aside for those separated from the division. Unless there was some special problem, such as making treasonous statements or urging others to resist American military authority, the aliens would remain in the army; they were to be sent to the 40th Infantry Division at Fort Sheridan, Illinois.[5] According to the divisional history, over 1,400 enemy aliens were identified and left the division before it sailed for Europe.[6] Some aliens, close to naturalization, demanded a board of examination to declare their loyalty to the United States, and a number of these men were allowed to remain with their units and deploy to Europe.[7] They were classified as simply "aliens" rather than "enemy aliens," which satisfied the regulations.

Port authorities also insisted on a second certificate, that there were no conscientious objectors among the troops sailing for Europe. The official list of faiths which could claim objector status was very short, comprising the Amish, Quakers, Dunkers, Mennonites, and a few others.[8] However, a number of soldiers claimed objector status prior to the division's departure from the United States. These cases would have to be resolved quickly. Unless there were compelling reasons to transfer men as objectors they were ordered to perform their duties or be court-martialed for disobedience in time of war; the penalty for such an offense was usually a dishonorable discharge and up to five years in prison. The records reveal that when faced with disciplinary proceedings most who had claimed objector status chose to remain with their units.

There was a final physical evaluation of the troops of the 82nd Division at camps Mills and Upton to determine their suitability for the rigors of military campaigning. Within the 327th Infantry, for example, five soldiers were deemed unfit because of severe venereal infection.[9] In the 328th Infantry Regiment sixteen men were separated for physical reasons, the majority of them venereal cases.[10] The 321st Machine Gun Battalion reported only two men not fit for overseas service, both because of gonorrheal infections.[11] These three units, reports were representative of the reports going to division headquarters, and they indicate that a relatively small number of men could not make the voyage to France.

General Pershing and the AEF medical staff were adamant that no soldier be sent from the United States who was suffering from a sexually transmitted disease. In France the AEF was waging war against venereal diseases, with courts-martial for those who contracted them, official prophylaxis stations established in towns where soldiers might contract them, and stern lectures against the evils of sexual activity with prostitutes. Pershing was certainly no prude, and from his long years in the regular Army he knew that there would be easy contact between prostitutes and the men. Many of the men now in the AEF, despite having been in the regulars, the National Guard, or the National Army, had never been away from home, and temptations would be great. However, when the 82nd Division reported that about a hundred soldiers could not deploy to France because of venereal infection, the War Department wanted an explanation of what the division had been doing to prevent the infections.

More to the point, Brigadier Walter A. Bethal, the Judge Advocate General of the AEF, wanted a detailed report. Lieutenant Colonel William Taylor, the Judge Advocate General (JAG) of the 82nd Division, responded to Bethal. Taylor had been one of the first officers assigned to the 82nd in August 1917, and he had worked with camp and local officials on two difficult problems: liquor sales and prostitution. He reported to Bethel that every possible step had been taken to suppress both alcohol and prostitution, by coordinating with police officials near Camp Gordon and in the city of Atlanta. Out of a divisional strength of about twenty-six thousand officers and men there had been only 274 trials by courts-martial involving liquor. The situation for the 82nd however, became unclear when dealing with sex and venereal diseases. Newton Baker had issued an order that houses of prostitution within a five-mile radius of any army camp would be closed, and by and large the local authorities did their best to comply with the directive from the Secretary of War. Atlanta, however, with a population of over a quarter-million, had had a very difficult time closing brothels or keeping prostitutes away from establishments frequented by soldiers.[12]

Taylor observed that a number of soldiers had arrived at Camp Gordon with venereal disease; it had been assumed that a number purposely contracted diseases to avoid combat service. It was also assumed that of the six hundred cases examined at Camp Gordon, only a few soldiers—he could not speculate how many—had contracted the disease after induction. The War Department policy stating that an infected soldier could not be deployed to France was well known by the troops.[13] The division's Judge Advocate General believed that only rigid enforcement of War Department and AEF policies could reduce the number of cases of infection. He pledged to do everything in his power to punish miscreants and to work with the division medical authorities to implement regulations.[14]

While personnel matters were being handled, troops were moving to various ports of embarkation to make the dangerous crossing of the Atlantic. Some units had almost no time to complete their preparations. The 319th Field Artillery Regiment arrived at Camp Mills on 12 May and was scheduled to board British ships on 19 May. All of the regiment's personnel matters had been worked out at Camp Gordon, but some crated equipment was yet to arrive. Regardless, on the night of 18 May the regiment departed for the docks of New York City.[15] The same hectic schedule applied to General Rhodes, who boarded the British ship *City of Exeter* on the night of 18 May.[16] Sailing with the artillery brigade was the 307th Ammunition Train, on board the American ship *Louisville*.[17] General Burnham and a large portion of his staff had sailed on 25 April on the *Caronia*, a British transport. He wanted to be in England when the bulk of his division arrived at Liverpool in early May.[18] The last units of the 82nd Division left the United States for England on 3 June, arriving in Liverpool ten days later.[19]

It had been decided at AEF headquarters that Burnham's division would train under both British and French direction in France. The artillery brigade needed more attention than the other components of the division; it would be sent to the French artillery training school near La Courtine for an intensive six-week course.[20] The remainder of the division would be attached to the British Fifth Army for at least one month before reverting to AEF control.

But before the division could cross the Channel to France there was a round of parades and public appearances in Britain to welcome the Americans and to bolster British morale, sagging after four years of bloodshed. The 325th Infantry paraded in London before the king and Englishmen, who had never seen an American combat regiment before.[21] The 319th Field Artillery Regiment got a day of rest and sightseeing in Winchester before going on to France.[22]

There were also some disciplinary matters to attend to before the division crossed. The Royal Navy reported that members of the 325th Infantry had participated in a theft while aboard the transport *Karmala*. It was found that soldiers of the National Guard 137th Infantry and the 82nd's 325th Infantry had broken into the ship's store and had taken tobacco, liquors, candies, and cash. The loss to the ship amounted to $506.83. The captain of the ship was furious, and the two regimental commanders were embarrassed. An immediate search identified the culprits, but only twenty-nine dollars was recovered—the rest had been smoked, drunk, or eaten. Brigadier General Cronin, commanding the 163rd brigade and other soldiers on board ship, ordered that the sum be paid back and the thieves held for courts-martial once the ship docked in England.[23] While shipboard incidents were rare, military justice had to be served once the troops were on dry land.

Some units went to visit a large British hospital near the city of Winchester and found out quickly that the Great War was not all cheering crowds and tourist jaunts. Private First Class Thurmond J. Baccus, Company C, 307th Field Signal Battalion, was among those soldiers elected to go to the hospital to show that the Americans were indeed in the war. The sights were sobering indeed. Many of the maimed British veterans urged the doughboys to stick a hand or a leg above the trench to get wounded and evacuated quickly. A shocked Baccus remembered them saying that a crippling wound "was much better than living in the trenches."[24] This was a view of trench life that Baccus had not heard about at Camp Gordon.

There was precious little time to spend in England. It was of critical importance to get the 157th Field Artillery Brigade across the channel and then on to La Courtine. Once in France, the artillerists were given an introduction to two facets of the war. The first was a lecture on what to do if the Germans conducted an air raid. Many of the doughboys had never seen a combat aircraft, let alone been bombed or strafed by one. The second, and most enduring, introduction was to *vin rouge*, the potent French red wine, which the doughboys found in wonderful abundance in France.[25]

For six weeks in June and July the artillery learned its craft from the French. The remainder of the division was to be attached to the British Fifth Army from 17 May until 17 June. The infantry and machine-gun units moved to St. Valery-sur-Somme, where instructors from the 66th British Division began intensive training.[26] The 82nd Division learned very quickly that its staff was unprepared for combat and lagged behind even the artillery in solid training. General Pershing had recognized that the AEF did not have the enough staff officers to prepare and issue orders or to perform the vital intelligence functions required on a modern battlefield. To overcome this, the AEF had established a General Staff College at Langres, France, where, it was hoped, enough staff officers could be trained to fill positions in the arriving divisions.[27] The 82nd Division did not have a G2 (intelligence officer) or a G3 (operations officer) who could advise the commander and prepare the briefings and orders required for the division to conduct combat operations.

The root of the staff problem went back to the situation in the army prior to the war. The United States Army had only about two hundred trained staff officers in April 1917, and precious few of them had any experience above the regimental or brigade level. Those officers who served on the newly formed General Staff in Washington had received no training that would serve the needs of a twenty-eight-thousand-man division in combat. In the War Department there was almost no understanding of what a division would require. In August 1917, when the 82nd was activated, the War Department had sent to Eben Swift a list of officers that would be given him to make up the division staff. Ten newly promoted majors were assigned to the staff of every National Army division. The positions were: chief of staff, assistant chief of staff, adjutant, quartermaster, inspector, judge advocate, ordnance officer, signal officer, adjutant for the depot brigade, and an adjutant of the field artillery brigade. This list indicates that a divisional staff was administrative and logistical in orientation. The initial allocation by the War Department allowed no one for training, operations, or intelligence.[28]

When Pershing and his small group of staff officers arrived in England and France in the summer of 1917, the allies were aghast at how small the AEF staff was. It was clear to the British and the French that what the United States Army envisioned for the AEF was inadequate. Pershing's own staff structure would not be complete until the early months of 1918; it is little wonder that the newly arriving divisions were woefully undertrained at the staff level for combat. As soon as the General Staff School graduated officers they were sent to the divisions to try to correct this situation. But those graduates, while they had a solid theoretical grounding, had very little practical experience as combat staff officers. Two critical areas had to be addressed. First, staff officers had to be sent to the National Army units as soon as they were graduated by the General Staff College at Langres. Second, those officers had to undertake, with no time lost, the training of their subordinates.

On 5 June 1918, Major General James McAndrew, chief of staff at the General Headquarters of the AEF, informed the 82nd Division that Major J. H. Lee, a recent graduate of the Staff College at Langres, was to report to the division as the G2.[29] The next day the division was informed that Major Jonathon M. Wainwright was detailed as the G3.[30] Wainwright had excelled at Langres, graduating from the Second Course in May 1918. He had done so well that he attracted the attention of Colonel Alfred Bjornstad, the director of the Staff College. Bjornstad informed Wainwright that he would write to Burnham to recommend him as a staff officer and for consideration as a divisional chief of staff if the position came open.[31] Wainwright certainly impressed Lieutenant Colonel Beebe, the 82nd's chief of staff, with how quickly he took over his duties as G3.[32]

Major Lee, a 1909 West Point graduate, was also an alumni of the Second Course at Langres. Lee had been the aide to Major General Leonard Wood at Camp Funston, Kansas, observing all of the difficulties in forming and training a National Army division. Leaving the 89th Division, Lee went to France and entered the Langres school. During his tenure as G2 of the 82nd he worked closely with his General Staff College classmate, and they made a good team.[33]

As soon as Wainwright and Lee arrived, they began the training of their sections. To remedy the shortage of trained staff officers, the AEF mandated that staff section leaders begin training what were known as "understudies." Each division commander was obligated to find in his division young, intelligent, and ambitious officers who could come to the general staff of the division and begin training.[34] In the 82nd Division, AEF guidance in this matter was forwarded to each brigade and regiment with the mandate that they begin the understudy process. By August Wainwright had built a G3 section with six good officers whom he had trained. Lee did the same thing with the G2 section.

Not all was G3 section training for Wainwright, however; one problem which had been brought to Wainwright's attention had nothing to do with preparing orders or maintaining battle maps. A number of officers at the division headquarters were not very good horsemen, and some who had been raised in a city had no horsemanship at all. Wainwright, a cavalryman, organized two classes in equitation, to meet from four to five a.m. and from five to six p.m., to teach them the skills they needed if they had to carry out their duties from horseback.[35] The AEF was always short of motor transport—automobiles and trucks—and many officer duties had to be conducted on horseback. This was a vital skill for any officer on Burnham's staff.

In early June, General Pershing visited the 82nd Division to see its progress in training with its British instructors. Pershing was a very hard man to please, and he had already relieved and sent back to the United States a number of division commanders who did not measure up to his standards. He was determined that the AEF would soon be its own army, fighting in its own sector under American commanders; there was little tolerance for error. On 8 June General Burnham received a letter from Colonel Carl Boyd of the AEF staff: the general "was much pleased to note the excellent personnel which composes [*sic*] your division. He feels that you have possibilities for producing a command which will be a credit to the American Expeditionary Forces and to our country."[36] From Pershing this was high praise and indicated that despite the language problems, the 82nd was doing well.

Pershing might well have been pleased with the progress of the training, because the British had prepared well for the arrival of the Americans. From liaison teams in the United States and from American evaluations, they were familiar with the areas in which the 82nd had received little or no training, and they assigned the 66th Infantry Division the responsibility of working with the All-Americans. At a conference held on 9 April 1918, the British decided that the trainers would consult with the Americans about training and send officers to serve with and direct the staffs of the American brigades. The April meeting produced a policy statement in line with the direction of American training: "The policy will be to train as many instructors as possible in order that the Americans may take over their own training as soon as possible."[37]

Training guidance sent by the AEF directed that the Americans put their rifles in storage and draw British military rifles and bayonets. British gas masks would be issued to every man for intensive gas-defense training. Automobiles and trucks, in such short supply in the AEF, would be issued to the 82nd Division for use while in the British sector. Also, the 82nd would receive their steel helmets from English stocks.[38]

The training schedule presented to the 82nd Division was intense, with no time for anything but training. Twenty separate training activities were set up by the 66th Division for everything from rifle practice (trench oriented), to the Stokes mortars, to Vickers and Lewis machine gun schools. The 307th Field Signal Battalion was sent to two locations to learn the most modern techniques in signaling. The division's cooks and bakers were sent to the British cookery school at Pont Remy, where the cooks were taught how to provide for the men in the trenches in combat.[39] Not only did the British provide camp kettles, butcher knives, and field rations, they also had to provide the ammunition, for which the Americans promised to reimburse the British.[40]

The 66th Division, under the command of Major General H. K. Bethell, threw itself into the work of training the Americans. Of course, for the British it was a respite from the miserable life in the trenches, from the boredom and constant danger. In some areas, such as drill, the 82nd had good skills; gas defense, mortars, sniping, etc., there was much to be done. The British went about simple combat training for the troops who would carry the rifles and fire the machine guns. They instituted two courses, each eight days long, for battalion intelligence personnel. The weakness in intelligence sections, which were not ready to perform combat functions, was obvious to both the English and the Americans; and the courses were a modest starting point.[41]

The various schools, however, placed strains on the American units. The situation with the 321st Machine Gun Battalion serves as a typical example of what was happening to the 82nd Division while training with the British. There were schools which required officers and NCOs to be in two places at once. Major E. J. Pike, commanding the battalion, informed division headquarters that five NCOs were ready to go to the intelligence school, but three of the five were already enrolled in the liaison school. Of the 115 NCOs in the battalion, every one, except for five company clerks, was in school. "Attention is called to the fact that another call for Noncommissioned Officers for school purposes can hardly be filled by this Battalion."[42] Beebe instructed his personnel officers to issue no more school orders until there had been an evaluation of what the division could do to fill the schools. The problem was that there was so much to do with so little time to overcome the shortfalls in training that had occurred in the United States.

The British envisioned training ten American divisions between 9 June and 30 August 1918, with each of the ten receiving one month's training. Between 15 July and 15 August four divisions would be trained at the same time. Often arriving American battalions would be sent directly into training and formed into "independent brigades."[43] The task was daunting, given the uneven status of training within those divisions.

By and large the Americans and British got along well. The Americans were impressed by the professionalism of the British, who seemed determined to prepare their new allies for service in the trenches.[44] If there was a constant complaint among the troops of the 82nd Division it was over food. British field rations were plain, prepared with little or no seasoning. Bread was mainly hard crackers. One infantryman recalled how after leaving the British they were fed by their own cooks and "got thick slices of white bread, we treasured every crumb."[45]

Near the end of the one-month training period some of the 82nd got to see the trenches and stay in them for a while, but the training was not to orient Americans in trench fighting—it was to teach basic skills. The 157th Field Artillery Brigade had no opportunity to see the trenches of the Western Front. Its time was spent in intensive range firing and learning the artillerist's craft from the French. The French had agreed to train the brigade from 5 June to 5 August, with the first two weeks spent in drawing all of the equipment and guns that the brigade's three regiments would need for active service.

While the regiments were learning the mysteries of the 75mm and the 105mm guns from French instructors who spoke English with varing degrees of proficiency, Rhodes was organizing his staff. Like every other AEF unit that arrived in France, the 157th Brigade had to build a staff from the ground up. The major additions were in operations, with the assigning of Captains E. C. Gwaltney and J. K. Fornance to the section, and intelligence, headed by Captain J. F. Brown. The telephone officer was First Lieutenant E. R. Watts.[46] The French made it clear that soon the brigade would have to work with an aero observation squadron and a balloon company. There was much for the brigade staff to learn before it would ever see active combat service.

The French had structured training from the individual gun crew to a final exercise, which would be a brigade-level field problem. The field training would end with the three regiments, the 319th, 320th, 321st, and the 307th Trench Mortar Battery firing under brigade orders and control. Through July training focused on what the 82nd's artillerymen called their final examination. On 1 August the 157th they passed with flying colors.[47] They were ready for front line service, or so the French indicated.

General Rhodes got along well with the French, because he was eager to learn how to command an artillery brigade and he was not afraid to ask questions of the battle-wise Frenchmen. On 22 June the French invited Rhodes to a lunch. It lasted two and a half hours, with fifteen courses and three different wines. After the generous repast, Rhodes, stuffed and sleepy, spent three hours in a conference on the employment of artillery in the offensive.[48] A few days later he was taken to a local chateau to meet the owner, Madame Marguerite de la Chaze, a woman over sixty years of age but, as Rhodes observed, "as young and sprightly as a woman of forty." At the end of the social visit, the woman gave Rhodes a rose, kissed him on the cheek, and pronounced herself his "godmother."[49] It seems, however, that her thoughts were far from godly; the next day she appeared at the firing range and pursued a thoroughly flustered Rhodes. "Try as I would to escape, she would trek me to my hiding places," recalled the general.[50] The French officers were amused by this unmilitary activity; Rhodes allowed that it would be safer to fight Germans than be near Madame de la Chaze.

A couple of weeks later Rhodes got his chance to be near the Germans, when the French introduced him to one of the technological innovations of the war. The general made a balloon ascension at the front, from eight hundred meters he observed that "the ground spread out exactly like an aerial photograph . . . guns and targets very plain . . . distant points visible probably fifty miles away."[51] While Rhodes overestimated distance, he learned a valuable lesson about artillery in the Great War: with air observation, particularly balloon observation, indirect fire on targets unseen from the ground was possible, with a high degree of accuracy. Aerial observation would change the employment of artillery on the modern battlefield, and the balloon was a distinct advantage to the artilleryman.[52]

The infantry and the artillery were making great strides in preparing for combat. Also of concern, however, to the British and the French were the American engineers. The 307th Engineer Regiment would have to function well on the battlefield if the 82nd Division was to fight either in the trenches or in open warfare. The engineers not only prepared roads and bridges but cut wire to open lanes for the infantry and built firing positions for machine guns. The combat engineering tasks were many, and when fighting was severe the regiment could serve as a reserve for the infantry. The British gave priority to training the 307th and indicated that the engineers would go through the firing range and bayonet course before any other units.[53] Once that was accomplished the regiment moved on to engineer-specific training.

> No part of the 82nd Division was neglected during the training period with the British and the French. The World War One division was designed to be a combined-arms formation, with infantry, artillery, and all other sections—from engineers and quartermasters—working together. The 307th Ammunition Train received practical training when it was assigned to support the artillery practice at La Courtine. Artillery bombardments during the Great War tended to be intensive, lasting long periods of time, and to support these fires there had to be a continuous supply of ammunition. At La Courtine the 307th Ammunition Train used French vehicles, because it had none of its own. Near the end of the training period the Train was informed that it would get new trucks once it left the area.[54]

The infantry was moving toward the end of their training with the British, and the AEF directed that the 82nd Division continue preparation for combat under the French Eighth Army's XXXII Corps on the line in the Toul area, which was fairly quiet. It would give the All-Americans a chance to serve in the trenches under the tutelage of battle-hardened French veterans. The division move into the trenches without the 157th Field Artillery Brigade, which still had a month of work to do at La Courtine; it would have to rely on the French for artillery support. While Burnham would certainly have wanted to have his division intact for this first contact with the Germans, it would have been impossible to hurry the 157th's valuable training program.

The 82nd Division would relieve the American 26th Division on the night of 25–26 June. The area the 82nd was to occupy was known as the Lagney sector, on the southern tip of the St. Mihiel salient. The St. Mihiel salient had been a quiet sector since the French had tried to take it in 1915 and 1916, with no success and heavy losses. The area had seen so little action that the Germans had allowed their barbed wire defenses to deteriorate. This was a good place for the Americans to learn the basics of survival in a trench war enviroment while taking few casualties. The French believed that there would be no major activity in the area, and they planned to bring a number of troops out of the trenches and send them to automatic rifle school. Battalions not actually in the trenches but held in reserve would continue rifle, bayonet, and gas-defense training. The AEF informed the division that it was to send selected officers and NCOs to the AEF's gas schools at Gondrecourt and Chaumont while in the Lagney sector.

The orders for the movement of the 82nd into the line and the departure of the 26th Division were prepared by the French, but the writing of orders moving divisional units into their locations fell to the division staff, mainly to Major Wainwright and his G3 section. The staff of the 82nd now had to learn exactly what the word "coordination" meant. The relief was to take place over two nights, and it involved noise and light discipline, which the division had only slightly practiced. Now, only a few hundred yards away were armed enemy soldiers listening for any noise, and noise could well bring down a deadly rain of German artillery or gas shells. The second night would be even more tense, because the Germans might have sensed the departure of the 26th Division. To cover the relief the French 154th Infantry Division sent teams to guide the soldiers through the connecting trenches and to oversee security. Complicating matters, the 82nd's 325th Infantry would be replacing a regiment of the French 65th Infantry Division on the left of the line of trenches. The twenty-eight-thousand-man American division, even devoid of artillery, took up more space than the usual twelve-thousand-soldier French division. Watching over this movement were large numbers of machine gun and automatic-rifle teams from the French 154th Division.[55]

The French had no intention of allowing an untested American division to hold a large section of the line without close supervision. The overall commander was Major General Breton, commander of the 154th; Burnham's divisional headquarters was nearby. The line was divided into two subsectors each with both French and American units. To the right of the line was subsector Minorville, with the 325th, the French 414th, and the 326th regiments. Overall tactical command there was in the hands of a French officer. To the left was subsector Ermitage, with the 416th French regiment, the 327th, the 413th, and the 328th regiments. As in Minorville, an experienced French officer maintained operational control. Both the 163rd and 164th brigade commanders of the 82nd were to be colocated with their French counterparts. French artillery would support the entire line, since the 157th remained at La Courtine.[56]

The All-Americans found the trenches held all the horrors that they had feared. Like all trenches, they were damp, and a stench from unburied bodies, rotting food, and unbathed men filled the air. Trees had been ripped from the ground, and though it was late spring there was no vegetation save for a few scrub brushes. The French had told the Americans that they would be under constant observation by the Germans, who had high ground behind their own trenches. In the area held by the 327th Infantry there was heavy sniping and artillery fire day and night. During hours of darkness the men of the 327th began a program of active patrolling in No Man's Land. On 29 June it suffered its first casualty, when Second Lieutenant William M. Walton of Palatka, Florida, was severely wounded by enemy shell fire.[57] The remainder of the division's infantry conducted the same type of deadly operations all along the front.[58] The All-Americans were finally in combat on the Western Front.

The 82nd Division had come a long way since leaving Camp Gordon, Georgia. The one month's training by the British had filled in a number of critical gaps for the infantry and machinegun units. The artillery exercises at La Courtine were realistic training at last for Rhodes's 157th Field Artillery Brigade. Most of the artillerymen had never seen a 75mm or a 105mm gun prior to arrival in France. They had had simulated drills at Camp Gordon, and they had fired antiquated guns at the firing range, but that was all, and until they had extensive firing with the guns they were to use they had been worthless to the division.

The 307th Engineers had gone from being ditch diggers to having combat engineering skills; more importantly, they saw what would be required of them in combat. Colonel J. L. Schley's engineers were impressed to learn that they had priority on the rifle ranges because they had to get on to even more important business. The 307th Ammunition Train, now partially supporting the infantry in the sector, saw firsthand what it would take to keep three artillery regiments and one trench mortar battery firing in actual combat.

Of equal importance was the divisional staff training that the 82nd had conducted while its units were in training. The addition of a competent G3 and G2, and the invaluable staff college experience they brought to the divisional staff, turned a stateside, logistics and personnel-oriented group of officers into a staff prepared to write and issue orders, make reports, and direct the operations of subordinate elements. None of this would have been possible had not Pershing and the AEF staff made the decision to devote three months to officers training at the General Staff College at Langres. Majors Wainwright and Lee made the difference in the 82nd's staff, but they had yet to be really tested in the crucible of actual combat.

Burnham's relationship with Pershing seemed to be on firm ground, and General Pershing, a hard commander to please, had been complimentary of the 82nd Division. It now depended on the division itself to live up to Pershing's expectations, and the trenches were a hard introduction to combat on the Western Front. John J. Pershing preached the doctrine of maneuver, or open warfare, and believed the infantryman with his rifle and bayonet, properly supported, to be the ultimate factor in victory. Regardless of Pershing's gospel of maneuver warfare, however, the 82nd was in the trenches, in a lethal enviroment. Only time would tell if the training would pay off and the 82nd Division was ready to fight.

NOTES

1. HQ, 82nd Division, AEF, General Orders No. 3, 8 April 1918, in Records Group 120, Records of the AEF, 82nd Division, National Archives, Washington, DC, carton 111 [hereafter cited as RG 120 with appropriate carton].

2. HQ, 82nd Division, List, Organizations and Commanders, 19 June 1918, ibid., carton 68.

3. American Battle Monuments Commission, *82nd Division: Summary of Operations in the World War* (Washington, DC: Government Printing Office, 1944), 3–4.

4. HQ, 82nd Division, Memorandum No. 10, 20 April 1918, RG 120, carton 118.

5. Ibid.

6. *Official History of 82nd Division, American Expeditionary Forces, 1917-1919* (Indianapolis, IN: Bobbs-Merrill Co., 1919), 2–3.

7. HQ, 82nd Division, Memorandum to 327th Infantry Regiment, Disposition of Enlisted Men (Aliens), RG 120, carton 72.

8. *Second Report of the Provost Marshal General to the Secretary of War on the Operations of the Selective Service System to December 1918* (Washington, DC: Government Printing Office, 1919), 56–62.

9. HQ, 327th Infantry Regiment, 23 April 1918, RG 120, carton 72.

10. HQ, 328th Infantry Regiment, 25 April 1918, ibid., carton 71.

11. HQ, 321st Machine Gun Battalion, 23 April 1919, ibid.

12. Taylor to Bethal, 3 July 1918, RG 120, Records of the Judge Advocate General, General Correspondence, carton 31.

13. Ibid.

14. Taylor to Bethal, 7 July 1918, ibid.

15. Typed copy, "Regimental History of the 319th Field Artillery," 21 December 1918, RG 120, carton 25.

16. Typed copy, "History of the Brigade Headquarters, 157th Field Artillery Brigade," c. March 1919, ibid., carton 22.

17. War Diary of the 307th Ammunition Train From May 19, 1918, to August 15, 1918, 17 August 1918, ibid., carton 29.

18. Burnham to Adjutant General of the Army, 6 May 1918, ibid., carton 91.

19. *Official History of the 82nd Division*, 4–5.

20. Typed copy, "History of the 320th Field Artillery from 18 May, 1918 to August 15, 1918," 27 August 1918, RG 120, carton 26.

21. *Official History of the 82nd Division*, 5–10.

22. Typed copy, "Regimental History of the 319th Field Artillery," 21 December 1918, RG 120, carton 25.

23. HQ, U.S. Troops Aboard the *Karmala*, 3 May 1918, ibid., carton 93.

24. Memoir by PFC Thurmond J. Baccus in the U.S. Army Military History Institute's World War One Survey, Carlisle Barracks, PA. This document is found in folders for the 326th Infantry, carton 3, [hereafter cited as MHI with appropriate collection].

25. Typed copy, "Regimental History of the 319th Field Artillery," 21 December 1918, RG 120, carton 25.

26. HQ, 82nd Division, Armies and Corps in Which the 82nd Division Has Served, c. January, 1919, ibid., carton 1.

27. For a full discussion of this problem and the AEF solutions see my *Pershing and His Generals: Command and Staff in the AEF* (Westport, CT: Praeger, 1997).

28. War Department to Swift, 27 August 1917, RG 120, carton 69.

29. McAndrew to Burnham, 5 June 1918, ibid., carton 68.

30. McAndrew to Burnham, 6 June 1918, ibid.

31. Bjornstad to Wainwright, 29 May 1918 in the Wainwright Papers, MHI, carton 2.

32. Beebe to Burnham, 24 September 1918, ibid.

33. Lieutenant General John H. Lee, "Service Remeniscences," John H. Lee Papers, MHI, 37.

34. McAndrew to Beebe, 13 June 1918, RG 120, Carton 68. A copy of this document was forwarded by Beebe to every brigade, regiment, and battalion. Those copies are also found in carton 68.

35. HQ, 82nd Division, G3, Memorandum no. 43, 8 June 1918, ibid., carton 103.

36. Boyd to Burnham, 8 June 1918, ibid., carton 85.

37. Conference Proceedings, 9 April 1918, in Records Group 165, Records of the War Department, General and Special Staffs, British Military Records, National Archives, Washington, DC., carton 8, [hereafter cited as RG 165 with appropriate carton].

38. British Memorandum to AEF, 1 May 1918, RG 120, carton 6.

39. British Training Schedule for the 82nd Division, undated, ibid., carton 91.

40. HQ, 82nd Division, General Staff Memorandum no. 29, 30 May 1918, ibid., carton 1.

41. War Diary, 66th Division, British, RG 165, carton 8.

42. Pike to Beebe, 3 June 1918, RG 120, carton 91.

43. Memorandum to Field Marshall Douglas Haig, 28 May 1918, RG 165, carton 8. Those American units, in the order of their arrival, were: 77th, 82nd, 35th, 28th, 4th, 30th, 27th, 33rd, 78th, and 80th divisions.

44. George McIntosh Sparks, *The 327th under Fire* (n.p.: c. 1920), 22. *Official History of the 82nd Division*, 11–13.

45. Statement by PFC Julius Olsen Knud, 163rd Infantry Brigade, 82nd Division

Questionnaires, MHI.

46. Typed copy, "History of the 157th Field Artillery Brigade," c. March, 1919, RG 120, carton 22.

47. Typed copy, "Regimental History of the 319th Field Artillery, 21 December 1918, ibid., carton 25.

48. Diary entry, 22 June 1918, Rhodes Diaries, entitled, "Diary of the World War," Rhodes Papers, MHI.

49. Diary entry, 3 July 1918, Ibid.

50. Diary entry, 4 July 1918, ibid.

51. Diary entry, 19 July 1918, ibid.

52. This change in artillery spotting and firing was fully discussed in my *The U.S. Air Service in the Great War, 1917–1919* (Westport, CT: Praeger, 1996).

53. Conference proceedings, 9 April 1918, RG 165, carton 8.

54. War Diary of the 307th Ammunition Train.

55. G3, 82nd Division, Synopsis of 32nd Corps Order no. 3179/3, 23 June 1918, ibid., carton 1.

56. Ibid.

57. Sparks, *The 327th under Fire*, 23–25.

58. *Official History of the 82nd Division*, 14.

Chapter 4

In the Trenches at Lagney

By 27 June, 1918, the All-Americans were in the trenches under the watchful eyes of their French mentors. Four infantry battalions were in the forward trenches facing the Germans across no man's land. The 2nd Battalion, 325th Infantry; the 3rd Battalion, 326th Infantry; the 3rd Battalion, 327th Infantry; and the 2nd Battalion, 328th Infantry had moved quietly into the trenches at night. One of the other battalions of each regiment was in the second trench, and the other battalion was in reserve.[1] Relieving the 26th Division while in contact with the enemy was a tricky maneuver, which both divisions conducted quite well. It was a good start for the 82nd Division's introduction to the deadly environment of the trenches.

While the infantry acclimated to the miserable existence of the Western Front, some enterprising 82nd Division soldiers found ways to improve their conditions. While not actually in the trenches, the men were billeted in barns, houses, and vacant buildings behind the lines. Sergeant Major Benjamin Heath of Headquarters, 82nd Division, was assigned a room that to which he took an instant dislike. Being an enterprising senior NCO, he and another sergeant found a room, "at the rate of one franc (18¢) a night and now we have a soft down feather bed to rest our weary bones in at night."[2] Private Elmer T. Jones of Company I, 325th Infantry, was shocked to see no young people near the front. He told his parents that "everyone you meet is old."[3]

The month of July was very hot and dry, and dust was everywhere. The Germans across no man's land seemed content to let the Americans carry out patrols and periodic raids against their positions without severe retaliation. The French artillery supporting the 82nd and the French in the trenches was battle-wise, firing only when it was absolutely necessary to support a raid or a stranded patrol. Casualties remained light during the entire period at Lagney, except for 327 soldiers wounded by gas attacks. The division could well look upon the month in the trenches near St. Mihiel as a period of training under combat conditions.[4]

The 82nd Division had entered the trenches with a definite manpower shortage.

Brigadier General Harold B. Fiske, Pershing's G5, or chief of training, had calculated that the division was short thirty-eight officers and 3,425 enlisted men. Fiske was a hard-driving, no-nonsense officer who personally observed training and kept meticulous records. He felt that the shorthandedness hampered training in the 82nd Division, but in July he reported that the situation had cleared up somewhat: the division now needed only twenty-one officers and 1,321 enlisted soldiers to reach the number required for an AEF combat division.[5]

General Burnham took the opportunity to continue the organizing and training of his staff. Few National Army divisions would have the luxury of training in such a quiet area, and Majors Wainwright and Lee took advantage of the time to exercise their G3 and G2 sections in various combat functions. The first order of business was instituting a system for collecting reports from the infantry brigades. With activity at a minimum it was a good time to force the subordinate commands to adhere to a set procedure. Wainwright's G3 section received a standardized report from the 163rd and 164th Infantry brigades at 6:30 a.m. every day. A second daily report would be sent by courier to the divisional G3 at 3:30 p.m. The reports thus covered a twelve-hour period and gave the commander, chief of staff, and the staff members an up-to-date picture of the division. The G3 made it clear that the brigades were to establish a time schedule by which their regiments and other units would send reports to the brigade staff.[6] The commander's guidance to his subordinate unit was also clear in regard to any emergency or rapidly changing situation: the situation was to be reported by telephone. Wainwright designated a rotation of G3 officers to be present at all times to receive telephone calls from subordinate units.

Major John Lee's G2 section had the responsibility for maintaining the divisional situation map. This procedure had been established by Pershing's G2, Brigadier General Dennis Nolan, and was required of AEF divisional G2 sections. Lee did not require a separate report from the brigade intelligence officer but drew heavily from the situation reports submitted to Wainwright. Lee's written guidance was to report all changes in position of friendly troops during the twelve-hour reporting period, down to platoon level. Reports had to be as detailed as possible, giving the old and new coordinates of units.[7] Once that information was received it was posted on the map used by the commander and the entire staff.

This reporting may sound mundane, representative of an army's desire for paperwork, but it was not. The day of a commander mounted on his horse watching his units in combat with the enemy was over. The modern battlefield required instant communication between the general and his subordinate commands. The depth of defense at Lagney was over five kilometers, and one infantry battalion covered a front of half a kilometer. The entire divisional frontage could be over six to ten kilometers in length. Artillery fired from unseen guns directed by balloon and observation aircraft made dispersal a life-saving necessity. The addition of a field signal battalion to a division was a clear indication that communications had a high priority on the World War One battlefield. Sometimes in severe weather or when wires were torn by artillery fire, couriers, pigeons, and the like had to be used, but the divisional and brigade commanders relied on the telephone for instant battlefield communications.

A standing operating procedure for reports and activities had to be established as well. The staffs of the American divisions were too large to be haphazard about the acquisition of operational and intelligence information. The divisional commander and his staff could not see the battlefield and could not rely on piecemeal information. They would have a difficult time absorbing the battlefield reports and field messages that would pour into a division headquarters in the heat of battle. The twelve-hour reports were the foundation upon which the division commander built his grasp of the battlefield; the special messages were placed on that foundation. Lieutenant Colonel R. E. Beebe, chief of staff, constantly reinforced his commander's insistence that all reports be submitted on time. To do otherwise was to risk confusion and misunderstanding in the combat information center of the division. Pershing's General Headquarters, AEF, required reports from the divisions, and when the first United States Army was activated for combat, reports to that headquarters would be required promptly, with no toleration for lateness.

To add importance to the training at all levels of command and staff was the fact that the French Eighth Army Commander intended to turn the entire Lagney sector over to Burnham's 82nd Division in early July.[8] The French XXXII Corps commander had agreed to turn over the sector, leaving artillery in place until the 157th Field Artillery Brigade could move from La Courtine to Toul and then to the divisional area. There was no time just to allow procedures to evolve. They had to be set and followed before the handover to the 82nd Division. Once the transition was completed the 82nd would have to rely primarily on its own commanders and staff officers to function in the face of the enemy, and there would be little margin for error.

Once Burnham was certain that the French 154th Division would be withdrawn he began to fret about his division. On 7 July formal orders arrived that the French would indeed turn over the entire Lagney sector to the 82nd Division. After a conference with his staff, Burnham wrote to U.S IV Corps commander to point out the problems that faced the division. The All-Americans occupied the entire frontage occupied by the recently departed 26th Division plus about 3,500 extra meters. He was short a full company of infantry and a full company of military police (they had been detailed to procure horses for the division), as well as the entire 307th Supply Train. In addition, a hundred infantrymen had been detailed to move supplies. Six out of nine machine gun companies were in training, and of course, the 82nd Division had no artillery or trench mortars. While the French had promised to assign artillery to the division, Burnham did not know the number of personnel or guns that the allies would leave. What Burnham wanted was a return of all troops, especially the 307th Supply Train; he told the corps chief of staff that the matter was urgent.[9]

A few days after Burnham's correspondence the French designated three artillery regiments to support the 82nd Division. The three regiments were combat veterans, and the French corps commander had every confidence in his troops. Colonel Pierre Gillette, commanding the 247th French Field Artillery Regiment, was designated by XXXII Corps as the chief of artillery for the 82nd Division. While

Burnham would have naturally preferred to have Rhodes's 157th Artillery Brigade in support, he now had some good, experienced gunners. The 82nd Division complied with the directives of the French XXXII Corps, and Gillette moved into division headquarters.[10]

The French also continued to feed intelligence reports to the division's G2, giving the staff section important information based on French intelligence expertise. Combat patrolling to obtain information about the enemy, terrain, obstacles, and the like was new for the Americans, and the French knew it. Their intelligence reports were detailed, especially as far as enemy order of battle and artillery was concerned. The G2 of the division had to rely heavily on this flow of important information.[11]

Realistically, the All-Americans were better off with experienced artillery than with the 157th, which was still in intensive training at La Courtine. The French also required the Americans to improve their positions constantly, by digging new trenches, constructing new firing positions for machine guns, and adding new wire obstacles. This constant work kept any complicated operations across no man's land at a minimum, which was wise.[12]

Colonel Schley's 307th Engineers received special attention from the French. The French wanted the 307th to build strong points, what they called Groupes de Combat. The strong points would be covered by machine gun fire from positions also prepared by the engineers. The reasoning was simple: if the Germans attacked in mass the strong points and supporting machine guns would provide concentrated or massed fires. The strong points would be in a new line of trenches just behind the old first trench, and they would be protected by new lines of barbed wire and other obstacles. A Company, for example, constructed six of those Groupes de Combat, dug three thousand yards of new trench, and prepared twelve thousand yards of new wire and obstacles. Other units did the same type of work, including constructing pillboxes and new command dugouts. Schley's engineers prepared the work plans, and the French corps and army headquarters approved them. Experienced French combat engineers monitored the work, making suggestions and adding much- needed expertise.[13] With all this work going, Burnham continued to request the return of detached troops to the division.

Burnham's urgent requests fell on deaf ears at corps and at AEF headquarters. The Lagney sector was quiet, and troops were simply not going to be returned from such critical details as procuring horses. Harold B. Fiske had noted the shortages, but his reports acknowledged that Lagney was a quiet sector that should be devoted to realistic training. To be sure, the allied high command, including Maréchal Ferdinand Foch, Marshall Sir Douglas Haig, and General Pershing, was certain that another German offensive was imminent, but the chances of a strong German blow falling on the Americans in training opposite the St. Mihiel salient seemed nil. Pershing began to have serious questions about Major General Burnham's command ability and judgment. The attitude at corps and at the AEF headquarters at Chaumont was that the 82nd should continue to train for that time when the First U.S. Army was activated for combat operations.

Questions of grand military strategy were of little consequence to the men in the trenches learning the hard lessons of war, and learning many of them the hard way. On the night of 5–6 July a patrol from Company A, 327th Infantry, blundered into the German wire and was discovered and fired upon. At the end of the brief fire-fight two Americans were dead and two wounded. The firing prompted a German artillery barrage of both gas and high- explosive shells aimed at the American trenches.[14]

While in the trenches the 82nd had its first contact with hostile aircraft. The division was not different from any other American unit in that at first it regarded airplanes as a novelty. The men quickly found out that the arrival of a German *avion* usually meant that an artillery barrage would follow. Sometimes German planes bombed the Americans. Sergeant Major Benjamin Heath of the division headquarters wrote to his sister,

> These beautiful moonlight nights are very tempting to Fritz and nearly every night now you can hear the hum of planes overhead and the shells bursting in air. Its lots of fun to see them [allied aircraft] chasing them around. There are anti-aircraft guns all around us on the hills and they don't mind waking us up out of a sound sleep. But we have gotten so used to them that we wake up, grunt, turn over and to sleep again and hope they won't drop any bombs on us.[15]

One suspects that Heath's description of the lackadaisical attitude of the doughboys to planes was for his sister's comfort. On the night of 15–16 July German recon-naissance planes directed a heavy gas and high-explosive bombardment on the forward trenches.[16]

At division headquarters Burnham and his G2 and G3 were increasingly concerned over the air war. Few American officers prior to 1917 had had any experience with air as a combat weapon. General Pershing, who devoted a good deal of time to the AEF's Air Service, had used the 1st Aero Squadron on his Mexican expedition of 1916–1917, but the squadron had flown antiquated aircraft unsuited for operations even south of the border. The AEF was building its Air Service into a respectable and formidable combat force, but few ground soldiers had ever worked with airplanes or balloons. Major Jim Wainwright constantly re-corded all friendly and enemy air activity, and it did not take him long to figure out that when "the balloon goes up" accurate artillery fire was not far behind.[17]

In Wainwright's operations reports the activity of enemy infantry usually merited a sentence, but aeronautics accounted for several detailed paragraphs. Wainwright also took care to report all antiaircraft fire. The 82nd Division was learning that the World War One battlefield was a three-dimensional one, with height being as important as width and depth. However, until the 157th Field Artillery Brigade rejoined the division there would be little opportunity actually to see friendly air fully integrated with ground forces.

The operations reports detailed the patrol activities of the division, but they did not reveal that Burnham was fuming again over an old problem. There had been a number of injuries due to soldiers' incomprehension of the English language. These incidents usually occurred when patrols came in through the wire or sentinels challenged soldiers who could not properly respond. A serious incident on the night of 1 July angered Burnham considerably. A ten-man combat patrol had been sent from Company E, 325th Infantry, to gather information about enemy wire and obstacles. Nothing went right; six soldiers became lost as soon as they were beyond the wire obstacles guarding the 82nd's trenches. When the lost soldiers approached the American trench the sentinel challenged one of them three times, with no response forthcoming. The worried guard threw a hand grenade, and the figure in the night ran.

A few minutes later another guard challenged a man who also did not respond. This guard, a Private Adamson, opened fire, hitting the presumed infiltrator. The wounded man called out "Me American!" whereupon Adamson asked several questions in English but got responses that sounded Italian. An Italian-speaking soldier was found who called out to the wounded man and discovered that he was Private Frank Billota of Company E, 325th Infantry, who could speak only Italian. The remainder of the patrol, found in a confused state, could not speak English either. Once they had become separated from their English-speaking lieutenant they had had no way of safely returning to the American trenches.[18]

A few days later, after an investigation into the shooting of Private Billota, Burnham fired an angry letter directly to the Adjutant General in Washington protesting that the division still had over a thousand soldiers who could not speak English. Specifically citing the Billota incident, Burnham wrote, "Their presence in the division, as well as being a menace to the safety of themselves and their comrades, tends to reduce the morale of their organizations."[19]   This letter went to the Adjutant General, who even before the 82nd Division had left the United States for duty in France had made his position clear in regard to separating soldiers from the division. There was no response to the letter.

Burnham was not content to let the matter rest, however. He resurrected the issue in late August with AEF General Headquarters, citing the various incidents and the lack of any response from the Adjutant General or the War Department. General Burnham now suggested that over a thousand soldiers be transferred from the 82nd Division to the Service of Supply for duties behind the front lines.[20] This request came at a time when the 82nd Division was forty-one officers and 1,378 enlisted men short of full strength.[21] With the recent formation of the First United States Army under the command of General Pershing, and with plans being made for the first American-planned and commanded offensive, against the St. Mihiel salient, any request to weaken a combat division met an icy response from Chaumont. The letter to GHQ, AEF, added to a growing suspicion at Pershing's headquarters that Burnham was not up to the job of commanding the 82nd Division in combat. It also appears that the G1 at both First Army and GHQ, AEF, regarded Burnham's problems with non–English speakers as in the same category as soldiers who were illiterate. It seems that higher headquarters did not understand fully what Burnham's problems were. But of course a division commander's complaints came at a very hectic time for the St. Mihiel planners.[22]

Possibly Burnham was also aggravated about the slow pace of patrolling no man's land and the enemy wire. The daily operations reports show that patrols were sent out on a regular basis, but little seemed to be accomplished. Certainly not every problem could be charged to language difficulties. There was very little detailed information from patrols to help Major Lee's G2 section construct a coherent picture of the enemy's order of battle. On 15 July, to end this state of affairs Burnham offered a reward of a thousand francs to the soldier or patrol that captured the first German prisoner.[23] Even the lure of a sizeable number of very spendable French francs had no effect.

Weeks went by, and no enemy prisoners were taken. Neither Burnham nor Wainwright could figure out why there was such a dismal record in patrolling. Certainly such negative reports to GHQ, AEF, would not inspire confidence in the All-American division. On 31 August, with the St. Mihiel offensive less than two weeks away, Burnham sent a blistering memorandum to his subordinate commanders. He began by pointing out that the 82nd had been in the trenches for eight weeks and had captured no enemy soldiers. On the other hand, the division had lost men to the Germans. GHQ, AEF, had been provided no useful information about the enemy; all Pershing's G2 had were question marks as to what faced the 82nd Division. "You are directed to obtain prisoners," Burnham ordered.[24]

Having ordered the taking of prisoners, the obviously irritated commander declared that the men were being improperly prepared for their missions. Battalion intelligence officers had to be involved in the process of patrol planning, because it was they who first received patrol reports, saw enemy prisoners and documents, and assisted the battalion operations officers in preparing for the missions. Each brigade was required to submit to division headquarters a plan for a substantial raid on enemy trenches, and the 307th Engineers were directed to obtain information as to enemy wire, obstacles, and terrain.[25] General Burnham's intent was unmistakable and his guidance was clear, but operations and intelligence reports show little concrete results. It had done Burnham little good to issue such a memorandum, because his subordinate commanders had already detected problems with aggressive patrolling, in early July. Marcus D. Cronin, commanding the 163rd Brigade, and Julian R. Lindsey, commanding the 164th Brigade, were solid, if unspectacular, professional soldiers, and their regimental commanders were also good, but there was something lacking as far as the troops were concerned. Brigadier General Lindsey investigating a penetration of his lines by a German patrol on the night of 5–6 July, found that there had been little reaction by the Americans. The patrol had focused on a group of demolished buildings that had once been the village of Xivray. The Germans had taken the town with almost no effort, the Americans firing only two shots at the aggressive enemy. One outpost of seven soldiers, bypassed by the Germans, had slept through the entire incident. Lindsey was furious that only two shots had been fired when the German movement could have been at least contested. His report ended,

> There is no reason whatever to believe that the hostile patrol failed to accomplish what they intended—not the slightest. There appears to be no ground whatever for any self-congratulations on this little affair.[26]

During the action at Xivray, an American lieutenant had called for artillery fire on the ruined town. This request had gone to battalion headquarters at 2 a.m., but the French had not fired their barrage until after 4 a.m. This delay of two hours had been caused by poor liaison. The lieutenant had wanted the artillery in order to attack the Germans and retake Xivray, but with no fire support he had been unable to advance.[27] Needless to say, Lindsey was angry at the lack of response to a proper request for artillery. Lindsey did not mention language difficulties in the 328th Infantry Regiment as having contributed to the fiasco. It appeared to be a poor application of what had been taught by both the British and French. Obviously more had to be done to instill aggressiveness in officers, NCOs, and the troops.

To bolster the confidence of the troops who were to undertake patrols, the division decided to shift machine gun units to support the operations. On the night of 17 July, for example, the 319th Machine Gun Battalion and two companies of the 321st Machine Gun Battalion were allocated to the 164th Brigade. On the same night, two companies of the 320th Machine Gun Battalion arrived to support the 163th Brigade.[28] During the less-than-effective performance of General Lindsey's troops on 5–6 July there had been only one machine gun in the Xivray area, and it had done nothing. There would now be no lack of firepower for the brigades.

Aggressiveness among the soldiers of the 82nd would have to be achieved over time. It could come only through continual patrolling and raids against the enemy. While Burnham and his subordinate commanders pondered the best methods of instilling a "killer instinct" into the troops, other valuable training went on. Throughout July selected officers and NCOs were sent to the two AEF gas defense schools, at Chaumont and at Gondrecourt. The officers attended more specialized courses at Chaumont, while the NCOs went to Gondrecourt, where the emphasis was on "training the trainers." Only six officers and ten noncommissioned officers at a time were sent to the week-long schools.[29] The division encouraged brigade and regimental personnel officers to select qualified men from units not in the forward trenches. Consequently, no leaders were absent from their posts while their men were in the trenches.

The troops may still not have been comfortable with their individual weapons. Lindsey and others noted that when contact was made with the enemy there was little rifle fire. By the end of July the 82nd had established, with the agreement of the French, a firing range near the town of Menil-la-Tour, near division headquarters. The range was set up as a combat firing range; it was meant to be as realistic as possible. On the range each soldier drew a hundred rounds for his rifle and two hand grenades, soldiers armed with the pistol drew twenty-one rounds per man and two hand grenades. Each company had a machine gun platoon of one machine gun with three hundred rounds, to add realism. The combat course was designed to last for four hours for each infantry company.[30] It was one thing to train soldiers on a fixed range where the distance was known, such as the one at Norcross, Georgia, but the confusion, sounds, and movement of actual combat made it another matter. The troops had been introduced to such a course while training with the British, but there they had concentrated on accurate firing more than on combat operations.

There was no question about Burnham's intent or his guidance as far as the

Menil-la-Tour range was concerned. The infantry companies would adhere to the schedule, and no one would miss going through the course. Time would not be wasted; the troops would be transported to the course by train so as to take full advantage of the time allocated to them. Range guards would be posted at least an hour before the firing began, and mounted troops would sweep the area to ensure that no soldier or civilian had wandered into danger. The division G1 was to have all required transportation in place. The G4 would provide food, and the division munitions officer had the responsibility of seeing that ammunition was on hand.[31] It must have been clear that Burnham meant deficiencies to be corrected as quickly as possible, through well planned and realistic combat training. From all reports the range worked well; it operated from 26 July to 2 August and all companies completed it. Perhaps now the time and effort would pay off for the All-Americans.

The time was growing near when the 157th Field Artillery Brigade would rejoin the 82nd Division. The final brigade-level firing exercise would be complete by the end of July, and the brigade would leave La Courtine some time during the first week of August. General Burnham had requested in early July that the brigade be sent immediately to join the division, but Brigadier General Charles Rhodes resisted; Rhodes informed his division commander that the unit had only just received its guns and that until training was complete and equipment was allocated the 157th Brigade could not be of much help to the 82nd.[32] General Rhodes was being diplomatic with his superior officer, but it was clear that he had no intention of moving his artillerymen and their newly issued French guns until they were ready. Rhodes's predicament was also known to observers and inspectors from General Headquarters, AEF. It added to the feeling at Chaumont that perhaps Burnham was not the man to take the All-American Division into battle.

While at La Courtine, Rhodes restructured his entire staff, obtaining the services of Major D. M. Beere as the brigade Chief of Staff. Beere had graduated from the General Staff College at Langres, France, in the same class as Jonathon M. Wainwright, and he had been assigned to the 321st Field Artillery Regiment for a short period. As an assistant Beere had First Lieutenant S. W. Farnsworth, a graduate of Yale University and of the first officer's training course at Fort Oglethorpe, Georgia. Beere felt comfortable with Farnsworth, who was intelligent and required little direction or supervision. In the operations section Rhodes had Captains E. C. Gwaltney and J. K. Fornance, both experienced officers who had been with the brigade since Camp Gordon. The intelligence officer was still First Lieutenant John F. Brown, who had receive solid training from both the British and French.[33]

The 157th Brigade finally had two regiments of 75mm guns and one regiment of 155mm guns, supplied by the French. Firing was going well, and the French trainers were enthusiastic with the rapid progress of the artillery. Rhodes worked with his staff to build a solid foundation of standard procedures for reporting, receiving fire missions, and deploying the brigade's three regiments. It was obvious that the staff was using time wisely at La Courtine. Rhodes organized his staff into three functional areas, administration, operations, and supply. Of the three areas, the operations section was given the highest priority for personnel and training.[34]

Rhodes and Beere identified combat tasks essential to the brigade's mission. The first was relieving another artillery brigade in a sector. This required close coordination with the unit being relieved, and obtaining maps, firing data, and all available intelligence information about the enemy, especially the location of his guns. The second task was submitting standard reports to higher headquarters and receiving them from the regiments. The intelligence section had the task of ground and air observation and maintaining the battle map in the division headquarters. The divisional communications officer was in charge of all links within the brigade and with higher headquarters.[35] The brigade communications officer was First Lieutenant E. R. Watts, who had first been with the 26th Division. He had been in France since the fall of 1917 and was familiar with all types of communications equipment. A civilian telephone expert, Watts was a valuable member of the staff, but his battle tasks were daunting.[36]

The artillery brigade had to develop a well defined intelligence system, because of the nature of artillery combat in World War One. Most fire missions were indirect fire–against targets which the gunners could not see, but that could be plotted on a map. A constant flow of information from ground observers, aircraft, and balloons dictated that maps be constantly and accurately updated. Five separate maps were maintained by the division intelligence section: a sector map, an enemy artillery activity map, a regimental and battalion map showing all friendly positions, a map depicting all missions fired or to be fired, and one showing the front-line "trace" of the entire 82nd Division.[37]

The brigade intelligence officer was also responsible for the flow of information to and from the regiments and battalions, and that meant that he had to monitor the activities of intelligence personnel at lower levels. Also, the brigade developed a training program for observers. It included map reading, reporting, sketching, observing fire missions, scouting, identification of enemy uniforms and equipment, and recognition of friendly and enemy aircraft. All this training reflected Rhodes's basic guidance, which was simply, "Remember, open warfare may come."[38] For the intelligence personnel at brigade level there was little time for rest, and certainly little margin for error.

Charles Rhodes had every reason to be pleased with the overall progress of the brigade staff and the artillery regiments, but there were personnel problems which the general had to deal with. On 19 July the assistant provost marshal of the brigade was passing the Hotel Moderne in La Courtine when he heard raucous laughter. Although it was after the AEF- established curfew hours, he found inside Lieutenant Colonel Osmun Latrobe, executive officer of the 307th Ammunition Train, drinking with three subordinates. The officer requested him to leave the café, but Latrobe refused and remained in the bar, drinking, for another hour.[39]

Rhodes was furious at such a flaunting of established regulations and demanded that Latrobe explain his behavior. His defense was basically, "If we violated orders, thousands are violating orders daily throughout France and doing so as unconsciously as we did."[40] In Rhodes's mind a second lieutenant might make such an excuse, but certainly not a senior field-grade officer commanding a unit about to go into combat. He called Latrobe to his office and gave him a strong verbal reprimand. Rhodes pointed out to Colonel Ferdinand W. Kobbe, commander of the 307th Trains, that this was a serious breach of AEF orders and military discipline. He suggested that Latrobe's conduct be considered in regard to future promotion.[41]

Like any other commander in the AEF, Rhodes had to balance retaining officers against keeping a less-than-effective one. Knowing that in a very short time the 157th Field Artillery Brigade would leave La Courtine for active service with the division, Rhodes was particularly concerned that inefficient officers be weeded out. On the other hand, a replacement might be hard to find. The activation of the First U.S. Army and the planning for an American offensive made manpower a high-priority item for the AEF.

A good example of how Rhodes handled this sticky area is the relief and reassignment of First Lieutenant Thomas Ambrose of Battery B, 321st Regiment. Ambrose had been an enlisted man in the regular Army artillery for fourteen years, rising to the rank of first sergeant. When the United States entered the war, Ambrose had been commissioned and assigned to the 321st, but he did not have the necessary skill in mathematics to command a firing battery. Colonel Clarence Deems, commanding the regiment, had requested that Ambrose be transferred to the 307th Ammunition Train, where he could oversee the care of the train's rather sizeable number of horses.[42] General Rhodes simply said that the regiment, being a horse-drawn unit, could itself use Ambrose in that capacity. There would be no officer replacements until mid-September. In any case, "the 321st will be put to the limit of its resources very soon to properly care for the large number of untrained and sick horses which will be assigned to it." Rhodes stated that he would reconsider Ambrose's retention when the regiment was motorized, but for the time being Colonel Deems would keep and use Lieutenant Ambrose.[43]

By the first week of August, the 157th Field Artillery Brigade began its movement to rejoin the 82nd Division. The division had been given orders to prepare to be relieved by the 89th Division and to take up positions in the area of the city of Toul, a more active part of the line. Once at Toul the 82nd would have to be a complete combat division, ready for action. Toul was a staging area; when the division was totally assembled it would occupy trenches in the Marbache sector just north of the city—and (though the division knew nothing about it as yet) near the sector assigned to the 82nd Division in the upcoming St. Mihiel offensive.[44]

The preparation for handing over the Lagney sector to the 89th went well, as far as planning was concerned. The staff, under R. E. Beebe's supervision, produced a clear and coherent plan for the disengagement—a tricky business at best with the ever-watchful Germans only a few hundred yards away. To distract and deceive the Germans as to their intent, the 82nd became very aggressive, giving the impression that the All-Americans were conducting a series of trench raids. On 3 August the 307th Engineers fired seven and a half tons of various types of gas from ground-based projectors into the German lines, and the next night companies K and M of the 326th Infantry carried out a large and successful trench raid. The 320th Machine Gun Battalion gave good covering fire as the two companies penetrated deeply into the German lines.[45] There was no problem with aggressiveness in these well planned and commanded operations.

During the night of 4 August, while the massive trench raid was in progress, the men of the 82nd were treated to a remarkable sight. As the Germans returned artillery fire, Bernetta A. Miller of the YMCA, with the 82nd, brought the troops hot chocolate, cakes, and cigarettes. Despite the heavy artillery and small-arms fire she continued to bring these supplies. By dawn she was back at her YMCA hut making more hot chocolate for the soldiers in the trenches. For her service that night she was cited, along with some combat soldiers, for her "devotion to duty and disregard of personal danger," in the General Orders of the 82nd Division.[46]

These efforts made to mask the relief of the 82nd Division spurred the Germans to retaliate. While 89th Division doughboys were replacing the All-Americans on the night of 7 August, the Germans fired a massive bombardment of high-explosive shells mixed with large numbers of mustard gas rounds. It could not have come at a worse time. The 82nd's men had been under gas attack and artillery fire before, but the 89th's soldiers had never been under fire. The German attack cost the 89th Division over seven hundred casualties the first night it was in the trenches.[47] Experience paid off for the 82nd Division, which reported only seventeen casualties from the bombardment.[48] A useful comparison can be made between the two units. Despite Burnham's well-founded concern over the lack of patrolling skills and aggressiveness, the division had learned some valuable lessons in the Lagney area, as shown in its reaction to the German barrage on 7 August. These were skills which would serve the 82nd Division well in the battles of the fall of 1918. The trench raids, which were a success, must have been a reassurance for Burnham that the division was developing a solid combat attitude.

Despite some nagging problems, Burnham may well have left the trenches at Lagney with confidence in his division. The fighting during the last week before the handover to the 89th Division had shown great improvement in the infantry regiments and machine gun battalions. The men had shown themselves to be fairly competent combat soldiers in the trenches. The 157th Field Artillery Brigade was about to be reunited with the division, and there was every indication that Rhodes had a very proficient unit.

Burnham had not given up his idea of having a large number of non–English speaking soldiers transferred from the division, and accordingly there were growing doubts at Pershing's headquarters about Burnham's aptitude for combat command. The 82nd was short forty-one officers and 1,378 enlisted men when it entered the Marbache sector. Since the 82nd Division would be one of the divisions designated by First U.S. Army to make the initial assault into the St. Mihiel salient, it was not the time to surface old problems or try to shrink the division even more. The training period was over for the All-American division, and it was were about to embark on a new and even more deadly phase.

NOTES

1. *Official History of the 82nd Division, American Expeditionary Forces, 1917–1919*

(Indianapolis, IN: Bobbs-Merrill, 1919), 13–14.

2. Heath to his sister, 7 July 1918, in U.S. Army Military History Institute Archives, World War One Questionnaires, Carlisle Barracks, PA, 163rd Infantry Brigade, carton 1 [hereafter cited as MHI with appropriate collection or carton cited].

3. Jones to parents, 8 October 1918, ibid.

4. *Official History of the 82nd Division*, 15–16.

5. Training History of the 82nd Division for the Months of June and July, 1918 in the Harold B. Fiske Papers, Records Group 200, National Archives, Washington, DC, carton 2 [hereafter cited as RG 200 with appropriate collections and cartons].

6. HQ, 82nd Division, General Staff Memorandum no. 73, 27 June 1918, in Records Group 120, Records of the AEF, 82nd Division, National Archives, Washington, DC, carton 1 [hereafter cited as RG 120 with appropriate carton].

7. Ibid.

8. Proceedings of a Conference held approximately 1 July 1918, ibid., carton 3.

9. Burnham to IV Corps Chief of Staff, 8 July 1918, ibid., carton 91.

10. HQ, 82nd Division, General Orders No. 12, 25 July 1918, ibid., carton 111.

11. G2, 154th Infantry Division (French) to HQ, 82nd Division, Memorandum No. 110, 30 June 1918, ibid., carton 8.

12. *Official History of the 82nd Division*, 14–15.

13. Typed copy, Chronological History—307th Engineer Regiment, 28 February 1919, RG 120, carton 28.

14. George McIntosh Sparks, *The 327th under Fire* (n.p.: c. 1920), 28. Also HQ, 82nd Division, Operations Report no. 9, 6 July 1918, RG 120, carton 7.

15. Heath to sister, 23 July 1918, Questionnaires, 163rd Infantry Brigade, MHI, carton 1.

16. Sparks, *The 327th under Fire*, 29. Also HQ, 82nd Division, Operations Reports nos. 19 and 20, 15 July and 16 July 1918, RG 120, carton 7.

17. These daily operations reports, compiled by Wainwright and Lee, approved by Beebe, contain detailed information giving an accurate account of the division's activities at Lagney. The reports went to the U.S. IV Corps and to the French. The G3 at Chaumont, Brigadier General Fox Connor, and the G5, Brigadier General Harold Fiske, also saw them. These reports appear in RG 120, carton 7.

18. HQ, 82nd Division, Special Order no. 3, 5 July 1918, RG 120, carton 73.

19. Burnham to Adjutant General, 12 July 1918, ibid.

20. Burnham to GHQ, AEF, 26 August 1918, ibid.

21. Training History of the 82nd Division for the Month of August, RG 200, carton 2.

22. Marginal note made by G1 Section, First U.S. Army on Burnham's letter of 26 August 1918, RG 120, carton 73.

23. HQ, 82nd Division, General Staff Memorandum no. 110, 15 July 1918, ibid., carton 1.

24. HQ, 82nd Division, General Staff Memorandum no. 187, ibid.

25. Ibid.

26. Brigadier General Julian R. Lindsey, Report of "That Little Affair at Xivray," 5 July 1918, ibid., carton 16.

27. Brigadier General Julian R. Lindsey, Preliminary Report on the 2nd Affair at Xivray, 6 July 1918, ibid.; HQ, 82nd Division, Operational Report no. 9, 6 July 1918, ibid., carton 7.

28. HQ, 319th Machine Gun Battalion, Bulletin no. 1, 16 July 1918, ibid., carton 22.

29. HQ, 82nd Division, General Staff Memorandum no. 98, 9 July 1918, ibid., carton 1.

30. HQ, 82nd Division, General Staff Memorandum no. 144, 27 July 1918, ibid., carton 10.

31. HQ, 82nd Division, General Staff Memorandum no. 141, 26 July 1918, ibid.

32. Rhodes to Burnham Memorandum, 8 July 1918, ibid., carton 25.

33. Typed copy, History of the Brigade Headquarters, 157th Field Artillery Brigade, c. March 1919, ibid., carton 22.

34. HQ, 157th Field Artillery Brigade, Report on Staff Organization, 16 August 1918, ibid., carton 22.

35. Ibid.

36. History of the Brigade Headquarters.

37. HQ, 157th Field Artillery Brigade, Information Memorandum no. 3, 23 July 1918, ibid., carton 22.

38. Ibid.

39. First Lieutenant A. P. Ringressy, Memorandum, 20 July 1918, ibid., carton 93.

40. Latrobe to Rhodes, 23 July 1918, ibid.

41. Rhodes to Kobbe, 27 July 1918, ibid.

42. Deems to Rhodes, 6 July 1918, ibid., carton 68.

43. Rhodes to Deems, 7 July 1918, ibid.

44. HQ, 82nd Division, Field Orders no. 10, 15 August 1918, ibid., carton 9.

45. *Official History of the 82nd Division*, 14–15: Chronological History—307th Engineer Regiment, 28 February 1919, RG 120, carton 28.

46. HQ, 82nd Division, General Orders no. 1, 13 January 1919, ibid., carton 85.

47. C. J. Masseck, *Official Brief History of the 89th Division, U.S.A.* (n.p.: War Society of the 89th Division, c. 1919), 7–8. The 82nd Division tried to assist the hard-pressed men of the 89th; see, Sparks, *The 327th under Fire*, 30–31.

48. *Official History of the 82nd Division*, 16.

Chapter 5

The Marbache Sector

A few days before the 82nd began its move from the Langey sector to the new positions at Marbache in the Moselle Valley, Major General William P. Burnham announced that insignia for the division had been approved: a red square with a blue circle on which was a double A in white, standing for the nickname of the division—the All-American.[1] General Pershing had so far forbidden the wearing or display of any unit-distinctive insignia for operational security reasons, but at some point in the future the men of the 82nd Division would be able to wear the square red, white, and blue double-A patch, a visual reminder that this division, with so many soldiers who could not speak English, was the All-American, the epitome of the American ideal, the melting pot.

While morale builders were important, the 82nd Division had other serious matters to concern itself with. The division was shifting to the Marbache sector, and the 157th Field Artillery Brigade and the majority of the 307th Ammunition Train were leaving La Courtine for Marbache. En route, however, the artillery brigade was diverted to the vicinity of the fought-over city of Chateau Thierry.[2] The First U.S. Army had decided to use it to support combat operations along the Vesle River; the brigade went into position as an artillery reserve for III Corps. Combat operations there went well, however, Rhodes received orders to prepare his unit for a movement to the Marbache area.[3] No sooner had Rhodes's staff prepared the movement orders than word reached it that two battalions were to be sent to the 89th Division, holding the Lagney sector. On the afternoon of 20 August, accordingly, Battery A of the 1st Battalion, 319th Field Artillery, opened fire on German trenches at Lagney.[4] The 157th Field Artillery was finally in combat with the enemy, at least two of its battalions were. Given the quietness of the Marbache sector, the temporary separation of two battalions would not present much a problem for Rhodes. At any rate the gunners were gaining valuable experience, and the division would have the 2nd Field Artillery Brigade of the first-class 2nd

Infantry Division in support at Marbache.[5]

For Burnham and the 82nd, things had to go well at Marbache. The division had been selected to participate in the offensive to reduce the St. Mihiel salient; this operation was the first real American combat mission of the war. When General Pershing had left Washington for France he had been given a simple set of orders: he was to go to France, take command of the American Expeditionary Forces, and form an American army under American commanders to fight in an American-designated sector of the Western Front. "Black Jack" Pershing never deviated from these instructions, given to him by Secretary of War Newton Baker with the full blessing of President Woodrow Wilson.[6] The allies were continually frustrated by Pershing's focus on building up the AEF and on training it. The general and his headquarters constructed an American force comprising infantry divisions, a massive supply system, an Air Service, a tank corps, and all the other components of a contemporary army. When the United States had entered the war in April 1917, it had not possessed a functional combat division. A little over a year later Pershing had almost two million soldiers and a modern and technologically integrated—albeit untried—army.

John J. Pershing had been stubborn with the allies and ruthless with his subordinates. He had set a standard for command and sent back to the United States a number of generals who could not measure up to his intellectual and physical guidelines. Pershing constantly demanded that the AEF be prepared for "open warfare"; he firmly believed that only when the infantrymen left their trenches and maneuvered against the enemy could the stalemate of the Western Front be broken. While he got along personally with Maréchal Ferdinand Foch of France and Marshal Sir Douglas Haig of Great Britain, Pershing made it irritatingly clear that he believed that four years of trench warfare had sapped the fighting spirit of their armies. Pershing's orthodoxy was open or maneuver warfare, and generals who deviated from or did not fully believe in it were liable to find themselves on a nearly empty troopship going back to the United States.

On 6 August combat operations ceased along the Vesle River, where nine American divisions and support units, totaling 300,000 troops, had fought on the ground and in the air. Bowing to the inevitable, Foch now agreed to the formation of the First U.S. Army; Pershing took command on 9 August. The next day Pershing's brilliant chief of staff, Brigadier General Hugh A. Drum, began planning for the St. Mihiel operation, scheduled to begin on 12 September.[7] St. Mihiel would, he hoped, prove the Pershing orthodoxy, when American soldiers swept from two sides into the salient and faced the Germans on open ground. During the heavy fighting along the Vesle and Ourq rivers in July Pershing had committed the 1st, 2nd, 3rd, 4th, 26th, 28th, 32nd, 42nd, and 77th divisions.[8] Of these nine, only one, the 77th, had been a National Army division. The 77th had arrived in France about the same time as the 82nd, but because of its organization it had been thrown into the Vesle fighting. If the St. Mihiel operation was to be a success, and if the First U.S. Army was to prepare for the subsequent major operation in the Meuse-Argonne area, more National Army units would be needed for the fight.

Once First Army was operational, Pershing's standing demands for high-quality commanders were implemented in corps and divisions. Brigadier General Malin Craig, chief of staff of I Corps, notified all subordinates commanders that they were to evaluate their own subordinate commanders; if any were found incompetent or physically not up to the demands of the upcoming offensive, they were to be replaced. A suitable replacement might not be found in time for the offensive, but it was better to have a subordinate in command than an inefficient officer.

Then Craig added a warning for General Burnham:

> One of the objects of these reports is to enable the Corps Commander [Hunter Liggett] to confirm his ideas of a very unsatisfactory state of discipline which, as far as outward appearances go, applies to several elements of the 82nd Division which have been visited by officers from these headquarters.[9]

Major General Hunter Liggett, commanding I Corps, was a no-nonsense officer who had the distinction of having faced down General John J. Pershing. When Liggett arrived in France Pershing had been ready to send him back to the United States because of his obesity. Liggett confronted Pershing and in effect told him to withhold action until he saw him in command. Pershing never had reason to regret backing down; Liggett became an important, and imposing, figure in the AEF. Like Pershing, he could be rigid in his enforcement of the regulations, but more importantly, he was a staunch advocate of the Pershing orthodoxy. A number of inefficient officers were relieved and reassigned from the 82nd Division in compliance with I Corps orders. The most severe housecleaning came in Brigadier General Julian R. Lindsey's 164th Infantry Brigade, where both regimental commanders were deemed to be inefficient and incompetent. General Lindsey recommended that Colonel Hunter B. Nelson, commanding the 328th Regiment, be reclassified: "lack of energy, no initiative, no force, poor administrator, incapable of training a regiment for combat." The commander of the 327th fared little better; Lindsey stated that Colonel Frank D. Ely had failed to bring his regiment up to standard. Lieutenant Colonel Richard Wetherill, who had begun his service as the division's machine gun officer and who was now serving in the 328th, was to be assigned to replace Nelson in command of the 328th.[10] Ely, however, remained in command of his regiment through St. Mihiel and into the Meuse-Argonne offensive.[11]

Lindsey also asked that the regiment's chief medical officer, Major H. B. Burnett, be relieved for inefficiency. Burnham balked, because Burnett had rendered good service as commander of the division's Sanitary Train before being assigned to the 328th Infantry. Lindsey was told only that Burnett's case would be investigated.[12] It would not be a good idea, reckoned Burnham, to have a complete turnover in the 164th Infantry Brigade with the St. Mihiel attack only a few days away.

In striking contrast was the report of Brigadier General Marcus Cronin, commander of the 163rd Brigade. If nothing was right with Lindsey's command, everything was going well with Marcus and his regimental commanders. Cronin wrote that Colonel Walter M. Whitman, a regular commanding the 325th Regiment, was "an excellent officer . . . a good leader of men . . . qualified for tactical command of a regiment or brigade." Colonel John C. McArthur, also a regular, commanding the 326th Infantry, was equally qualified to take command at a higher level. As Cronin pointed out, each commander had eleven months' experience as a commander and had shown promise as a leader of men in combat. Cronin had no one who he believed was incompetent or should be relieved.[13]

Colonel Bryan Conrad, commanding the 307th Trains, requested the relief of one of his supply majors who had a drinking problem and had made false statements to his commander. The officer had been a regular Army NCO for eighteen years; in 1916 he had applied for a commission in the Reserve Officer Corps as a captain and had begun commissioned service upon the outbreak of the war in 1917. In Conrad's opinion, his drinking was intolerable in a unit preparing for a major combat operation. Conrad had also believed that after so many years in the ranks as a sergeant, this officer lacked the education and skills to command men in combat.[14] Burnham agreed to the transfer, considering no major better than one who might stagger into a battle drunk.

A few days before the command screen, the 82nd Division had undergone a detailed inspection by officers from the Inspector General's office at Headquarters, 1st Army. The inspection had been directed by the Inspector General of the AEF, Major General André Brewster, a hard-nosed regular Army officer whose service with Pershing went back to early 1917. (Brewster had little tact and was known as one of the men John J. Pershing listened to. To fall afoul of General Brewster meant a short career in the AEF.) The inspection team was under Colonel J. C. Johnson, who had a reputation as Brewster's most demanding officer. Johnson had been personally selected by André Brewster to take the position of inspector at First Army. This was basically a pre-combat inspection, and Burnham understood clearly what was at stake for himself and the 82nd Division.

The inspection team arrived on 26 August and departed four days later after looking at every aspect of the division. The troops appeared to be in good physical condition, and their marks of discipline—saluting, wearing the uniform, and military courtesy—were noted as good. There seemed to be few problems that would require courts-martial, and the actual number of trials had been quite low. Johnson found that less than 1 percent of the troops in the division had been involved in courts-martial action. Obviously the troops had made progress with the basic skills of a soldier.[15] Military courtesy and a low incidence of major courts-martial were good indicators that the 82nd's command structure had stressed the small but important things that, when put together, made for an at least efficient, if not spectacular, combat unit.

Johnson was bothered, however, by shortages in key leadership positions within the division. Men had been sent back to the United States to help train the new National Army divisions being formed for service in France. For example, on 28 August, while Johnson was inspecting, each brigade lost two battalion intelligence officers and four intelligence NCOs in that way.[16] In addition to this levy, Captain John B. Thornhill, the division's assistant G2, was selected to be G2 in a newly formed division. On 2 September, only ten days before the St. Mihiel offensive,

Thornhill and other selected men departed for a troopship at Brest, France, for the trip home.[17] All divisions had been informed by Pershing's headquarters that after 1 October all regular Army officers who did not hold general staff positions or command of a battalion or regiment would be taken from their divisions and sent to tactical command positions.[18] How these critical shortages were to be made up was never spelled out by Pershing's headquarters. The only guidance from Chaumont was, "You will take steps at once to provide suitable substitutes not of the Regular Army for the positions mentioned."[19] This was again a process of robbing Peter to pay Paul, at a time that would be very critical in any division's history.

Regardless of the loss of key personnel, Johnson observed morale was high and soldiers were eager to patrol. When the inspecting officers talked with the troops there were no complaints. It seemed to Johnson that there were no pressures on the division due to language difficulties, and that all the men were capable of performing their combat missions. There was a spirit of confidence that the division could hold its trenches against an enemy attack or mount an offensive using open warfare techniques. Colonel Johnson believed that only the test of battle could really determine whether the 82nd was a functioning combat unit, and he recommended that it be given the chance in the upcoming offensive.[20]

While with the 82nd, Johnson took the opportunity to talk to Brigadier General Charles Rhodes about conditions within the division. Rhodes was considered by Pershing's headquarters to be a man destined for higher rank, probably the best general officer in the entire All-American Division. Johnson began asking probing questions, "feeling the pulse of the general officers," especially about Burnham's capacity for combat command. Rhodes was somewhat uncomfortable with the line of questioning, and he "recommended that he be given the opportunity to demonstrate his fitness to command in battle."[21] The cavalryman turned artillery brigade commander had no idea that Pershing had marked him for higher duties, and his loyalty to his present superior officer showed Johnson that Rhodes was a man of the highest military principles—a finding that would be relayed to "Black Jack" Pershing.

There were some problem areas that disturbed Johnson and his inspection team. One critical issue was the lack of combat ambulances in the 307th Sanitary Train. There simply were not enough motor vehicles to take care of wounded soldiers. While Johnson noted this in his report, the 82nd Division would not have a full ambulance section until a few days before going into battle in the Argonne Forrest in October.[22] The whole question of critical shortages in transportation merited special mention. The division was allocated 479 trucks to haul ammunition, food, cargo and the like; it had only 218, less than 50 percent of the number authorized. Of forty-five General Motors and Ford ambulances required for the division, there were only eleven. The Table of Organization and Equipment stated that the division was authorized 301 motorcycles, but only sixty-one were serviceable and ready for combat operations. There were almost no spare parts available to repair even the vehicles on hand.[23] Like almost all other AEF divisions, the 82nd would go into the St. Mihiel and the Meuse-Argonne offensives with a large number of horse-drawn vehicles.

Johnson's report to Malin Craig and Hunter Liggett was both fair and detailed. He felt that Burnham could indeed command the 82nd in combat. As Johnson said, the commander was, "quiet, fair minded, not excitable or nervous, capable of grasping the military situation and not favoring snap judgement." The inspector also felt that the staff was highly capable, and he gave high marks to Jonathon Wainwright as a first-class divisional G3. He felt that Brigadier General Lindsey had a tendency to be overly critical, while Cronin, the other infantry brigade commander, was a good, if unspectacular, commander. Of all the general officers of the All-American division, he felt, Brigadier General Charles Rhodes was perhaps the best, and in Johnson's opinion would give the best account in the upcoming offensive. In short, the 82nd Division, despite shortfalls in vehicles and spare parts, was ready for combat.[24]

Brigadier General Harold B. Fiske, Pershing's G5, visited the 82nd Division area to observe training and preparations for combat. His major concern was the shortage of troops. Fiske's reports indicate that the 82nd was short forty-one officers and 1,378 enlisted men.[25] That would not be a hindrance as far as the division's participation in the St. Mihiel operation was concerned. While the month in the Marbache sector had not been spent strictly training, in that soldiers had been in constant contact with the enemy through small arms fire, patrols, and artillery action, it was fairly clear that the division had been preparing and training for open warfare. Of particular importance was the guidance all commanders had given to be prepared for the time when they would leave the trenches and maneuver against the Germans. Rhodes's guidance to his subordinates was simple "It must be constantly borne in mind that it will be open warfare which will win the war."[26]

In the Marbache sector, the infantry regiments carried on aggressive patrolling. Plans were very specific, and unlike patrols in the Lagney sector, these involved large-unit actions and well-planned and executed raids. On the night of 25–26 August platoon-level or larger patrols went into no man's land to ambush the enemy and reconnoiter enemy defenses. During the night of 27–28 August two officers and fifty enlisted men made a lengthy reconnaissance of enemy positions on a hill behind enemy lines. Even larger patrols were dispatched during the night of 30–31 August to inspect enemy defenses and to bring in German prisoners for interrogation.[27] All of these patrols accomplished their missions with a minimum of casualties. This was a far cry from the hesitant actions in the Lagney sector, when Burnham had had to offer a reward for any German captured by a patrol.

While in the Marbache sector an old problem surfaced again. Regimental commanders were ordered to ascertain how many soldiers could speak no English at all. Within the 326th Regiment, for example, Colonel McArthur reported that over three hundred soldiers were "so ignorant of English and so incapable of learning it that they are a distinct menace to the efficiency of the Regiment."[28] If that were the case for all regiments, over a thousand soldiers would be lost, with little chance of replacement. Finally, after guidance from a frustrated Burnham, the number was pared down to a little over a hundred per regiment. When the 82nd Division sent a request to GHQ, AEF, that those soldiers be transferred to the Service of Supply for labor, the response was that that action would be taken.[29] However, the St. Mihiel offensive was nearing its start, and the General Headquarters at Chaumont never addressed Burnham's request. The All-American division would go into combat whether all could speak English or not. Probably the army had heard enough about language problems in the 82nd Division.

With First U.S. Army plans for the St. Mihiel offensive in high gear, there was little time for minor issues. The 82nd Division was part of Hunter Liggett's I Corps, which also had its requirements for planning. Liggett had decided to shift the 1st Division to a new attack position and replace it with the 90th Division. The 90th would thus be on the left flank of the 82nd, and new coordination measures would be required. The 90th Division, under the command of Major General Henry T. Allen, one of Pershing's favorite generals, was made up of well-schooled troops, mainly from Texas and Oklahoma. Once fighting began, the 90th, the "Tough Ombres," could be expected to be aggressive, driving hard toward any objective. This would place extra pressure on the 82nd to keep in contact with it and to maintain an equal aggressiveness in the attack. To complicate matters for Wainwright, who as G3 had the main responsibility for the divisional plans, the 82nd was astride the Moselle River. An infantry regiment—all there was room for be-tween the Moselle and the divisional boundary on Allen's right flank—would have to be especially well commanded to maintain contact, carry out its mission, and not lose sight of the sister regiments on the eastern side of the Moselle. This would be a delicate operation for a division like the 82nd, and it would require some detailed plans.

It was necessary that all the attacking divisions carry on routine operations while preparing for St. Mihiel. The defending enemy had to be kept in the dark as to intentions; any sudden change in the actions of a unit might signal that something was up. Obviously unit commanders would have preferred to rehearse their troops and stockpile ammunition and equipment, but that was not to be. The 2nd Division's artillery brigade was replaced by Rhodes's 157th starting on 22 August. Civilians observed the arrival of the troops and their guns, and no doubt some information found its way across the lines to the Germans, but that fitted in well with the scheme of things for the 82nd Division. Would the Germans suspect that a major offensive was in the offing if a combat division had just swapped out its artillery support?

The nature of the Marbache sector greatly irritated Rhodes and his artillerymen. It was truly a quiet zone and had been so since the French failed to reduce the St. Mihiel salient earlier in the war. "It was permitted to fire for registration but artillery must be careful not to hit any Germans. In fact, with the exception of our forward platoons, the guns were placed so far to the rear that it was impossible to clear our own lines," wrote a disgusted brigade staff officer.[30] Being fresh from their training at La Courtine, the gunners went to work and fired their guns as they were expected to do, registering targets and getting used to the terrain. Battery A of the 319th Field Artillery Regiment was the first to fire. The only variation was the firing of several short battalion and regimental barrages, but that was about as much as the entire brigade was allowed to do. [31]

Burnham and his staff could not have handled anything more than patrols and periodic artillery registration missions. The general and his adjutant and G1 were in the process of trying to juggle numbers and to shift officers around between various units. The two infantry brigades had reported that they were short of key personnel at the regimental and battalion level. While this was nothing new for the 82nd Division, the needed officers were not authorized by the Table of Organization and Equipment for a combat infantry division. All of the regiments needed gas officers, as did all of the battalions. Every regiment and battalion needed a munitions officer, to ensure the flow of ammunition, grenades, and the like to the troops. This officer would coordinate with the 307th Ammunition Train to arrange the prompt delivery of munitions, and he would continually inform the division munition officers and the commander of the 307th what the requirements would be. Not only were the infantry units affected by this shortage, but the three machine gun battalions were as well. The machine gun battalions requested that an officer be assigned as a battalion intelligence officer.

Burnham had to make hard and unpleasant choices as far as officers were concerned. He had either to let those critical positions go unfilled or assign second and first lieutenants from the combat units to fill them. Given the upcoming St. Mihiel operation, Burnham felt that it was more important to have soldiers moving ammunition and coordinating anti-gas efforts than to have platoon leaders in the infantry and machine gun companies. This meant that nearly twenty commissioned officers who had some training in munitions or anti-gas defense (and intelligence) left their units for service at a staff level.

Never one to suffer in silence, Burnham informed General Pershing of his decision and requested that those positions not now authorized on the Table of Organization and Equipment be added. This was perhaps not the time to drop this information on General Headquarters, AEF, but the general did.[32] Headquarters chose not to respond to his request for an increase of officers' billets within a division with the St. Mihiel operation only a few days away. In fairness to Burnham, Colonel Johnson's inspection had noted the critical shortage of trucks within the division. Coordination of ammunition deliveries would be difficult under the best of circumstances, but the attention of an officer might well be justified with hauling capabilities diminished.

The 307th Ammunition Train would have a task which was made more difficult by the fact that half of its transportation was horse-drawn. It had served mainly with the 157th Artillery Brigade during training at La Courtine and had undergone a great number of intensive, realistic exercises. While ready for service, it was hampered by a lack of vehicles and by the requirements for fodder and shelter. The horse-drawn elements needed to be near woods to conceal the animals, because once German aircraft or balloons spotted large concentrations of horses and mules they either called in artillery fire or sent aircraft to strafe the position. On 22 August the train headquarters began the process of relieving the 2nd Division's ammunition train, which had served its artillery in support of the 82nd Division. By the 27th of that month the relief was completed, and the 307th began the work of establishing a corps ammunition dump for the All-Americans to be used by the division in the upcoming offensive.[33] It remained to be seen, however, how effective the train would be once the division was engaged in open warfare, using large quantities of ammunition. The 82nd was not alone, however, in its heavy use of horse-drawn units; the entire AEF would suffer from this motor-horse mix in the following months.

Burnham had another real concern on the eve of the St. Mihiel offensive. Colonel Julien Schley, commander of the efficient 307th Engineer Regiment, was in Field Hospital No. 1 near Toul. On the night of 14 August, with the entire regiment on the move into new positions, Schley and his aide had been driving between units, overseeing the movement of the regiment. The roads had been crowded, as the 2nd Engineer Regiment of the 2nd Division was also on the march. With blackout conditions in effect, Schley's vehicle had an accident with another AEF vehicle. Schley, his aide, and his driver had been rushed to the field hospital. While the injuries were not life-threatening, there was no way to tell when Schley, whose unit was vital to combat operations, might return to his command. Lieutenant Colonel H. C. Mower, who had been with the 307th since September 1917 and who commanded the 1st battalion of the regiment, had to assume temporary command.[34] Mower was a good officer who would prove himself in combat, but both his battalion and the regiment would suffer from his having to divide time between the two jobs. Luckily for Burnham and for the 307th Engineers, a battered and bruised Schley was able to rejoin the 82nd Division in early September, a few days before the St. Mihiel offensive was due to commence. Once Schley returned to duty he retained Mower as his second in command, placing Major Eugene Kelly in command of the 1st Battalion.

In 1917 a twenty-eight-thousand-man infantry division called for a combat engineer regiment of over three thousand soldiers. This regiment was required to carry on all of the normal engineer functions of such a regiment and also to serve as an infantry reserve. The French XXXII Corps directed many of the activities of the regiment, which included fortifying trenches, building new, concrete-reinforced pillboxes, and roads into the Marbache line. With the growing emphasis on open warfare, the engineers were frustrated with the defensive, trench warfare–oriented nature of the work. As time drew near for the St. Mihiel offensive, however, pontoon-bridge instruction began, using an American-made "floating foot bridge." If doughboys were to advance against Germans over terrain crisscrossed with rivers and streams, such training was necessary. At the same time engineers were assigned to artillery batteries of the 157th brigade to instruct the artillerymen in hurried digging of gun emplacements. If artillery was to be displaced forward to support an American advance during St. Mihiel, temporary gun pits to protect troops would be vital.[35]

St. Mihiel began to occupy the attention of every unit in the 82nd Division. On 6 September Liggett's planners delivered the corps attack order to the major subordinate commands, setting the assault for 12 September. Almost immediately the division began to evacuate civilians from its area of activity. Concerned about enemy espionage and worried that civilians might get in the way of troop and supply movement, the 82nd's military police and other troops began the process of clearing the region.[36] Plans also called for shifting units into attack positions over a three-night period, but normal activities such as patrolling had to continue, to give a semblance of business as usual.[37]

Infantry patrols were assigned the task of mapping in detail enemy defenses in front of the 82nd Division. As the day for the attack approached, daylight patrols left the American trenches to test German positions. The Germans, or so the All-Americans found out, did not take this patrolling in stride. There was an increase in enemy air observation and counter-air-observation activities, and on the nights of 10 and 11 September, when the moon was full, the Germans launched several bombing and strafing raids all along the 82nd Division's sector. Enemy resistance to American reconnaissance also stiffened during the days prior to the attack.[38]

While the artillery was restricted as to what it could do, the brigade did carry on a vital intelligence function. Captain John F. Brown, the 157th's intelligence officer, kept meticulous logs detailing German activity all along the front. From air and ground observers Brown traced German tendencies in artillery firing, finding that the heaviest firing was around the Point-à-Mousson area on the west bank of the Moselle River.[39] That was of critical importance, because the 82nd would be active in that zone once the St. Mihiel operation began. Across the division's frontage, Brown reported, there were no less than four German balloons observing what the 82nd Division was doing. It was not until a few hours before the St. Mihiel offensive began that an allied plane downed one of the German balloons.[40]

Wainwright and the division G3 section had their St. Mihiel orders, and they prepared orders for the subordinate commands. This was going on all along the line for the divisions that would assault the salient. Infantry regiments sketched their objectives; the 307th Engineers parceled out companies to the regiments and to the artillery brigade, but priority went to the infantry. Everyone knew how much Pershing counted on this operation's going well, and General Burnham was aware that this was his own personal test of leadership in combat.

Charles Rhodes's preparations for the offensive were detailed and clear. His brigade had two problems: there had to be a continuos flow of ammunition to the guns, and Rhodes's artillery regiments and batteries had to be prepared to move forward to support the infantry advance. Given the shortage of artillery in an AEF division, planning had to be careful. Rhodes required that calculations be made and that two days' worth of ammunition be stockpiled. Once the ammunition fell below one day's supply the ammunition officer was to see that a full two days' resupply was received. There had to be close coordination between the brigade ammunition officer and elements of the 307th Ammunition Train designated to support the artillery.[41]

The operational planners set time periods for different types of fire. Once the battle began, priority went to the destruction of enemy artillery batteries and observation posts. This would continue for three hours. After the third hour, priority would be given to firing a mixture of high-explosive and gas shells against enemy artillery positions. After seven hours of bombardment the 157th Brigade's regiments would fire missions in predetermined sectors to support infantry operations. The batteries could fire at targets of opportunity or respond to calls for fire in volley at enemy positions. There was time for both controlled and flexible operation built into the fire plan.[42] How the 157th Brigade would function in the offensive, with air assets attached, was another matter, and only actual operations could really determine the competence of the brigade. Planning had been completed by Wainwright and his G3 section. The artillery and infantry brigades plus the engineer regiment had a clear idea of how the first day of the St. Mihiel offensive was to be conducted. The 163rd Infantry Brigade had the 320th Machine Gun Battalion attached, and the 164th the 321st Machine Gun Battalion. Brigade and regimental munition officers had a good supply of ammunition, including grenades and mortar rounds.[43] Unit commanders reported that all soldiers had steel helmets, gas masks, food rations, and all of the equipment necessary to carry out their assigned missions.

The 82nd Division had shown steady, if unspectacular, improvement since its arrival in France. The All-Americans at Marbache were very different from the soldiers who had had to be coaxed by a substantial cash award to get one German prisoner. The division was now intact with the arrival of Charles Rhodes's efficient 157th Brigade. Officers and noncommissioned officers had gained valuable training and experience, and the troops that served under them showed aggressiveness and tactical experience. It remained now for the All-American division to put all of the training and trench experience into practice in the upcoming St. Mihiel offensive.

NOTES

1. HQ, 82nd Division, Notice of Approval of the Official Insignia of the 82nd Division, 1 August 1918, in Records Group 120, Records of the AEF, 82nd Division, carton 1 [hereafter cited as RG 120 with appropriate carton].

2. Typed copy, History of the Brigade Headquarters, 157th Field Artillery Brigade, c. March 1919, ibid., carton 22; War Diary of the 307th Ammunition Train, 17 August 1918, ibid., carton 29.

3. *Official History of the 82nd Division, American Expeditionary Forces, 1917-1919* (Indianapolis, IN: Bobbs-Merrill, 1919), 228–29.

4. Typed copy, Regimental History of the 319th Field Artillery, 21 December 1918, RG 120, carton 25.

5. American Battle Monuments Commission, *82nd Division: Summary of Operations in the World War* (Washington, DC: Government Printing Office, 1944), 8–9.

6. See James J. Cooke. *Pershing and His Generals: Command and Staff in the AEF* (Westport, CT: Praeger, 1997) for a full discussion.

7. John J. Pershing, *My Experiences in the World War*, II (Blue Ridge Summit, PA: Tab Books Reprints, 1989), 225–26.

8. Ibid., 210–12.

9. HQ, I Corps to HQ, 82nd Division, 6 September 1918, RG 120, carton 68.

10. Lindsey to Burnham, 7 September 1918, ibid.

11. George McIntosh Sparks. *The 327th under Fire* (n.p., c. 1920), 40–41.

12. HQ, 82nd Division to Commanding General, I Corps, 10 September 1918, RG 120, carton 68.

13. Cronin to Burnham, 19 August 1918, ibid., carton 15.

14. Conrad to Burnham, 20 August 1918, ibid., carton 68.

15. Inspection Report by Colonel J. C. Johnson to First Army, 1 September 1918, RG 120 (First Army Reports), carton 3410.

16. HQ, 82nd Division to Brigade Commanders, 28 August 1918, RG 120, carton 68.

17. HQ, 82nd Division, Special Orders No. 201, 2 September 1918, ibid.

18. Adjutant General, AEF, to HQ, 82nd Division, 13 August 1918, ibid.

19. Ibid.

20. Inspection Report by Colonel J. C. Johnson to First Army, 1 September 1918, RG 120 (First Army Reports), carton 3410.

21. Diary entry, 29 August 1918, in the Rhodes Diaries entitled "Diary of the World War," in the Rhodes Papers, U.S. Army Military History Institute Archives, Carlisle Barracks, PA, [hereafter cited as MHI with appropriate collection].

22. Typed copy, History of the Ambulance Section Headquarters, 307th Sanitary Train, 2 November 1918, RG 120, carton 29.

23. Inspection Report by Colonel J. C. Johnson to First Army, 1 September 1918, RG 120 (First Army Reports), carton 3410.

24. Ibid.

25. Training History of the 82nd Division for the Month of August 1918, in the Harold B. Fiske Papers, Records Group 200, National Archives, Washington, DC, carton 2.

26. HQ, 157th Field Artillery Brigade, Training Memorandum No. 1, 22 August 1918, RG 120, carton 25.

27. All patrol orders issued by HQ, 82nd Division, can be found in ibid., carton 3.

28. McArthur to Burnham, 6 September 1918, ibid., Carton 73.

29. G1, GHQ, AEF to Burnham, 19 September 1918, ibid.

30. Typed copy, History of the Brigade Headquarters, 157th Field Artillery Brigade, c. March, 1919, ibid., carton 22.

31. Typed copy, Regimental History of the 319th Field Artillery, 21 December 1918, ibid., carton 25.

32. Burnham to Pershing, 7 September 1918, ibid., carton 68.

33. War Diary, 307th Ammunition Train, 1 September 1918, ibid., carton 29.

34. Chronological History of the 307th Engineer Regiment, 28 February 1919, ibid., carton 28.

35. Ibid.

36. *Official History of the 82nd Division*, 18–19.

37. James G. Harbord, *The American Army in France* (Boston: Little, Brown, 1936), 422–23; Pershing, *My Experiences*, II, 225–28, 260–62, 265–66.

38. Sparks, *The 327th under Fire*, 32–33.

39. HQ, 157th Field Artillery Brigade, Operations Reports, 9–10 September, 10–11 September, and 11–12 September, 1918, RG 120, carton 24.

40. HQ, 157th Field Artillery Brigade, Operations and Intelligence Summary, 11–12 September 1918, ibid.

41. HQ, 157th Field Artillery Brigade, General Instructions, c. 10 September 1918, ibid., carton 23.

42. Ibid.

43. *Official History of the 82nd Division*, 20.

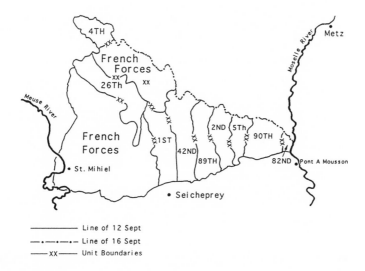

St. Mihiel Offensive.

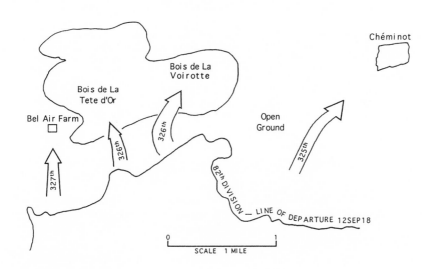

82nd Division, St. Mihiel.

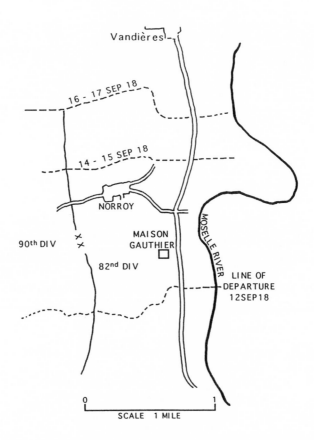

Vandières

16 - 17 SEP 18

14 - 15 SEP 18

NORROY

90th DIV

82nd DIV

MAISON
GAUTHIER

MOSELLE RIVER

LINE OF
DEPARTURE
12 SEP 18

0   1

SCALE 1 MILE

328th Infantry, St. Mihiel.

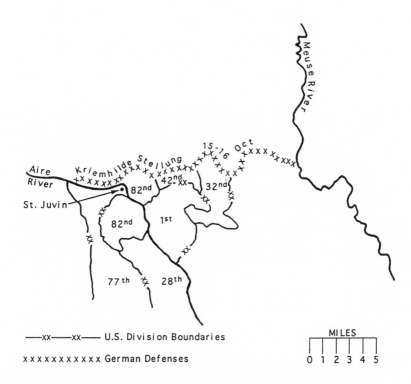

82nd Division Sector, Meuse-Argonne.

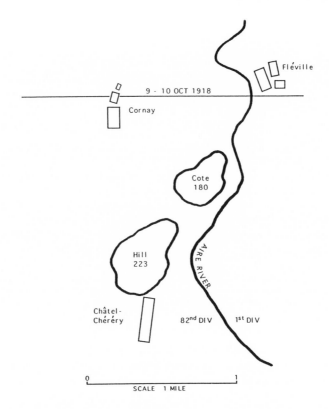

Meuse-Argonne: The Battle for Cornay.

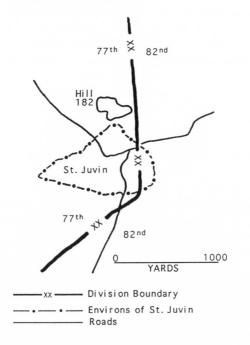

Boundary Confusion at St. Juvin.

Chapter 6

St. Mihiel

With preparations for the St. Mihiel operation completed, and with troops waiting for the artillery bombardment to open the first United States offensive against the enemy, Major General John Burnham had other worries in addition to battle. The senior chaplain of the AEF had just informed Burnham that military police and chaplains had observed soldiers, including men from the 82nd Division, in red-light districts near the front. Since the AEF's arrival in France a battle had been waged against venereal disease, and General Burnham had to take steps to see that his soldiers did not fall victim to the various diseases caused by contact with prostitutes. Colonel Johnson, the First U.S. Army inspector, had found the incidences of venereal disease to be low in the division, but the campaign against VD in the AEF was monitored by General John J. Pershing himself and by his staff.

Frankly, there was not much a commanding general of a division could do to stop men from consorting with prostitutes. The best thing was to turn the whole thing over to Major John Paul Tyler, the senior chaplain of the 82nd Division. At any rate, in twenty-four hours the division would be in the opening stages of the St. Mihiel offensive, and the soldiers would not be anywhere near brothels or street walkers. In a short note to Tyler, Burnham wrote, "it has been brought to the attention of the Senior Chaplain [of the AEF by the military police] that soldiers are openly solicited by lewd women on the streets of Nancy. It is requested that steps be taken to protect our men from this temptation."[1] Lieutenant Colonel Troupe Miller, the G1 of the 82nd, had to be able to inform the G1 of the First Army that steps were being taken by the division.

Major Tyler also had much on his mind preparing for the upcoming battle. He had had complaints about the services of the Young Men's Christian Association (YMCA), the Knights of Columbus, the Red Cross, and the Salvation Army. Tyler had to figure out how to get these groups to work in harmony to supply the troops with the little niceties which the army did not provide, such as tobacco, candy bars, writing paper, and the like. Of more importance, however, were the classes conducted with all of the 82nd's chaplains. The Protestant, Roman Catholic, and Jewish chaplains had to learn how to minister to a dying soldier of a different faith. Hebrew chaplains had to carry a crucifix in order to minister to a dying Catholic. Non-Jewish chaplains learned the proper Hebrew prayers. Given the expected violence of the offensive, it was obvious that time could not be wasted in trying to find a cleric of a dying soldier's faith. In a draft division like the 82nd there would be a wide variety of religious faiths, just as there was a very diverse selection of languages. The chaplains had to be prepared to do those sad but vitally necessary duties on the field of battle.[2]

While Burnham and Tyler had serious matters to deal with, the busiest man in the 82nd Division was Major Jonathon M. "Jim" Wainwright, the G3. He was now face to face with the realities of modern warfare. While the World War One division was a powerful organization, independent companies and detachments were sent from corps, army, and AEF assets to give extra strength to the division in combat. Wainwright had to integrate into the battle plans the 307th and 308th Salvage Squads, Sales Commissary Unit 30, a graves registration unit, the 307th Mobile Veterinary Section, the 307th Mobile Ordnance Repair Shop, and the 340th Machine Shop Truck unit.[3]

The 82nd Division would share the services of the 50th Aero Squadron, an efficient observation unit, with the 90th Division. The two divisions would also have to use the 42nd Balloon Company. The 50th Aero Squadron would be required to divide its time between aerial observation for the infantry and the artillery, while the balloon company would spot targets for the artillery brigades of both the 82nd and the 90th.[4] It was not an ideal utilization of forces, but it was the best that I Corps could do given its allocation of air assets from Colonel William D. "Billy" Mitchell at First U.S. Army.

Jim Wainwright had graduated from the AEF's General Staff College at Langres, but nothing taught at the three-month school could have prepared him for the magnitude of the battlefield of the Great War. As a G3 he was orchestrating infantry and artillery brigades, supply trains, and attached units. Wainwright had only five officers working under him to coordinate and to prepare orders. He had been informed that his own promotion to lieutenant colonel would arrive soon, and he worked for a good and knowledgeable chief of staff in Colonel Royden E. Beebe. Major Lee was a solid G2, and the division's chief signal officer, Lieutenant Colonel Dailey, could be counted on to see that radio and especially telephone communications continued to function during the offensive operation: it was time to see now if it could all be put together and made to work. No American division, corps, or army had ever faced the complexities of such a modern battlefield, and the tasks were never-ending.

What made this operation so intense was the fact that John J. Pershing had struggled so long and hard to get an American army, under American commanders, committed to battle in open warfare. In late August, with the offensive less than two weeks away, Maréchal Foch had visited "Black Jack" Pershing at his First Army headquarters at the town of Ligny-en-Barrois and tried to change the whole plan. Pershing was aghast; he quite rightly refused to scrap the offensive, and he would not turn AEF divisions over to the French.[5] Planning for St. Mihiel had been completed, and the G3 at First Army had turned his attention to the upcoming Meuse-Argonne operation, due to begin in late September. The British and French had grave doubts that the AEF could complete one operation and move forces to begin another in so short a time. There was, however, a brilliant group of staff officers at both AEF and at First Army, including Fox Connor at GHQ, AEF; Hugh A. Drum, chief of staff, First Army; and as an assistant G3, George C. Marshall.[6] These officers were just as determined as Pershing that the Americans could fight at St. Mihiel and be ready to attack in the Meuse-Argonne immediately after. "Black Jack" Pershing always believed that the American officer equaled any professional officer in the world, and he believed that St. Mihiel and the Meuse-Argonne would prove that once and for all.

Jim Wainwright had been well trained at the staff school at Langres. He knew that combat orders were just so many words on paper until the commander and staff read, reread, and analyzed those orders. There were countless subtasks to be considered. The commander would have to communicate to his operational planners his intent—how he wanted to fight the battle and what missions and submissions were vital to achieving what the corps order had defined as missions for the division. The division then had to set missions for the subordinate brigades. As the I Corps order was passed to subordinate divisions, planners had to subdivide large objectives, focus on the terrain over which the division would fight, what enemy there was before them, how to array their combat and support forces, and learn what units were on their left and right and where divisional boundaries had been established. Once the corps order was digested, the divisional order could be written by the staff. Unlike I Corps headquarters, the 82nd could not see the whole corps frontage, only that area over which it would fight. The divisional order had to be prepared, approved by Burnham, and given to the subordinate brigades and other units, where the process would begin again. A divisional order could not be delayed because the subordinate units, those who would actually fight the enemy, needed time to analyze the missions, subtasks, and the like. Wainwright was too well trained to deprive the subordinate brigades of the time they needed. The order, Field Order No. 9, was completed and was sent to the subordinate commands on the morning of 10 September.[7]

The St. Mihiel operation (see map) presented some serious challenges to untried staffs at all levels. The St. Mihiel salient was a triangular-shaped bulge jutting into the allied lines. As the late Donald Smythe wrote, "[The St. Mihiel salient] cut the Paris-Nancy railway and served as a jump-off line for a possible German flanking attack against Verdun to the west or Nancy to the east. It also served as an effective German bulwark against any allied advance against Metz or the vital Briey iron mines."[8] The salient, which was about twenty-five miles wide and about fifteen miles deep, was bordered on the east by the Moselle River and on the west by woods and rolling hills. Pershing had been focused on St. Mihiel since early August; he believed that this attack would prove that the AEF had matured, that it would lift the morale of the American and allied populations, and that it would show the Germans that United States forces were a factor of prime importance in the war.[9] The French had been bloodied in 1915 trying to take the salient, and there was every indication that the Germans would fight to hold this area, because of its critical iron mines, rail lines, and the important city of Metz. John J. Pershing was convinced nonetheless that a successful reduction of the St. Mihiel salient would be a vindication of Pershing's insistence on his orthodoxy—open, or maneuver, warfare.[10]

Every commander knew Pershing's intent as far as St. Mihiel was concerned. There could be no room for failure in this first American offensive based on open warfare. To ensure that every officer understood what was expected, Wainwright sent two teaching teams to all battalion headquarters to deliver lectures on the upcoming operation between 3 and 6 September. Every officer was required to attend these presentations, so that all would have a common understanding of tactics and procedures. The series of lectures took an entire afternoon and consisted of four main items: organization of a position, passage of lines, artillery support, and employment of machine guns.[11] Wainwright, Burnham, and the divisional staff were doing everything possible to prepare for 12 September, the start of long-awaited American offensive.

Unknown to Pershing or his planners at First Army, the Germans had decided to evacuate the St. Mihiel salient. Unlike what the AEF would encounter in the Meuse-Argonne a few weeks later, the defenses in the salient had been allowed to deteriorate, with wire becoming rusty and broken, and defensive positions crumbling. The area had been considered of minor importance since the bloody French reverses in 1915.[12] German troops there were not first-class combat forces, and there were dug-outs with carpets, electric lights, beer halls, and the like. However, the Germans were expert at using terrain to position machine guns and artillery to inflict maximum damage on an attacker at a low cost to the defenders. On the eastern side of the Moselle River the Germans owned the high ground, and their artillery could provide deadly enfilading fires on any attacker. The American planners also had to be concerned about the possibility of a German counterattack once the AEF moved into the salient. The flanks of the First U.S. Army thus became a concern to the operational planners.

The 82nd Division rested astride the Moselle River, and that dictated its participation in the St. Mihiel offensive. The I Corps plan, initially issued on 6 September, envisioned no attack by the 82nd Division as a whole, but the 328th Infantry Regiment, west of the Moselle, would be drawn into the fighting. The concept as seen by I Corps was for the 82nd to act as a flank guard for the corps' advance.[13] The divisional order stated, "The 82nd Division will hold its present front, exerting pressure on the enemy with all its means, maintaining contact with him. The Division will not advance."[14] If the enemy on the flank of the overall advance was kept occupied with the 82nd Division to their front, the possibility of a counterattack would be greatly lessened. This was the main mission of the All-Americans, and for a division with limited experience at the staff and combat unit level it was the best possible situation. The greatest problem to be faced by the division was maintaining contact with the right flank of the 90th Division. This task fell to the 328th Regiment of the 164th Brigade, but Wainwright had taken this into account.

The Field Order directed the 164th Brigade to push "mobile combat groups" forward from the positions just north of the town of Point-a-Mousson. Also, a group from the 327th would aggressively patrol forward on the east bank of the Moselle.[15]

Brigadier General Charles Rhodes's 157th Field Artillery Brigade was prepared to begin firing the initial bombardment of German positions. In fact Rhodes's gunners had been ready since 5 September. All ammunition was in place. Twenty-five percent of all shells were gas shells, of the nonpersistent variety; if infantry patrols or combat groups moved into enemy areas, their movement would not be hindered by persistent chemicals. Gun positions and ammunition dumps had been totally camouflaged.[16] At Rhodes's headquarters there was a liaison officer from the 42nd Balloon company to assist in transmitting important data to the firing batteries. Of particular importance to the 157th was balloon observation of the area around Metz. If there was a counterattack into the 82nd Division or 90th Division area of operations the balloon would be quick to spot it and give the information to the artillery.[17]

Captain John F. Brown, Jr., the intelligence officer of the 157th, increased observation of the area of operations beginning on 10 September. He carefully assembled every report from artillery and infantry observers on enemy activity between the front and Metz. Of concern to Brown were thirty-three trains that pulled into Metz on the morning of 11 September; twelve more trains arrived by the late afternoon. From air observation it was known that the train station in Metz was lighted and that there was unusual German activity at that location. Another observer reported that enemy artillery seemed to be on the move.[18] These were obvious causes for concern for the 82nd and the 90th divisions; unknown to the Americans, however, were these movements of the Germans pulling back to a new defensive line.[19] Regardless of German intent, the observation and reporting was both timely and informative, giving Brown a good idea of conditions in the enemy area. This information was published in the twenty-four-hour intelligence summary which went to division and to I Corps.

Major General Burnham had prepared his division for the upcoming operation quite well, but he had continually to reinforce the concept of the operation for his brigade commanders, who were not happy with the role assigned to the 82nd Division. On 11 September Burnham had been called to General Hunter Liggett's I Corps headquarters for a final coordination meeting. Liggett was worried about I Corps's right flank and the possibility of a German flanking attack while the corps was advancing into the St. Mihiel salient. The divisional frontage held by the 82nd was thirteen kilometers in length, and on the All-Americans' right was the French 125th Division. Security for the corps thus rested with the 82nd Division, and Liggett was adamant that nothing be done to jeopardize that security. Burnham, who well understand the corps order and had reinforced it in Field Order No. 9 just the day before, was taken aback by Liggett's strong language. When he returned to his headquarters he was so concerned about Liggett's fears that he called Brigadier Generals Cronin, Lindsey, and Rhodes to his headquarters to warn them personally of Liggett's concerns, and he restated in no uncertain terms the mission assigned to the 82nd Division.[20] Burnham knew that Julien Lindsey, commanding the 164th Brigade, was openly disappointed at having no role in the general advance into the St. Mihiel salient. Lindsey would bear watching during the operation.

The terrain over which the 82nd Division would have to fight had a number of natural and man-made obstacles. The ground itself was rolling, with a number of fairly high ridge lines on both sides of the Moselle River. On the east side of the Moselle the high ground and good observation belonged to the defending enemy, 370 to 400 meters high. These positions, about three to four miles north of the 82nd's line of departure offered to enemy artillery spotters a good view of American operations on the west side of the Moselle. This was especially critical for the 82nd's 328th Infantry Regiment and the entire right flank of the 90th Division (see map). The hills and ridge lines were covered with trees and scrub, which favored the defender's carefully emplaced machine gun positions. The 328th was separated from the rest of the 82nd by the twisting, slow-moving Moselle River. Field Order No. 9 gave to the 328th the task of sending combat patrols north on both sides of the Moselle, but by the second day of the battle this would prove to be impractical, and the regiment's actions would be restricted to the west bank of the river.

Julien Lindsey's 164th Brigade (327th and 328th regiments) had the left side of the 82nd's line, while Marcus Cronin's 163rd Brigade (326th and 325th regiments) had the right. While the 164th moved north along the Moselle, the 326th was to move into two heavily wooded areas—Bois de la Tete d'Or and Bois de la Voivrotte. The 325th would move in a generally northeasterly direction, across farms toward the shattered town of Chéminot, about two miles from the regiment's line of departure. All of the regiments would run into fortified farms which the Germans had turned into machine gun positions and strong points. These farms were constructed of stone, with houses and walls in places several feet thick. As the doughboys of the AEF had found out in the fighting in July and early August along the Vesle and Ourq rivers, these fortified farms could be hard nuts to crack for infantry. Usually these mini-forts were in clearings in the woods, near open fields that offered to the Germans excellent fields of fire for machine guns in the woods, the farm houses, and the yards themselves. Taking these farms would be reduced to man on man, bayonet on bayonet, determination against determination. Pershing had preached the gospel of open or maneuver warfare, and the terrain and enemy positions in the 82nd Division area of operations (see map) offered an opportunity to put it into practice.[21]

Operation plans had been written and distributed to subordinate commands, artillery shells had been stacked, doughboys had drawn their ammunition and now smoked and conversed in several languages, and chaplains prayed with the devout. All that man could do to prepare for battle had been done, and the 82nd Division had done it well. What soldiers could not control was time and weather; as the clocked ticked down to H-Hour the skies opened up, and it rained heavily. For the divisions who would use Colonel George S. Patton's tanks this was unwelcome to say the least, but since the 82nd had been allocated no tank support the rain was a simply a discomfort for the infantryman and an irritant for the artillerymen and the airmen. At 9:05 p.m. Jim Wainwright sent a message to all brigades and other units that the time for H-Hour was set at 1 a.m., 12 September 1918.[22]

At the designated time thousands of artillery pieces opened up all along the line, sending high-explosive and gas shells at a rate of three per minute into target areas. It looked as if the St. Mihiel salient was bathed in a strange sunlight. The ground seemed to roll under the soaked infantrymen waiting to advance as patrols or mobile combat groups. Once the skies passed from black to light gray the artillery slackened, and the infantrymen of the All-American division began their deadly work.

At about 5:30 a.m. the first combat patrols pushed forward from the 82nd's positions. It was oddly quiet after the four or five hours of artillery fire, and the Germans seemed content to allow the doughboys to push forward. Reports began to filter into the division's operation center to Jim Wainwright that "little resistance has been encountered. Patrols continue to advance. No casualties reported."[23] At 9:30 of the first day everything seemed to be going well, and the 328th Infantry Regiment, on the western side of the Moselle, seemed to be having no difficulty in maintaining contact with the right flank of Major General Henry Allen's 90th Division.[24] By mid-morning there was a general euphoria at corps and at First Army headquarters over the speed of the advance into the salient. It appeared that objectives set for the second day of the advance could well be in American hands by early afternoon of 12 September. To relieve Hunter Liggett's worried mind, there appeared to be no concentration of enemy forces on the corps's right flank. The operation could not be going any better. It even appeared that the Germans were confused by the speed of the offensive; they were shelling towns still in their hands.[25]

Messages poured into the G3 section reporting an almost unhindered advance forward by patrols and mobile combat groups. The 327th's combat group reached the fortified Bel Air Farm, about one mile north of the line of departure, about 11 a.m. with no serious casualties.[26] Observers from the 328th Infantry, from across the Moselle, reported at the same time Germans were evacuating the farm, retreating north, offering no resistance to the oncoming Americans.[27] Colonel Frank D. Ely, commanding the 327th, consolidated his position at Bel Air, ordered his men to put on their gas masks, and prepare for a German counterattack to retake this important observation point.[28] At the same time, about 1 p.m., General Lindsey reported that a combat group was about to take Maison Gauthier, a fortified farm complex, a mile north of the 328th's line of departure.[29] Once Maison Gauthier was secured, Lindsey could push more groups forward toward the town of Norroy, a mile and a half to the north.

It certainly appeared that the careful preparation for the St. Mihiel operation was paying off. The coordination between the infantry and the artillery was working well. In General Marcus Cronin's area of operations the 325th Infantry was poised to send groups to just south of the town of Chéminot, a large town on a major highway two miles from the 325th's line of departure. Cronin was able to report at 1:50 p.m. that, as requested, the artillery had ceased firing so that his doughboys could move forward.[30] But there was a disturbing note in Cronin's situation report to the G3: that "a patrol once started shall not return. . . . Patrols shall be reinforced to maintain continuity in the patrol itself, and in its forward progress."[31] Cronin was obviously pushing larger numbers of troops forward than had been anticipated; for practical purposes, both Cronin and Lindsey were interpreting their orders with the widest possible latitude. Cronin made clear the nature of his advance when he wrote of his patrols going north, "As they progress, supports are pushed across behind them." Hunter Liggett had made it plain that the 82nd, as a division, was not to advance, but this is exactly what was happening. Instead of smaller, platoon-sized, patrols, entire companies were being sent forward. Battalions were beginning to surge forward, because German resistance was so slight during the first eight hours of the attack. The 82nd's command structure had heard the gospel of open warfare often, and these men, by the nature of their training, were aggressive. The opportunities appear to have been irresistible.

By 2:30 p.m. Lindsey was about to occupy the area around Maison Gauthier with the full 328th Infantry Regiment.[32] That was certainly no combat patrol or mobile combat group. Even the headquarters got caught up the advance. At 4 p.m. General Burnham instructed Cronin to send a full company to the northern end of the Bois Voivrotte and hold it.[33] Of course no commander would push a full company of infantry forward without arranging for more infantry in its support. While not stated, it was clear that at least a full battalion of the 326th Infantry would now be moving to the north, at least two miles from the regimental line of departure.

Not every German, however, was content to pull back from his position. Patrols from the 326th Infantry plunging into the Bois de la Tete d'Or found gray-clad machine gunners willing to contest every foot of ground. The U. S. regimental commander had the woods swept with high-explosive and mustard gas shells.[34] Colonel Frank Ely had pushed Company L and two platoons of Company M plus Company D of the 321st Machine Gun Battalion to Bel Air Farm and was in the process of bringing up Company F to support the operation. Ely's patrol now consisted of nearly a full battalion of the 327th Infantry.[35]

The German army of 1918 might well be bruised and battered, but it certainly was not finished. German forces began to stiffen by late afternoon of 12 September. If the Americans intended to take the city of Metz, the doughboys on either side of the Moselle posed a serious threat. Counterattacks fell upon Bel Air Farm and Maison Gauthier; the All-Americans beat back both attacks, but Bel Air Farm could not be held, and the units of the 327th were forced to withdraw.[36] Major Benjamin Moore, commanding the 321st Machine Gun Battalion, had three machine gun companies near Bel Air Farm, and at times he served as an infantry commander, moving troops toward the fortified farm. During the withdrawal from the farm, Moore took command of the defense while the infantry pulled back to new positions.[37] The 328th beat off a small counterattack against Maison Gauthier and moved forward to occupy German trenches near the town of Norroy, where they engaged German troops. By dusk, the 328th had pulled back from the positions near Norroy, preparing for a move on the town the next day.[38]

Julien Lindsey was straining for a general advance in his sector. He told

Burnham, "Am convinced that a general advance today would have gained considerable ground."[39] The attack of the 90th Division, with which the 164th Brigade was to maintain liaison, would give Lindsey his chance to move his whole brigade into the fight on the next day.

Marcus Cronin's troops ended the day with some sharp fighting. The 326th was still moving slowly through the Bois de la Tete d'Or against well placed enemy machine gun and artillery fire, and the 325th met with resistance near Chéminot. Cronin had coordinated with the 157th Field Artillery Brigade and the trench mortars to begin the 13th of September with heavy fire on both the Bois de la Tete d'Or and Bois Voirotte, as well as on enemy positions near Chéminot.[40] During the day Cronin had also pushed elements of the 325th toward the town of Eply, which was about one and half miles from the line of departure and was the easternmost town facing the 82nd's lines. Cronin was determined to take Eply as well. A problem for Cronin was the inactivity of the French 125th Infantry Division on his right flank. A drive toward Chéminot and Eply might well create a gap between the Americans and the French. This would have to be handled with care; the French division showed no inclination to get into the fight.

Early the next morning Lindsey threw the 328th Infantry against the German defenses at Norroy, which they found to be formidable but unoccupied. The town was taken; the German commander had evacuated civilians to the town of Vandières, about three miles to the north.[41] Of more importance, however, was a message received at 82nd Division headquarters from the 90th Division that the "Tough Ombres" were advancing quickly through the Bois le Petre. Since German resistance was nonexistent, Henry Allen's Doughboys were pushing their attack.[42] At 11:45 Burnham ordered Lindsey to move the 328th forward to conform to the movements of the 90th Division.[43] By 7:30 that night the 90th and the 328th were a mile beyond Norroy.[44] At dark on 13 September another attack on Bel Air Farm took place with a number of German prisoners taken.[45] The 328th, however, now had an exposed right flank, and German artillery spotters on the high ground directed heavy fire against the regiment which was preparing to push on to Vandières in the morning.

Lieutenant Colonel Richard Wetherill, in command of the 328th Infantry for only a few weeks, ordered his men forward but encountered German machine gun and artillery fire. Lindsey, on the scene overseeing Wetherill's slow advance toward Vandières, recognized the increasingly heavy fire as coming from German artillery batteries on the high ground east of the Moselle.[46] Wetherill decided that Major G. Edward Buxton's 2nd Battalion would continue the advance toward Vandières; about 4 p.m. Buxton gathered his company commanders and artillery liaison officers to discuss how the battalion was to maneuver against the town under heavy fire. While he was explaining his concept of the operation to his subordinates, liaison officers from the 360th Infantry Regiment, 90th Division, and several officers from the 90th division artillery arrived to coordinate movements.[47] The day had been frustrating because of the slow nature of the advance, and the soldiers of the 328th reported that enemy fire had increased as the day went on.[48]

By the afternoon of 14 September division headquarters had become concerned about the artillery and machine gun fire coming from the high ground east of the Moselle. The focus of Wainwright and the staff was now the progress of the 328th Infantry. The lines for the other three regiments had basically not changed, nor had the 90th Division advanced during the day.[49] It was decided that during the morning of the 15th a number of divisional staff officers, including Colonel Beebe and Lieutenant Colonel Emory Pike, the division machine gun officer, would go to the 328th sector to observe its advance on Vandières.

Lieutenant Colonel Wetherill decided to use 3rd Battalion to continue operations on the 15th. He pulled Major William Boyle's 1st Battalion back to just south of Norroy and placed 2nd Battalion just behind Colonel Johnson's 3rd Battalion. Boyle's unit was given the task of maintaining, by way of company-size patrols, liaison with the 360th Infantry Regiment of Henry Allen's 90th Division.[50] Companies A and C of the 321st Machine Gun Battalion supported the entire advance on Vandières, but they spent most of the day firing across the Moselle, trying to suppress German machine guns that were causing casualties in the 328th Infantry.[51]

While Johnson's 3rd Battalion was moving north under heavy fire from east of the Moselle and from enemy machine gunners in Vandières, Colonel R. E. Beebe, the chief of staff, arrived to observe. With him was Colonel Raymond Sheldon, who had just been assigned to relieve him as chief of staff for the 82nd Division. Beebe, who had made a fine record with the All-Americans, was to go to the G3 section of the AEF at Chaumont. Colonel Julian L. Schley, commanding the 307th Engineers, and Lieutenant Colonel Emory Pike, the 82nd's machine gun officer, were also on the scene. As they left Norroy they came under heavy German artillery fire, which also pounded Johnson's battalion.[52]

Beebe found a serious situation when he reached the PC (Command Post) of 3rd Battalion. Johnson had severely sprained his ankle and could not walk. The town of Vandières had to be taken to reduce the fire now hitting the exposed flank of the 90th Division.[53] The 3rd Battalion was being swept with artillery fire and was taking heavy casualties, almost three hundred in the space of a few minutes.[54]

The 82nd and the 90th were now paying a price for I Corps's decision not to advance the 82nd, east of the Moselle, against the high ground north of Bel Air Farm. Beebe, Schley, and Pike were good soldiers and recognized that with Johnson immobile and in great pain, his units were becoming disorganized.[55] Pike went forward to help get soldiers moved from exposed positions and dug in as well as conditions would allow. Pike then moved into the ruined town of Vandières, where there was even more chaos as artillery rained down on the 328th infantrymen. Sometime in mid-afternoon Pike was severely wounded, but he continued to work with the disorganized troops. Despite the obvious loss of blood he was able to remain on the scene, calming the soldiers and getting them in to foxholes or other shelter. Weakened by the loss of blood, Pike was carried to a dressing station in Vandières, where he died of his several wounds.[56] For his extraordinary courage under fire, Emory J. Pike of Des Moines, Iowa, was awarded the Congressional Medal of Honor, the first 82nd Division soldier to receive the decoration.

Major Johnson of the 3rd Battalion, 328th Infantry, did not fare so well. Having been in pain all day, unable to command the troops he had trained, Johnson was almost incoherent. Captain Charles F. Lewis of the 307th Engineers, who saw Johnson that night, later wrote, "He was in a rather demoralized condition and could answer none of the questions I and the adjutant of the 328th asked."[57] (Rumors circulated that Johnson had lost his nerve in the heat of battle, but Wetherill discounted the rumors, and Johnson remained in command of his battalion during the Meuse-Argonne operation).

Colonel Beebe recognized the dire condition of the battalion and informed Lindsey that "Major Johnson's battalion was badly shot up today. Investigation of trenches and dugouts near Norroy showed gas in all. Lt. Col. Wetherill ordered them (the [battalion]) back to Point-à-Mousson as the best place to recover. They would be of little use up there and I approved the action."[58] It was the devastated condition of the battalion, not Johnson's conduct, that caused concern for the division. Notwithstanding of the vote of confidence from Wetherill, however, Johnson's reputation continued to suffer from rumors, and Colonel Beebe was to report in 1926 that "Johnson [had] committed suicide because his sprained ankle was misunderstood."[59]

On the afternoon of 16 September, units from the 90th Division relieved the 82nd north of Vandières, and the division's activity in the St. Mihiel offensive slowed down. General Allen's "Tough Ombres" of the 90th Division continued to experience trouble with enemy artillery on the east bank of the Moselle, where the enemy had the distinct advantage in holding high ground perfect for unimpeded observation of the area around Vandières.[60]

General William Burnham could now take a long look at what the 82nd Division had accomplished during the St. Mihiel operation, and he had every reason to be satisfied with the troops under his command. Hunter Liggett sent a personal telegram to Burnham praising the division.[61] But the success on both sides of the Moselle had come at a cost. Thirty-six officers and 998 enlisted men were listed as killed, wounded, or missing.[62] The worst casualties had come in the 328th Infantry, because of the heavy enemy shelling on 15 September. Emory Pike's death necessitated the appointment of a new division machine gun officer, and with a new offensive looming it was necessary to find an experienced one. Major Benjamin Moore came to the division and was promoted to lieutenant colonel prior to the Meuse-Argonne fight. Major G. Edward Buxton, who commanded a battalion in the 328th Infantry, was brought to division headquarters to be the division inspector, a position for a lieutenant colonel. Colonel Beebe departed for General Headquarters at Chaumont, and his place was taken by Colonel Sheldon, a regular Army officer who had been trained at Langres. Sheldon was a very different type, very demanding of the staff. The even-tempered Jim Wainwright was so frustrated by Sheldon's close supervision and domineering personality that he confided to Brigadier General Rhodes that he was thinking of asking for a transfer.[63]

Burnham's brigade commanders—Lindsey, Cronin, and Rhodes—had proven themselves to be first-rate, aggressive combat commanders. Anticipated difficulties with Lindsey had not materialized, and Burnham's reports on those generals' efficiency were highly complimentary. The troops had performed well in combat, showing an offensive spirit that had not been evident during their time of training with the British and the French. Combat service support units, such as the supply, ammunition, and sanitary trains, had also rendered good service. All in all, this division had passed its first test in combat.

Pershing visited the division on 16 September and was highly complementary of Burnham's troops and officers. "Black Jack" spent a good bit of time with Rhodes, because Pershing had been Rhodes's cadet captain at West Point. When Pershing left, Beebe pulled Rhodes aside and informed him that he (Rhodes) was being considered strongly for his second star and an assignment at a higher level.[64] At the same time Beebe tried to protect Wainwright, who was angry over Colonel Sheldon's methods; Beebe recommended to Burnham that every step be taken to keep Wainwright in the division.[65] It appeared that Pershing was quite pleased with the 82nd Division and was elated over the progress in reducing the St. Mihiel salient. There did not seem now to be any problem between Burnham and Pershing, and the commanding general indicated that the 82nd would have a major role to play in the upcoming Meuse-Argonne operation, scheduled to begin on 26 September.

Orders came to the 82nd Division to prepare to move to staging areas near Verdun to prepare for the new offensive. The division, now about twenty-six-thousand strong, would be relieved by the French 69th Infantry Division and driven by French trucks to its new area. The turnover of the division sector was completed by 21 September, and the trucks, with Indochinese drivers, began to arrive en masse on 25 September. As the division departed the St. Mihiel area it could hear the opening guns of the last great offensive of the war. It was a confident group of All-Americans who left in a driving rain for Verdun.

NOTES

1. Burnham to Tyler, 11 September 1918, in Records Group 120, Records of the AEF, 82nd Division, National Archives, Washington, DC., carton 92 [hereafter cited as RG 120 with appropriate carton].

2. Report from Tyler to Senior Chaplain, AEF, 10 September 1918, in Records Group 120, Records of the G1, Chaplain's Office, AEF, National Archives, Washington, DC, carton 3822.

3. HQ, 82nd Division, Statistical Section, to Statistical Section, I Corps, 16 September 1918, RG 120, carton 1.

4. See James J. Cooke, *The U.S. Air Service in the Great War, 1917–1919* (Westport, CT: Praeger, 1996), 132–33.

5. John J. Pershing, *My Experiences in the World War II* (Blue Ridge Summit, PA: Tab Books Reprint, 1989), 234–51. James H. Hallas, *Squandered Victory: The American First Army at St. Mihiel* (Westport, CT: Praeger, 1995), 49–54. James G. Harbord, *The American Army in France, 1917–1919* (Boston: Little, Brown, 1936), 418–23.

6. Forrest C. Pogue, *George C. Marshall: Education of a General, 1880–1939* (New York: Viking, 1963), 169–79. See James J. Cooke, *Pershing and His Generals: Command and Staff in the AEF* (Westport, CT: Praeger, 1997), 118–20.

7. HQ, 82nd Division, Field Order No. 9, 10 September 1918, RG 120, carton 6.

8. Donald Smythe. *Pershing: General of the Armies* (Bloomington: Indiana University Press, 1986), 179.

9. Pershing, *My Experiences*, II, 225–26.

10. Harbord, *American Army*, 408, 424–25.

11. HQ, 82nd Division, G3, Schedule of lectures, General Staff Memorandum No. 190, 2 September 1918, RG 120, carton 1.

12. Hallas, *Squandered Victory*, 2–4.

13. *Official History of the 82nd Division, American Expeditionary Forces, 1917–1919* (Indianapolis, IN: Bobbs-Merrill, 1919), 18–19.

14. HQ, 82nd Division, Field Order No. 9, 10 September 1918, RG 120, carton 6.

15. Ibid.

16. HQ, 157th Field Artillery Brigade, Operations Memorandum No. 5, 30 August 1918, ibid., carton 23.

17. HQ, 82nd Division, Field Order No. 9, Annex No. 2, Plan of Air Service, 10 September 1918, ibid., carton 6.

18. HQ, 157th Field Artillery Brigade, Operations-Intelligence Summaries, 11 and 12 September 1918, ibid., carton 24.

19. Hallas, *Squandered Victory*, 76–77.

20. R. E. Beebe to American Battle Monuments Commission, 6 December 1928, in Records Group 117, Records of the American Battle Monuments Commission, National Archives, Washington, DC, carton 248 [hereafter cited as RG 117 with appropriate carton].

21. The terrain information has been taken from the maps included in American Battle Monuments Commission, *82nd Division: Summary of Operations in the World War* (Washington, DC: Government Printing Office, 1944), Map Sheet: St. Mihiel Offensive. I have employed the modern technique of "Intelligence Preparation of the Battlefield" to analyze the terrain.

22. HQ, 82nd Division, Field Message Log, 11 September 1918, RG 120, carton 4.

23. HQ, 82nd Division, Field Message Log, 9:30 a.m., 12 September 1918, RG 120, carton 4.

24. *Official History of the 82nd Division*, 19.

25. HQ, 82nd Division, Field Message Log, 9:35 a.m., 12 September 1918, RG 120, carton 4.

26. HQ, 82nd Division, Field Message Log, 1:05 p.m., 12 September 1918, ibid.

27. Ibid.

28. HQ, 82nd Division, Field Message Log, 1:20 p.m., 12 September 1918, ibid.

29. Ibid.

30. Cronin to Burnham, Field Message Log, 1:50 p.m., 12 September 1918, ibid.

31. Ibid.

32. Lindsey to G3, 82nd Division, Field Message Log, 1:40 p.m., 12 September 1918, ibid.

33. Beebe to Cronin, Field Message Log, 3:50 p.m., 12 September 1918, ibid.

34. Lindsey to G3, Field Message Log, 2:30 p.m., 12 September 1918, ibid.

35. George McIntosh Sparks, *The 327th under Fire* (n.p.; c. 1920), 34–36. HQ, 82nd Infantry Division, Division Machine Gun Officer [Major B. Moore], After Action Report, 19 September 1918, RG 120, carton 7.

36. Operations Officer, 164th Brigade to G3, 82nd Division, Field Message Log, 6:05 p.m. and 6:10 p.m., 12 September 1918, Ibid., carton 4.

37. Moore to Operations Officer, 164th Infantry Brigade, 5:30 p.m., 12 September 1918, ibid., carton 22.

38. *Official History of the 82nd Division*, 22–23.

39. Lindsey to Burnham, Field Message Log, 6:05 p.m., 12 September 1918, RG 120, carton 4.

40. Cronin to Burnham, Field Message Log, 10:10 p.m., 12 September 1918, ibid.

41. *Official History of the 82nd Division*, 23–24.

42. G3, 90th Division to G3, 82nd Division, Field Message Log, 11:15 a.m., 13 September 1918, RG 120, carton 4.

43. Beebe to Lindsey, Field Message Log, 11:45 a.m., 13 September 1918, ibid.

44. Operations Officer, 328th Infantry to G3, 82nd Division, Field Message Log, 8:00 p.m., 13 September 1918, ibid.

45. Report from 327th Infantry to G3, 82nd Division, Field Message Log, 9:30 p.m., 13 September 1918, ibid.

46. HQ, 164th Infantry Brigade, After Action Report by Brigadier General Julien R. Lindsey, 16 September 1918, ibid., carton 16.

47. HQ, 2nd Battalion, 328th Infantry, After Action Report for 13–14 September 1918, by Major G. Edward Buxton, 15 September 1918, ibid., carton 21.

48. Richard Douglas to American Battle Monuments Commission, 24 July 1926, RG 117, carton 248.

49. American Battle Monuments Commission, *82nd Division: Summary*, 12.

50. HQ, 1st Battalion, 328th Infantry, After Action Report for 15 September, by Major William Boyle, 18 September 1918, RG 120, carton 21.

51. HQ, 321st Machine Gun Battalion, After Action Report for 15 September 1918, by Captain I. C. Holloway, 20 September 1918, ibid., carton 22.

52. Beebe to American Battle Monuments Commission, 6 December 1926, RG 117, carton 248.

53. Ibid; notes by Beebe on the Taking of Vandières, c. 1919, ibid.; George Wythe, *A History of the 90th Division* (n.p.: The 90th Division Association, 1920), 59.

54. Hallas, *Squandered Victory*, 209.

55. Beebe to American Battle Monuments Commission, 6 December 1926, RG 117, carton 248.

56. Wetherill to Burnham, 20 September 1918, RG 120, carton 85.

57. Charles F. Lewis to American Battle Monuments Commission, 12 November 1928, RG 117, carton 248.

58. Beebe to Lindsey, 16 September 1918, Field Message Log, 164th Infantry Brigade, RG 120, carton 16. The date of this message is correct, but Beebe is a day off concerning the heavy artillery pounding the battalion took.

59. Beebe to American Battle Monuments Commission, 6 December 1926, RG 117, carton 248.

60. Wythe, *90th Division*, 65–66.

61. *Official History of the 82nd Division*, 29.

62. HQ, 82nd Division, Memorandum No. 41, 6 March 1919, RG 120, carton 1.

63. Diary entry, 22 September 1918 in the Charles Rhodes Diary entitled "1918, Diary of the World War," Charles Rhodes Papers, United States Army Military History Institute Archives, Carlisle Barracks, PA.

64. Diary entry, 16 September 1918, ibid.

65. Copy, Letter from Beebe to Burnham, 24 September 1918, in the Johnathon Wainwright Papers, ibid., carton 2.

Major General William P. Burnham, 1918. Courtesy U.S. Army Military History Institute. Used with permission.

Major General George Duncan and Red Cross Workers, 1918. Courtesy U.S. Army Military History Institute. Used with permission.

Brigadier General Julian R. Lindsey, 1918. Courtesy U.S. Army Military History Institute. Used with permission.

Major General Charles D. Rhodes, 1918. Courtesy U.S. Army Military History Institute. Used with permission.

Sgt. Alvin C. York, Where He Earned the Medal of Honor. Courtesy U.S. Army Military History Institute. Used with permission.

325th Infantry Wounded, October 12, 1918. Courtesy U.S. Military History Institute. Used with permission.

319th Artillery Regiment Ammunition Supply, October 31, 1918. Courtesy U.S. Army Military History Institute. Used with permission.

82nd Division Headquarters, Prauthoy, France, 1919. Courtesy U.S. Army Military History Institute. Used with permission.

Italian-American Soldier of the 82nd from New York City, 1919. Courtesy of David M. McCoy. Used with permission.

Chapter 7

The Meuse-Argonne

On 20 September the 82nd Division relinquished direct control of the ground over which it fought during the St. Mihiel Offensive. The division was ordered to concentrate at the town of Marbache on 24 September, in staging areas, prior to being committed to the Meuse-Argonne, operation which was due to begin on 26 September. Once combat ended the division staff began the process of writing the orders for the movement. It was also a time for inspections, for preparation of after-action reports, and for replacing lost or damaged equipment. The machine gun battalions were concerned about the effects of continual firing on their guns and gun barrels. The battalion commanders reported that much of the rifling in the barrels was worn out and that before any future combat operations the barrels would have to be exchanged for new ones.[1]

Brigadier General Charles Rhodes faced a similar problem in the 157th Field Artillery Brigade. Rhodes was shocked to find that the 319th Regiment had fired 12,161 rounds during the St. Mihiel operation. The 320th had expended 29,903 rounds, since it had been in support of the 328th Infantry's fight on the west bank of the Moselle. The 321st had fired 21,057 shells during the same period. This meant the entire brigade had used 63,121 artillery shells of various types and calibers during the five-day battle.[2] It was obvious that the large number of rounds fired would have to be taken into consideration by the brigade and division ammunition and supply officers once the 157th began to support the division in the next fight.

For Rhodes and his gunners, however, the end of combat did not only mean counting empty shell casings. Rhodes and his staff felt the need of a good hot meal, and they decided to try a local restaurant. In his diary Rhodes wrote,

In the evening [20 September] most of the staff went in to Nancy to dine at the famous restaurant Liege-Oise, where they have good food. Also present, as usual, were a large number of comely French girls, who seem not adverse to being fed a good meal by American officers. Our aviators from a neighboring air-field appear to be the favorites. Boche planes bombed at 9:00 o'clock.[3]

The younger members of the staff liked the idea so much that the next night, without permission, many of them went back to Nancy, to the pretty French girls, to free-flowing wine, and they got rip-roaring drunk. Wearing his sternest face, Rhodes gave them all a dressing-down but took no further disciplinary action.[4] Perhaps Rhodes, the old professional soldier, remembered Madame Marguerite de la Chaze's attentions when the brigade was in training at La Courtine.

The lull in combat operations allowed staff officers to look at what had gone right for the division and what had gone wrong. Lieutenant Colonel John P. Hanson, division quartermaster (or G4), raised a point that impacted directly on the morale of the doughboy who had to fight the battles. When the division was preparing for St. Mihiel a sales commissary unit had been assigned. Second Lieutenant Carl P. Weyford, commanding Sales Commissary Unit No. 30, had appeared at division headquarters, but his supplies had not. The 82nd Division, and indeed the whole AEF, had problems providing the such nice-to-have items as tobacco, candy bars, cakes, etc., for the soldiers, who had no other way to buy those items. In modern terms this unit functioned like a mobile Post Exchange. John J. Pershing had asked the YMCA, early in the war, to assist by selling items to soldiers, and in some cases this worked well, but many soldiers never really understood the role of "that damned Y" in providing items at a cost. To supplement them the sales commissary units provided items. The unfortunate Lieutenant Weyford's truck never did arrive (it had been mis-routed to I Corps headquarters), and the 82nd had no access to those things that soldiers deemed so important. Soldiers in combat must rely on their officers not only for their well-being in battle, but also for the small things. Hanson enlisted the aid of Lieutenant Colonel Troupe Miller, the division G1, and they simply kept Weyford, hoping that his truck would show up. The Sales Commissary Unit did not function well; it became a very sore point for the 82nd Division, since it involved troop morale.[5]

No soldiers in a combat unit in any war have a comfortable existance. For the infantry of the 82nd Division the weather added to their normal miseries. Corporal Fred H. Takes from Bernand, Iowa, serving in Company A, 325th Infantry, had survived the action around Chéminot without a scratch, but he was not sure he would not be drowned by the heavy rains that began to fall after the St. Mihiel offensive ended. "It rained all night," Takes wrote in his diary on 29 September. "I did not go to the mess but I don't think there was any on account of the rain. . .I stayed in my tent until noon. It was raining almost all forenoon."[6] Takes and his buddies could hear the artillery thundering all along the Meuse-Argonne front, and they wondered when they would be thrown into the battle. Most of the common soldiers of the division seemed to be content to play the role of army reserve. Of concern, however, was the growing sick list from colds and from diarrhea, a sick list that got longer as the rains continued to fall and colder weather set in.[7]

The doughboys of the 327th Infantry were relieved by the French 182nd Infantry Regiment on 19 September. For six days, as heavy rains continued to fall, they camped, waiting for transportation to their staging areas. When the trucks arrived they were loaded on and began the long drive to a sodden woods that they were told was the beginning of the Argonne Forest. The next morning the regiment was shocked awake as the artillery began the great offensive, "the Big Push."[8]

The Meuse-Argonne offensive followed very closely on the heels of the St. Mihiel operation, and it was to be for Pershing, the great battle that would prove that the AEF had come of age. The St. Mihiel operation had gone very well; in four days, 12 to 16 September, the AEF had accomplished all of its tasks. First U.S. Army now did what the British and French doubted it could do, prepare twelve divisions to attack on 26 September in another area of operations. While those divisions moved to their line of departure, other units were on the move from the old St. Mihiel battlefield to take their places as army reserve, to be prepared to move on order into the fight. The staff work at First Army was first rate, because of some dedicated and well trained officers.[9] But there were some unsuspected problems in the plan for the 26 September attack. Many of the units scheduled to make the initial assault were divisions that had received a minimum of training. Some had been rushed to the Meuse-Argonne with staffs who had never planned for a battle and with a large portion of infantrymen who did not even know how to disassemble, assemble, clean, or fire their rifles.[10]

In the wake of the euphoria that followed St. Mihiel, the First Army staff over-looked some important points not only about the combat troops but also logistics. Already immense traffic jams were slowing down the flow of supplies and the movement of troops. The telltale signs were missed at Ligny-en-Barrois, where an aggressive, can-do attitude reigned supreme. Major General James Guthrie Harbord, head of the SOS, the AEF's supply service, visited Pershing's headquarters and was swept up by the optimism. Later, in more sober times he wrote, "To doubt audibly was to be a traitor."[11] Pershing visited every unit prior to the start of the attack, and he found that "they were all alert and confident and I returned [to headquarters] feeling that all would go well."[12] "Black Jack" Pershing, who had staked so much for the United States on this great offensive, was blinded by his faith in the troops and by his easy success at St. Mihiel.

The terrain over which all AEF units would have to fight was some of the worst on the Western Front. The Meuse-Argonne area was a box about twenty miles wide at the base and about fifty miles long. It was bounded by the thick Argonne Forest on the west and by the Meuse River on the east. There would be some American units east of the Meuse, but the main fighting would take place to the west. To make matters worse for the AEF, the Germans had three main lines of defense, and unlike in the St. Mihiel area the Germans had continually improved their positions with excellent machine gun positions, many strands of wire, and strong points. The enemy had the internal lines of communication and thus could move forces with relative ease. Observation and high ground belonged to the Germans, which would hinder the American's advance for weeks. In addition the weather refused to cooperate, and roads designated as supply routes were quickly turned into quagmires. Troops and supply trains became hopelessly bogged down, and forward movement slowed down to a snail's pace.

Regardless of the odds against the AEF, Pershing was committed and confident when the artillery began to fire its several hours' barrage. However, shortly after the infantry crossed the line of departure it became clear that not all would go as well as the First Army planners had hoped. The overall course of the battle at that point did not concern the command and staff of the 82nd Division, however. The main mission of the division was to move from the old St. Mihiel area to the base of the Argonne Forest. The orders issued by the divisional staff showed how far the All-Americans had come since landing in France. Troupe Miller, the G1, had prepared the basic order, which took into consideration everything from march discipline, to feeding of troops, to the disposition of band instruments. Since the division had a mix of motor vehicles and horse-drawn equipment, times had to be carefully planned. The three-to-five day operation was carried out with little difficulty.[13]

Colonel Sheldon, despite his irritating personality and tendency to micromanage the division staff, was a good soldier. Nonetheless, shortly after the St. Mihiel operation General Rhodes had a discreet conversation with Burnham, informing him of growing aggravation with Sheldon in the staff.[14] Burnham arranged a transfer for Sheldon and brought in Colonel Gordon Johnston, a well-trained regular, to be the new chief of staff. Johnston went to work immediately, preparing the division for combat operations. He worked well with Wainwright, something that Sheldon could not do, and what emerged was a smooth-running division staff that in the long run, contributed greatly to the successes of the division in combat.

Wainwright and Johnston understood that the St. Mihiel operation had put a fairly sharp edge on the division but that the experience on the Moselle could quickly be forgotten if not reinforced by training and by care for the troops, who were living in continual rain and constantly dropping temperatures. Morale and military discipline go hand in hand, and the two officers coupled inspections of uniforms and equipment and insistence on military courtesy with hot food. While the staff was working on keeping up morale, replacing equipment, and the like, the 82nd Division lost over ninety key noncommissioned officers. On 18 September the GHQ at Chaumont informed the division that NCOs would attend the ninety-day Officers Candidate School at Langres, due to open on 6 October. Many other AEF divisions were likewise effected by the order, which was very specific. It was certainly true that every AEF division which had seen any combat needed junior officers, but this was a terrible time to require the divisions to send men. The 325th lost five first sergeants, as did the 326th. The 326th sent two battalion sergeants-major to the school, and the division lost one senior mess sergeant.[15]

But the AEF school system was not through. From 6 to 27 October the 82nd Division was required to send two officers per week to the Gas Defense School at Chaumont. From 6 October to 20 October twenty-five noncommissioned officers per week were required to attend the NCO Gas Defense School at Gondrecourt.[16] While this selection process was taking place, GHQ at Chaumont directed the division to send a number of captains and majors to the General Staff School, a three-month course, at Langres.[17] These were major losses of key personnel at a time when the division was preparing for the Meuse-Argonne operation. While the division had talent in junior officers and NCOs, it would be difficult to maintain unit cohesion and discipline in battle with new, unproven soldiers. It would also prove to very difficult to pull junior officers and NCOs out of actual combat to attend a school. As far as gas defense was concerned, those soldiers had been learning such lessons in a very practical, live-or-die situation. On the other hand, Wainwright and Johnston had no choice but to designate soldiers to attend the various AEF run schools, but their absence would hurt rather than help the division in the upcoming fight.

Regardless of the irritation over losing key men at a bad time, the 82nd continued to prepare for combat. As a First Army reserve, the division had to be in a state of readiness to respond to any call, and for the 327th Infantry that call came rather quickly. The 82nd Division was bivouacked south of the historic city of Varennes, close to the original line of departure for the attacking divisions. The 82nd rested in reserve behind the 28th Division, from the Pennsylvania National Guard, and the 35th Division, made up of National Guard troops from Kansas and Missouri. When the battle began on 26 September it appeared that all was going well. Both the 28th and 35th took early objectives, including Varennes. Pershing had every reason to be pleased with the first few hours of the Meuse-Argonne offensive.[18] But then things seemed to go wrong for the 35th Division, which had little training and no real combat seasoning. Major General Peter E. Traub had an inexperienced staff, and he spent much time doing things that subordinates should have done, if they had been able. Pershing became concerned and went to the command posts of both the 35th and 28th divisions on 28 September. At the 35th Division he found that Brigadier Lucien Berry, commanding the 35th's Field Artillery Brigade, had become almost worthless. He was distraught, telling Pershing that he had, "become a millstone about the neck of General Traub." Pershing then visited Charles H. Muir's 28th Division, where he found conditions bad, if not nearly as dire as in the 35th Division. For all practical purposes the 35th Division was falling apart.[19] Now was the time to use the army reserve, and Pershing ordered that Major General Charles P. Summerall's battle-tested 1st Division relieve the 35th Division. The 28th needed help, not relief, and planners at First Army ordered the 82nd to send a regiment as a reserve for the 28th. This regiment was Colonel Frank Ely's 327th Infantry, which had performed well during St. Mihiel at Bel Air Farm.

At 4:30 p.m. Colonel Ely received orders from Brigadier General Julien Lindsey to move his regiment to a staging area a few kilometers north of Varennes. Ely assembled his battalion commanders: Major Frank Blalock, 1st; Major Harold Blanchard, 2nd; Captain Harwell G. Davis, 3rd. The mission was somewhat vague, in that the 327th was to be "placed at the disposal of the 28th Division." Leaving behind their machine gun company and their combat trains, the 327th moved quickly, despite road congestion, on the night of 29 September.

Ely found a critical situation. The 28th held a position north of a town named

Aprémont, and the 35th Division was supposed to be on line with the Pennsylvanians. But the 35th Division, however, was breaking up; its stragglers filled the woods. The 28th Division envisioned that the 327th would extend the line, taking over a section held by the now-ineffective 35th and participating in an attack by the 28th on 1 October. Blanchard's 2nd Battalion would lead with Frank Blalock's 1st Battalion following. Davis's 3rd Battalion remained at Varennes as the regimental reserve.[20]

Blanchard's position was on a ridge line near the destroyed village of Baulny. The All-Americans had seen the devastation of war, but they were not prepared for the chaos and confusion on Baulny Ridge. The battalion had been directed to drive back stragglers even at the point of bayonet; there were many confused, demoralized soldiers milling around the ridge when Blanchard arrived. He recalled that "We met, and turned back, a number of stragglers from the 35th Division. No extreme measures were necessary but the organizations of the 35th Division were very much intermingled with one another."[21] Lieutenant Guy T. Robinson, commanding Company G, believed that the situation was so bad on Baulny Ridge that the 327th was used to deceive the enemy into believing that fresh troops had arrived to take the place of the badly disorganized and dispirited 35th Division.[22]

The 327th had actually taken over a portion of the line held by a regiment of the 35th, stabilizing the situation until Summerall's "Big Red One" could assume responsibility for the entire 35th's sector. In the fog and friction of war, however, things can be overlooked, and Peter Traub, the 35th's commanding general, had not been informed that one of his regiments had been replaced. Visiting his units, he ran into Company F of the 327th and exploded; he sought out Major Blanchard to order the battalion to leave the area. Blanchard saw that Traub was "very wrathy," but he had his orders and told the angry Traub "that we were not under his orders."[23] German artillery continued to hit the area occupied by the 327th, and the troops used foxholes vacated by the fleeing 35th Division infantrymen.[24] By the morning of 1 October Ely's regiment had suffered nearly two hundred casualties, mainly from well placed German artillery fire.[25]

The situation was too uncertain for the 28th Division to launch any sort of attack before the entire 1st Division arrived to take over the 35th's sector. On the other hand, with Summerall's regulars moving into position there was no longer a need for the 327th to remain in the area. On 1 October, the day the attack was to be launched, the 327th was ordered to pull back to the location held by the 3rd Battalion near Varennes. There it was ordered to stay because, it appeared that First Army would move the entire division into the area. On 3 October, Lindsey's 164th Brigade was ordered to march north to Varennes. Colonel Julian Schley's 307th Engineer Regiment had been detailed, after St. Mihiel, to work with Colonel E. D. Peck, I Corps's engineer and Director of Light Railways and Roads. Once it was clear that the 82nd was moving up and would soon be in combat, Schley's regiment was released from road work and sent back to divisional control, to rejoin by 6 October.[26] To the division staff it was clear that 6 October had some significance for the planners at First Army.

On Thursday, 3 October, all brigade commanders and senior officers were called to division headquarters for a meeting. Everyone expected to receive marching orders, but what they got was a new division commander.[27] Major General George B. Duncan was scheduled, by AEF orders, to assume command of the All-Americans on 4 October; Burnham announced that he himself would become the U.S. military attaché in Athens, Greece.

In July, Major General André Brewster, Pershing's inspector general, had reported, "I have not had a chance to form an opinion of this officer's tactical ability. My opinion as to his merits must be negative. He does not make a great impression on me."[28] But that had been in July, and when Colonel Johnson inspected the 82nd Division in August he had recommended that Burnham continue to command. That was Charles Rhodes' input as well. The 82nd had done well during the St. Mihiel operation, earning the praise of Hunter Liggett, I Corps commander.

Pershing had wanted a divisional command for George Duncan for some time. Initially Duncan had been assigned to command the 77th Division, which was considered a highly desirable position. An old tropical infection, contracted when Duncan had served in the Philippines, caused him to be relieved from command of the 77th in August.[29] Pershing, who considered Duncan one of his oldest friends, had searched for a new divisional command for him, and in October had decided on the 82nd. While there had been some negative reports about Burnham, his combat record was very good and the division had just completed an efficient move from the old St. Mihiel battlefield to the base of the Argonne Forest. The 327th Infantry had responded well to orders to support the 28th Division. Pershing arranged for Burnham to leave divisional command with honors and with his rank and reputation intact. By 21 October Burnham was in Athens.[30]

Most of the senior officers of the 82nd Division knew Duncan either personally or by reputation, and there appeared to be no resentment over Burnham's relief. Duncan had been born in Kentucky in 1861 and graduated from West Point in 1886. One of the closest friends was Cadet Captain John J. Pershing. He served on the frontier, in Cuba during the Spanish-American War, and then in the Philippines. When the United States entered the war in 1917 Duncan was a colonel serving on the General Staff in Washington. Given command of the 26th Infantry regiment, Duncan made a good combat record in the 1st Infantry Division, and he had been rewarded with the command of the 1st Brigade in that division.[31] The critical André Brewster had considered Duncan "a good, rough soldier, a good general, fearless, aggressive and self-reliant."[32] Of course, Duncan had the advantage of coming to a battle-tested division with good brigade commanders, a steady chief of staff, and a well-run staff of professional soldiers.

There was no time to give thought to the change in divisional commanders. The 82nd was already on the move toward a new combat assignment. During the afternoon of 3 October, Rhodes and members of his staff made a reconnaissance of the roads into the next staging area, close to the artillery brigade of the 28th Division.[33] The nature of the assignment was not clear; planners were told that they would relieve either the 1st, 28th, or 77th division or would be fitted into a position between two of those divisions. What Rhodes found were congested roads made worse by continual rains and heavy traffic.[34] By the evening of 3 October Lindsey's 164th Brigade had closed on areas just west of Varennes. Its mission was to make a thorough reconnaissance of the road networks north of its staging area to the front.[35]

On the afternoon of 3 October the soldiers of the 325th were given some time off because the regiment would leave its bivouac area for a new location to the north. Fred Takes and his buddies decided to visit the town of Bar-le-Duc. On the way Takes and his friends "went through an American hospital grounds and saw the wounded coming in from the front. There was one ambulance after the other. We also went to the American graveyard where a large number were buried and quite a few in the graves and not covered. Others were in their coffins, piled up waiting for their graves to be dug. Today was my birthday."[36] The men of the 82nd were under no illusions as to what awaited them to the north, where the battle for the Argonne Forest raged.

While the 82nd was slowly shifting to the north, a drama was being played out in the Argonne Forest that would effect the All- Americans. The 77th Division, anchoring the left flank of U.S. First Army Meuse-Argonne attack, was driving into the heavily wooded, rolling hills of the Argonne. Major General Robert Alexander, a hard-fighting disciple of Pershing's gospel of open warfare, was determined that his division, "The Statue of Liberty" 77th, would prove its mettle. "To that battle the 77th Division brought the determination to *ADVANCE*, no matter what the obstacles in our road."[37] Certainly a good division, the 77th plunged into the woods, hills, and ravines of the Argonne, where a determined set of German defenders awaited them. Alexander's men experienced some problems maintaining contact with the French 1st Dismounted Cavalry Division on their left. By 2 October a dangerous gap had appeared in the lines between the 77th and the French, allowing German infantry to infiltrate behind the lead elements of the attacking Americans.[38]

Major Charles W. Whittlesley, commanding 1st Battalion, 308th Infantry, received a message from the regimental commander on 2 October to push forward "regardless of losses."[39] With the division moving forward the gap widened, and German troops were able to cut off Whittlesley and what became his "lost battalion." For several days the division attempted to locate and then relieve the battered soldiers; on 7 October Whittlesley's troops were extricated from the ravines where they had been pounded by the Germans. Because of the terrain and the German defense, the decision was made to clear the Argonne of the enemy.

The 82nd was about to attack into the Argonne, hitting the enemy in its left flank. The orders were issued at noon, 6 October, and things began to move quickly. Charles Rhodes's 157th had to be on the march as quickly as possible to support the infantry. The brigade moved rapidly forward, making surprisingly good time over muddy, shell-pocked roads. On 5 October Rhodes, Wainwright, and Lieutenant Colonel D. M. Beere, Rhodes's brigade adjutant, had made a reconnaissance forward to locate positions for the three regiments of the brigade.

Late that afternoon, Rhodes ordered his regiments to move north at dawn the next morning. After a tiring day Rhodes returned to his billets, but at 9 p.m. he received a telephone call from Colonel George C. Marshall, an old friend. Marshall, in the G3 section of First Army, had access to all types of information, and he had just seen a dispatch stating that eleven brigadiers had been approved for their second star. Among the eleven was Charles D. Rhodes.[40] However elated Rhodes might have been, the matter of his promotion was overshadowed by the hectic events of 6 October.

Lindsey's 164th Brigade would make the initial attack, with the 327th Infantry on the left and the 328th on the right (see map). The brigade would strike to the northwest with its right flank anchored on the Aire River. The 327th would move in a northerly direction toward the town of Cornay, while the 328th swept through Châtel-Chéhéry onto Hill 223, about one kilometer north of the town. The 327th would take a hill called Côte 180, less then a kilometer northeast of Hill 223. Once the hills were in American hands the assault would continue north westward toward the small town of Cornay.[41] The two assaulting battalions of the two regiments were to be in place to begin the attack at 5 a.m., 7 October. Moving toward the line of departure was the 321st Machine Gun Battalion.

The movement north turned into a nightmare. Rains continued to fall as the infantry and artillery moved forward. The roads were badly congested, and to make matters worse German shells continued to hit the road. It was clear that only the 320th Field Artillery regiment would be in position by dawn.[42] The 319th Field Artillery experienced heavy German artillery fire as it struggled over bad roads to get into position, and to add to its misery, German aircraft bombed it.[43]

Colonel Frank Ely had prepared his forces well for the upcoming fight. The regimental marching order placed Major Blalock's 1st Battalion in the lead, followed by a machine gun company and a Stokes mortar platoon. Coming behind the lead element was Major Blanchard's 2nd Battalion, with the 3rd Battalion in reserve. If the march took more time than planned the regiment was ready to go directly into the fight without needing to line up assaulting units.[44] As it turned out Ely's planning paid off for the 327th.

Richard Wetherill's 328th anticipated starting the attack at 5:30 a.m., but rain, dense fog, and delays in the artillery prohibited a movement toward Hill 223. German artillery hit companies A and C, but they held firm. Finally, at 8 a.m. the Doughboys of companies B and D moved against the hill, forcing the German defenders to pull back several miles. Enemy artillery continued to blanket the area, but Wetherill ordered the 1st Battalion to dig in on the hill and prepare for a German counterattack.[45] While the 328th was struggling to take its objective, the 327th, through heavy German machine gun and artillery fire, took Côte 180 at about 8:30 a.m. Like their comrades on Hill 223 the doughboys dug in and prepared for a German counterattack.

To maintain contact between the 164th Brigade and the 55th Infantry Brigade of the 28th Division, Lindsey directed Ely to send a company to the left of Hill 223.

Captain Leon T. Weaver of Brewton, Alabama, commanding Company H, led his troops to the west of Hill 233. They went forward in disciplined order as artillery hit the ranks. As men fell, gaps were filled, but they kept contact with the Pennsylvanians. Watching this attack, which looked like a charge from the Civil War, was Brigadier General Dennis Nolan, Pershing's former G2, now commanding the 55th Brigade. He sent a special message to General Duncan commending Weaver; for his leadership that day Weaver was awarded the Distinguished Service Cross.

At the divisional command post near Varennes it became clear that German artillery and well placed machine gun nests were making forward progress difficult. Gas shells were falling in unusual quantity, making operations in some areas a near impossibility.[46] The 157th Field Artillery Brigade had the services of the 1st Balloon Company, but the rain and fog hindered spotting. Charles Rhodes, the ex-cavalryman, was becoming quickly an expert on artillery fire, and he reckoned that the division needed more guns. He tried to get in touch with I Corps artillery, but with no success; he then tried to relay a message through the 1st Division's artillery brigade, but telephone lines had been cut by enemy shelling. Finally, word reached Rhodes through Brigadier General Malin Craig at I Corps that the French 239th Motorized Artillery Regiment would be assigned to his brigade.[47]

The Germans were not through, however; at 5 p.m. messages arrived at division headquarters that enemy artillery fire had intensified on Hill 223 and on Côte 180. Obviously the Germans were preparing for a counterattack against the defenders of those hills. Lindsey's headquarters reported that "there must be quite a scrap going on at that point."[48] Casualties began to mount, and Wetherill ordered all of what remained of 1st Battalion to move onto the hill. German infantry swarmed around the hill and less than a kilometer from Ely's command post. Gray-clad infantry began firing on the 327th's command post; and five Germans were killed behind it.[49] By late in the evening the situation around Hill 223 had been stabilized; the 1st Battalion held on throughout the night despite heavy shelling. Colonel Wetherill had ordered the 2nd Battalion to prepare to move forward to support the hard-hit 1st, but as the German counterattack slackened he ordered the 2nd to remain in position near the contested town of Châtel-Chéhéry.[50] General George Duncan had made it clear to Wetherill that Hill 223 had to be held and that if the enemy took it, the hill had to be taken back.[51]

Assessing his first day in command, Duncan had good reason to be pleased. The division had taken and held two key pieces of terrain, beaten back a determined counterattack, withstood heavy German artillery, and maintained contact with the 28th Division {through the brave, but costly, attack of Captain Weaver and H Company). The division would continue the attack on 8 October toward Cornay, cleaning out a number of German pockets of resistance around Châtel-Chéhéry. Throughout the night there was a resupply of ammunition, and where possible coffee was given to the troops. The artillery planners worked to prepare a fire plan to support the attack the next day. The brigade had fired twelve thousand rounds of high explosive and gas shells, and it had to resupply the guns. Rhodes's operations officer worked out a rolling barrage, two hundred meters in front of the troops, which would move toward Cornay at a rate of one hundred meters every three minutes. It was close, perhaps dangerously so, but the concept was based on the idea that the Germans must not be given time to recover from the initial one-hour-and-forty-five minute barrage.[52]

The 163rd Brigade was coming up as fast as road and weather conditions allowed. Corporal Fred Takes of Company A, 325th Infantry, later remembered the night march and the periodic German shelling. When the men of his company arrived they "sure were a fine sight this morning [8 October]. We were wet and full of mud from head to foot."[53] They passed by a destroyed American first aid station and saw dead doughboys from the 164th Brigade. A message from I Corps directed that the attack continue to the north to take Cornay by noon; the artillery began firing at dawn. As the artillery shifted to support the 82nd's advance, the 2nd Battalion of the 328th moved forward. The German opposition was furious, and casualties began to mount. Second Lieutenant K. P. Stewart, a platoon leader in G Company, was shot in the leg. He continued to drag himself behind his men, shouting encouragement, until a German bullet struck him in the head, killing him.[54]

There was an ample supply of courage in the 328th that day. Company G received a heavy volume of machine gun fire early in the attack, and a small patrol of four NCOs and thirteen privates was dispatched to silence some of the machine guns. In this group was a quiet young corporal from Pall Mall, Tennessee, named Alvin C. York. York had come to Camp Gordon in November, 1917, and had been in action at St. Mihiel. On 8 October, however, that unassuming, devout Tennessean found himself one of the few Americans standing; almost the entire patrol was dead or wounded. York began to fire at the German defenders, killing every member of a thirteen-man group. He then proceeded to capture three officers and 129 enlisted men. There were over twenty German bodies near York when the fight ended. That afternoon Privates Joe Kornatski, Percy Beardsley, Michael Sacina, George W. Willis, and Patrick Donahue told Colonel Wetherill what they had seen, and Wetherill recommended York for the Distinguished Service Cross.[55]

The day's fighting for Cornay ended with some gains made by the 82nd Division, at a high cost to the 327th and 328th infantry regiments. Elements of the 1st Battalion, 327th infantry, actually got into Cornay some time on the afternoon of 8 October, and there they stayed despite heavy German pressure to oust them. That night patrols moved north to locate German positions for the fighting that would resume on 9 October.[56] The usually energetic Charles Rhodes now felt the strain of the day's battle. He had been with the 321st Field Artillery when it was hit by German counterbattery fire, killing four and wounding six. Rhodes fell asleep near the firing guns, oblivious of the noise of the artillery pieces.[57]

In Cornay the small detachments of the 327th held on throughout the night as the Germans tried to push them out. German artillery blasted the Americans, forcing them to shift from one location to another. Second Lieutenant B. A. Shipp captured a German officer in the melee in Cornay; he found that the Germans were pushing down to the battle area a new division to continue the fierce counterattacks. Shipp reckoned that the enemy considered that pile of stone and rubble to be a key defensive position, and he immediately sent the information back to regimental headquarters. By then, however, the Germans had closed in on three sides around the small group of Americans. After dawn machine gun fire raked the All-Americans as the Germans closed the trap, calling on the doughboys to surrender. The captain in charge, believing resistance to be futile and having more American wounded than able-bodied men, decided to give up. Shipp, a regular Army officer, asked permission to try to make a break for American lines, and he was told to try it. Running like a madman through German rifle and machine gun fire, Shipp, bruised and bloodied, made it to American lines on the night of 9 October.[58]

In a small space of a few square miles (see map) there were numerous acts of heroism, and few ran away from German shells, gas, and machine gun bullets. Not every brave member of the 82nd Division was carrying a rifle or French Chauchat automatic weapon, however. Moving north of Varennes with their stoves, pots, pans, and ingredients were two sisters, Mary and Sunshine Sweeny, members of the YMCA attached to the All-Americans. Under shell fire, wearing steel helmets, the Sweeny sisters from Kentucky set up shop in ruined buildings and began to cook hot chocolate and coffee. With rain constantly falling, the two women rigged a shelter to protect the fires in the stoves, and as soldiers came by the thoroughly drenched, mud-spattered sisters served them a warming drink. Moved by patriotism and a devotion to their Lord, the two sisters cheered the troops and shared their miserable conditions and dangers. As the division fought northward Mary and Sunshine Sweeny packed up and followed the soldiers to new battlefields. For their service the Sweeny sisters were cited for gallantry and "exceptional meritorious service" in the general orders of the 82nd Division. For her gallantry under enemy fire Mary Sweeny was awarded the Croix de Guerre, as was Bernetta Miller.[59]

The night of 8 October was a time for Duncan and his staff to take stock of the progress of the fighting. The 82nd had continually moved forward, and the objective, Cornay, was in sight. There were some problems, however. It appeared that Richard Wetherill's 328th Infantry was used up. Casualties were well over three hundred in the regiment, and losses were particularly severe among lieutenants and captains at the company level. Duncan decided to pull the 328th from the battle and replace it with the 325th Infantry Regiment, under the command of the solid Colonel Walter Whitman. That commander moved his regiment into the line and immediately pushed patrols toward Cornay.[60] Corporal Fred Takes and his comrades noticed the increasing number of dead American and German soldiers as they moved toward the sound of the guns.[61]

Although it would have been hard to imagine at the time, all the regiments of the 82nd were to see much worse.

Frank Ely's 327th had just about reached the end of its road as far as combat effectiveness was concerned. No matter how well trained and physically disciplined a unit may be going into a battle, tension, stress, and lack of sleep eventually take their toll. Ely made the division aware of the condition of his troops with a number of messages that began after midnight on 9 October. At one point he told the division command post, "Find my men exhausted and gassed." Even the stalwart Major Blalock had simply collapsed from the continual operations. "All of my regiment," Ely communicated, "have been in continuously gassed area since midnight October 6th. About six gas alarms last night. All of us are more or less gassed and ineffective."[62] The gas mask was a device designed by some kin to the Marquis de Sade. There was a clamp for the nose and a tube running into the mouth; it was hot, and it often leaked gas. This certainly did not mean that the 327th was a poor unit; the stress of combat and the lack of sleep and food had final-ly caught with Frank Ely and his men.

It was not only the infantry regiments which were badly shot up. The machine gun battalions had experienced a number of casualties because of their daring in combat. Companies A and D of the 321st Machine Gun Battalion, commanded by Captain I. C. Holloway, were to support the assault on Côte 180. In the attack the troops of Company A got four machine guns on the hill to provide suppressive fire for the infantry surging up and around the hill, but they lost heavily when German machine gun and artillery fire hit the hill. In the fighting on 8 and 9 October, all companies recorded heavy casualties. By the time of their relief by the 320th Machine Gun Battalion, the 321st, now at about 50 percent strength, was in dire need of hot food and, more importantly, time to inspect barrels and to perform maintenance on its weapons.[63]

Even the tough Charles D. Rhodes was feeling the strain of the past few days. He was averaging about three hours of sleep or less per night. "The night strain of preparing for the daylight-support by artillery of a general infantry attack,—is *TREMENDOUS*," he confided to his diary.[64] Taking stock of the day, Wainwright figured that 1,184 soldiers had either been killed or wounded, and he noted the severe gas shelling.[65] It was a good time to bring up Marcus Cronin's 163rd Brigade with two fairly fresh regiments. I Corps intended for the momentum of the attack to continue northward toward the Kriemhilde Stellung, the German main line of defense, which was about five miles north of Cornay. The Stellung had a formidable series of defensive positions, massive strands of barbed wire, and other obstacles, all covered by machine guns and artillery. The enemy could not be allowed to rest and recover before the main American effort against the Kriemhilde Stellung.

By 7 a.m., 9 October, the 325th and 326th Infantry had moved into position to continue the attack toward Cornay. By 7 p.m. the artillery was firing on German positions near the objective.[66] What the 82nd Division did not know was that the Germans had decided to abandon the Cornay position and occupy new defensive lines closer to the Kriemhilde Stellung.[67] As the two regiments slowly moved forward to Cornay, new missions were being assigned to the 327th and the 328th, both units which badly needed some time to rest from combat.

The first few days of the 82nd's commitment to battle in the Meuse-Argonne had gone well. The division's planners had made good use of the terrain and allocated areas to the two attacking regiments that allowed them to make good use of their combat power, but the cost had been high. From General Duncan down, all senior officers were dedicated to the Pershing orthodoxy of maneuver warfare; what had emerged, however, was basically frontal assaults, man on man, bayonet on bayonet, with little real maneuver, except at the platoon or company level. Regardless of the type of battle being waged in the Argonne Forest, the All-Americans were ready to push forward to the Kriemhilde Stellung, which promised a hard fight for every American involved. Duncan, Wainwright, and the rest of the 82nd, however, faced the upcoming phase of the battle with optimism.

NOTES

1. HQ, 321 Machine Gun Battalion to G3, 82nd Division, 19 September 1918, in Records Group 120, Records of the AEF, 82nd Division, National Archives, Washington, DC, carton 22 [hereafter cited as RG 120 with appropriate carton].

2. Diary entry, 21 September 1918, in the Charles Rhodes Diary entitled 1918, Diary of the World War, Charles Rhodes Papers, United States Army History Institute, Carlisle Barracks, PA [hereafter cited as MHI with appropriate collection].

3. Diary entry, 20 September 1918, Ibid.

4. Diary entry, 21 September 1918, ibid.

5. John Hanson and Troupe Miller to Burnham, 30 September 1918, RG 120, carton 92.

6. Diary entry, 29 September 1918, Corporal Fred Takes Diary, Fred Takes Folder, MHI, carton 23.

7. *Official History of the 82nd Division, American Expeditionary Forces, 1917-1919* (Indianapolis, IN: Bobbs - Merrill, 1919), 31; HQ, 82nd Division, General Staff memorandum No. 227, 6 October 1918, RG 120, carton 4. This memorandum deals in large part with the health of the troops.

8. George McIntosh Sparks, *The 327th under Fire* (np.: c. 1920), 39.

9. See James J. Cooke, *Pershing and His Generals: Command and Staff in the AEF* (Westport, CT: Praeger, 1997), see chap. 9.

10. Paul Braim, *The Test of Battle: The American Expeditionary Forces in the Meuse-Argonne Campaign* (Newark: University of Delaware Press, 1987), 96.

11. James G. Harbord, *The American Army in France* (Boston: Little, Brown, 1936), 436.

12. John J. Pershing, *My Experiences in the World War II* (Blue Ridge Summit, PA: Tab Books Reprint, 1989), 294.

13. G1, HQ, 82nd Division, General Orders No. 16, 23 September 1918, RG 120, carton 9.

14. Diary entry, 21 September 1918, Rhodes Diary, MHI.

15. HQ, 82nd Division, Special Orders No. 227, 1 October 1918, RG 120, carton 88.

16. Memorandum, GHQ, AEF to 82nd Division, 21 September 1918, ibid., carton 11.

17. See Cooke, *Pershing and His Generals*, 124.

18. Pershing, *Experiences*, 296–97.

19. See Cooke, *Pershing and His Generals*, 132; Pershing, *Experiences*, II, 298–99.

20. Sparks, *The 327th under Fire*, 41–42.

21. Blanchard to the American Battle Monuments Commission, c. 15 August 1930, in Records Group 117, Records of the American Battle Monuments Commission, National Archives, Washington, DC, carton 250 [hereafter cited as RG 117 with appropriate carton].

22. Guy T. Robinson, "Narrative of the Experiences of Guy T. Robinson,

Meuse-Argonne Sept. 30 AM to Oct. 1st AM," c. August 1930, ibid.

23. Blanchard to American Battle Monuments Commission, c. 15 August 1930, ibid.

24. Guy T. Robinson, "Narrative," ibid.

25. HQ, 82nd Division, After Action Report (Meuse-Argonne Offensive), c. December 1918, RG 120, carton 7.

26. Ibid.

27. Diary entry, 3 October 1918, Rhodes Diary, MHI.

28. Report from Brewster to Pershing, 15 July 1918, RG 120, carton 2262.

29. See Cooke, *Pershing and His Generals*, 107–09.

30. Bound report, "In the Matter of Major General William P. Burnham, 82nd Division," Records Group 200, John J. Pershing Papers, National Archives, Washington, DC, carton 8.

31. Biographical files, "Major General George B. Duncan" (War Department, 1937), MHI.

32. Report from Brewster to Pershing, 15 July 1918, RG 120, carton 2262.

33. Diary entry, 3 October 1918, Rhodes Diary, MHI.

34. Typed copy, History of the Brigade Headquarters, 157th Field Artillery Brigade, c. March 1919, RG 120, carton 22.

35. HQ, 164th Infantry Brigade, After Action Report, 26 September–11 October 1918, c. 12 October 1918, ibid., carton 16.

36. Diary entry, 3 October 1918, Takes Diary, MHI.

37. Robert Alexander, *Memories of the World War, 1917–1918* (New York: Macmillan, 1931), 175.

38. Much has been written about this. See: American Battle Monuments Commission, *77th Division: Summary of Operations in the World War* (Washington, DC: Government Printing Office, 1944); 77th Division Association, *History of the 77th Division, 1917–1919* (New York: Wynkoop, Hallenbeck, Crawford, 1919); and James J. Cooke, *The U.S. Air Service in the Great War, 1917–1919* (Westport, CT: Praeger, 1996), 180–81, 189–90.

39. Much information can be gleaned about the situation of the battalion from the records of the court martial of Second Lieutenant Maurice S. Revnes, 306th Machine Gun Battalion, (1919). The testimony is found in the Hugh Drum Papers, MHI, carton 16.

40. Diary entry, 5 October 1918, Rhodes Diary, MHI.

41. HQ, 82nd Division, After Action Report (Meuse-Argonne Offensive), c. December 1918, RG 120, carton 7.

42. HQ, 164th Brigade, After Action Report, 26 September 1918–10 October 1918, c. 12 October 1918, ibid., carton 16.

43. Typed copy, Regimental History of the 319th Field Artillery, 21 December 1918, ibid., carton 25.

44. Sparks, *The 327th under Fire*, 49–51.

45. HQ, 328th Infantry Regiment, After Action Report, October 7 to October 31, 1918, c. November 1918, RG 120, carton 21.

46. G3, HQ, 82nd Division, Operation Report No. 80, 8 October 1918 and Operation Report No. 81, 9 October 1918, ibid., carton 6.

47. HQ, 82nd Division, Message Log, 8:30 p.m., 7 October 1918, ibid., carton 23.

48. HQ, 82nd Division, Message Log, 5:08 p.m., 7 October 1918, ibid.

49. HQ, 82nd Division, Message Log, 6:15 p.m., 7 October 1918, ibid.

50. HQ, 328th Infantry Regiment, After Action Report, October 7 to October 31, 1918, c. November 1918, ibid., carton 21.

51. HQ, 82nd Division, Message Log, 8:08 p.m., 7 October 1918, ibid., carton 23.

52. HQ, 157th Field Artillery Brigade, Field Order No. 7, 8 October 1918, ibid.

53. Diary entry, 8 October 1918, Takes Diary, MHI.

54. *Official History of the 82nd Division*, 59.

55. Wetherill to Lindsey, 23 October 1918, RG 120, carton 84; Wetherill to Duncan, 10 February 1919, ibid.

56. Blanchard to American Battle Monuments Commission, c. 15 August 1930, RG 117, carton 250.

57. Diary entry, 8 October 1918, Rhodes Diary, MHI.

58. Captain B. A. Shipp, "Brief Narrative of My Experiences, October 7–9, 1918," c. 15 August 1930, RG 117, carton 250.

59. HQ, 82nd Division, General Orders No. 1, 13 January 1919, RG 120, carton 85. Also see Lotti Gavin, *American Women in World War 1: They Also Served* (Boulder: University of Colorado Press, 1997), 152, 272, 273.

60. Whitman to American Battle Monuments Commission, 23 February 1927, RG 117, carton 248.

61. Diary entry, 9 October 1918, Takes Diary, MHI.

62. Sparks, *The 327th under Fire*, 62–64.

63. HQ, 321st Machine Gun Battalion, After Action Report, 3 November 1918, RG 120, carton 22.

64. Diary entry, 9 October 1918, Rhodes Diary, MHI.

65. G3, HQ, 82nd Division, Operations Report No. 81, 9 October 1918, RG 120, carton 6.

66. G3, HQ, 82nd Division, Operations Report No. 82, 10 October 1918, ibid.

67. Blanchard to American Battle Monuments Commission, c. 15 August 1930, RG 117, carton 250; *Official History of the 82nd Division*, 82–83.

Chapter 8

Meuse-Argonne, Phase II

Hunter Liggett's I Corps wanted Cornay taken as soon as possible, and the 82nd was poised to do just that. Of course, the All-Americans were helped by the German decision to pull back to the strong defensive line, the Kreimhilde Stellung, and abandon the Cornay area, but the enemy had too many good, experienced combat troops just to leave without exacting a price. They would make the upstart Americans pay for every inch of ground. As at St. Mihiel, well placed machine guns and expertly directed artillery could cause heavy losses for a pile of worthless rubble. Marcus Cronin's 163rd Infantry Brigade would make the final push against Cornay. When he and his two regimental commanders (Colonels Walter Whitman, 325th, and John C. McArthur, 326th) arrived at Brigadier General Julien Lindsey's command post for a conference, there was no question that Cornay would be taken.[1]

Both regimental commanders brought their battalion commanders to the meeting with Cronin. It was clear to everyone there that the attack on the morning of 10 October had to succeed. The initial artillery fire would begin at 5 a.m. with the infantry "going over the top" two hours later.[2] Whitman's 325th Infantry had the hardest job, with its 1st Battalion attacking directly north from Hill 233 toward Cornay and the 2nd Battalion moving north from Côte 180. Once near Cornay the doughboys would come under enemy observation and fire from the town of Fléville. Fléville, on the east bank of the Aire River, was in the 1st Division's area of operation, but the division had not yet taken the town. McArthur's 326th would be on the left of the 325th and would not have to contend with flanking fires from the enemy on the east side of the river.[3]

As Whitman's troops went forward they encountered little enemy opposition; First Lieutenant A. C. Slattery captured six Germans who seemed very willing to surrender. Once in Cornay, the doughboys went about the business of preparing positions for a counterattack, and then they scoured the ruins for war souvenirs.[4] The 164th Brigade moved up to support the troops in Cornay and made contact with the 77th Division on the left flank.[5] The day, 10 October, seemed to be going well, and there was no reason to believe that the 82nd would have much difficulty moving north from Cornay toward the town of St. Juvin, three miles away. To allow the movement of the 325th north to St. Juvin a bridge would have to be built across the Aire River. Company C of the 307th Engineers located several crossing sites and began the process of assembling a bridge for a hasty river crossing.[6] By dawn of 11 October a number of improvised bridges were complete, and Whitman's rain-soaked doughboys began to move across.[7]

On the surface it appeared that the attack was going well, but there were problems early in the day. The rain had slowed to a drizzle, but visibility was very poor, with troops able to see only a few hundred yards at best. Balloon and air spotting for the 157th Field Artillery Brigade was seriously reduced. General Rhodes was becoming alarmed at the state of his officers at brigade headquarters and in the regiments. Lack of sleep and continual firing had taken its toll on a group of usually energetic officers and men.[8] The 321st Artillery Regiment, equipped with French 75mm guns, was placed in direct support of the 163rd Infantry, but weather conditions made accurate firing impossible.[9] Rhodes also believed that the division's order prohibited barrage-firing on enemy positions prior to the attack. The mission, as interpreted by the brigade, was to fire harassing and interdicting fires when needed by the infantry.[10] For this operation at least, artillery support was not satisfactory, because the gunners were not clear as to what the mission was. Many doughboys believed that they were being thrown into a fight with no artillery support. However, during the morning Jim Wainwright at the 82nd's command post noted no unusual problems as the division's units moved closer to St. Juvin.[11]

Soldiers were simply slowing down from fatigue, hunger, and thirst. No matter how hard the 307th Supply Train tried, the amount of food and water which could be brought to the men was never enough. Poor roads, made worse by constant rain, and enemy shelling simply brought supplies to a standstill. If there was a priority, it was for ammunition to go forward. On the morning of the attack Corporal Fred Takes saw that his soldiers, like all of the others in the 325th Infantry, were suffering from thirst. The Aire River was obviously polluted by dead animals and men, and there was no drinkable water nearby. Takes did find some raw cabbage left by the retreating Germans, and he and his squad ate that. While moving forward Takes spotted a dead German soldier, and he "found a loaf of bread in his pack. It was very black and heavy. I cut the outside of the loaf off and I and a few others ate it. It was good, for the pack kept it dry."[12]

Another indicator of the mental and physical fatigue in the division was that artillery was firing short and hitting Americans while they were advancing. Julien Lindsey was livid about reports from the 327th and 328th that they were being shelled by friendly artillery. "Many reports have been received today [approximately 1 p.m., 11 October] of casualties from own artillery fire. Such reports were received when it was positively known that artillery targets were not closer than 2 kilometers of the front line."[13] Major Thomas Pierce, commanding the 3rd Battalion, 325th Infantry, complained to Colonel Whitman about poor shooting by the 157th. Major Pierce recalled that during the attack the Germans were firing from three sides and the American artillery was firing from the fourth.[14] Corporal Fred

Takes simply noted in his diary, "The shells were now falling all around us. Our barrage was falling short."[15] General Duncan made his displeasure known to Rhodes in no uncertain terms, and as nerves became frayed, the situation became worse between the two generals. A day later, Duncan, the old soldier, smoothed over the rift between the two tired commanders.

If Duncan was angry with his artillery, he was furious with the tank corps. General Lindsey had requested tank support for the attack on 11 October. Since his 164th Brigade was pretty badly shot up, he needed support in moving forward against the Germans. The tank park at Varennes had forty-eight tanks in running condition, and on that morning twenty-three left for the 164th Brigade. Three tanks arrived at Lindsey's command post, and these were in such doubtful condition that they were not used in the fight. An argument began over the tanks; the senior tank commander on the spot said that he had been ordered not to deploy less then five tanks at a time in combat. Julien Lindsey took his complaint to Duncan, who let Brigadier General S. D. Rockenbach, chief of the Tank Corps, know exactly how he felt. The situation simmered for months thereafter, and it did nothing to help Duncan's disposition on a day when things were going from bad to worse.[16]

To complicate matters the 327th Infantry was assigned to the 163rd Brigade, and the 325th was attached to the 164th Brigade. This conformed to unit locations before the attack, and on paper at least it made sense. However, the brigade commanders had not worked with those regimental commanders before, and unit integrity, so carefully built up through training, St. Mihiel, and the early phase of the Meuse-Argonne operation, was weakened. Cronin was not fully aware of the conditions within the 327th, which had taken such a heavy pounding only a few days before, and he had had little personal contact with Colonel Frank Ely or his staff.

The divisional battle plan was simple. The 163rd would attack northward, on the east, toward the Sommerance-St. Juvin Road, about three miles from Cornay. The 164th would also attack toward the north, aiming toward an area immediately east of St. Juvin. The 77th Division would move to the northeast, orienting on St. Juvin, which, it appeared, the Statue of Liberty division was to take and hold. On the right of the 82nd Division was the 1st Division, which had the mission of moving north toward the main German defensive line. Of concern to the All-Americans was the Big Red One's first major objective, the town of Sommerance. If the 1st Division did not take Sommerance, the Germans could pour a devastating flanking fire into the right flank of the 82nd. The plan was not complicated, but the execution would present great difficulties.[17]

Ely's 327th was given a tough job. It had to cross the Aire River at dawn to begin the attack north, and do so with no artillery preparation. The 3rd Battalion, under the command of a Captain H. Davis, was selected as the assaulting unit, but it was a hodgepodge of under strength companies, including what was left of the 1st Battalion. Major Harold Blanchard and his 2nd Battalion supported the assault, but Blanchard was the most experienced commander, with the strongest unit in the 327th Infantry.[18] Blanchard looked over the ground over which the 327th was to advance, and his experienced eye told him that the regiment had arrayed itself over too wide a front for the number of soldiers available.[19]

Captain Harwell Davis of Memphis, Tennessee, led his patched-up battalion across the makeshift bridges, and his troops came under heavy artillery and machine gun fire. Davis, who had recently commanded B Company, positioned himself with the lead companies, and the battalion pushed forward. Once it was even with the town of Sommerance, which had not been taken by the Big Red One, the Germans opened fire. Davis went down with several machine gun wounds. Troops were falling, and the attack was in serious trouble. With Davis down, Captain Courtney S. Henley of M Company took command, but in a few minutes Henley, from Birmingham, Alabama, was badly wounded.[20] Captain Leon T. Weaver, of Brewton, Alabama, in command of the support company, rushed to the front of the battalion, which had now fought its way into the first wire obstacles of the Kriemhilde Stellung. It had become obvious to Weaver that things were not going well: what he found was like a firestorm, and companies were being commanded by noncommissioned officers. A senior NCO was actually directing the assault of the battalion into the wire. Weaver did not last long; he was badly gassed. Nonetheless, he refused to leave the field until his company had come up.[21]

Not every act of courage that morning was performed by soldiers. Mr. H. B. McAfee, secretary of the YMCA contingent assigned to the 82nd Division, was not required to be in the middle of a terrible battle, but that day, when courage was commonplace, McAfee went forward with the troops and helped with the mounting number of wounded. The YMCA man grabbed his bag of chocolate candies, cakes, and cigarettes and went from foxhole to foxhole to hand out his wares, "in the face of continued shell fire, and sniping by rifles and machine guns, showing an entire disregard of his personal safety."[22] A prayer and a cigarette was as good as a bullet on that day.

To make matters worse, the 325th was not advancing. Colonel Walter Whitman was a solid commander and had gone forward with his lead battalion toward the German wire. Very quickly the 325th had come under heavy machine gun fire, and by 8:30 a.m. the attack had slowed.[23] Captain James R. Cooke, on Whitman's regimental staff, watched the colonel expose himself to enemy fire as he helped to stabilize the forward units.[24] The 3rd Battalion was to make the first attacks, but it was halted by heavy fire from the front and from Sommerance. By mid-morning Whitman had ordered Major David R. Hawkins, commanding the 2nd Battalion, to attack toward Sommerance to reduce those enemy machine gun positions, which were wreaking havoc for the 327th and 325th. Hawkins threw Company E into the fight, followed by the remainder of the battalion.[25] Company F was ordered to fall in on the left of the 3rd Battalion, but it made slow progress due to enemy machine gun fire; but once in position along a ridge line, German artillery opened up. The entire battalion had to withdraw behind the hill. Once the fire slackened the battalion surged forward again, only to be driven back. It had not reached the German wire.[26]

The toll in dead and wounded continued to mount throughout the morning. Recently promoted Major Warren Lott, commanding 1st Battalion, 325th Infantry, was ordered to take companies A and D under his personal command to reinforce the 327th. When Lott arrived he was told by Colonel Frank Ely to go back; the entire 327th, or what was left of it, was about to pull back. By noon the 327th was no longer capable of continuing the attack.[27] By 2 p.m. it was obvious to the division headquarters that strong German artillery and machine gun fire plus determined infantry counterattacks had driven the 325th and 327th regiments back.[28]

Duncan decided to relieve the exhausted, gassed Colonel Ely and replace him with Lieutenant Colonel Frank H. Burr. Burr's mission was to reorganize what was left of the depleted and worn- out 327th and renew the fight. That night Burr prepared to advance toward St. Juvin with what little he had left.[29] In fact, Burr had only twelve officers and 322 men left in the regiment. Major Harold Blanchard remained in command of his 2nd Battalion, but the 1st and 3rd were commanded by first lieutenants.[30]

By 4:30 p.m. the division had decided to pull its units back away from the ridge line near St. Juvin and dig in. What Duncan and Wainwright wanted was sunset, so that the brigades could make contact with others and prepare for action the next day.[31] Lindsey reported to division headquarters at 6 p.m. that most of the units were on line with each other. At the same time he complained that artillery fire from the 157th Field Artillery Brigade was again falling on the advanced units of the 82nd Division.[32] Charles D. Rhodes waited during the afternoon for a counterattack order, but by sunset it became clear that no such order would arrive, because of the battered condition of the troops.[33] As the battlefield darkened and a light rain began to fall, Corporal Fred Takes, who had survived the day without a scratch, could hear moans and shrieks from the American wounded. No one could venture out to bring them back to American lines. Despite the cold rain and the cries of the wounded, Takes fell into a deep sleep.[34]

Brigadier General Marcus Cronin's troops had made as little headway as the rest of the division. What he remembered most about that bloody day was the intensity of the German bombardment with high explosive and gas.[35] The 1st Infantry Division, the Big Red One, known in the AEF as "Pershing's Pets," was used up by the afternoon of 11 October and had to be relieved by the 42nd "Rainbow" Division, one of the AEF's oldest and most battle-tested divisions. Within three days the hard-fighting National Guardsmen of the Rainbow would be bled white. These doughboys were paying the price for the Pershing orthodoxy of open warfare which by mid-October had become basically a series of frontal assaults against the strongest of German positions on the Western Front, the Kriemhilde Stellung. Pershing himself recognized the perseverance and bravery of the 82nd Division when he acknowledged that the division, despite heavy opposition and crippling casualties, had pushed farther than even his beloved 1st Division.[36]

As darkness settled over the battlefield, Duncan, Wainwright, Johnston, Lee, and others met to discuss the day's events. The division command post had received a continuous flow of information and was well aware of the terrible cost of the day's fighting. It was also concerned about the state of logistics, that troops had not been fed a hot meal for days. To make matters more complicated, telephone lines were down between division and General Cronin's brigade headquarters. Communications had to be relayed by Colonel McArthur's 326th Infantry, which still had telephone communications with Cronin's command post. At 8:30 p.m. Wainwright told McArthur that Duncan had decided not to attack the St. Juvin line. He added, "No serious operations contemplated for tomorrow. Please transmit to Gen. Cronin"[37]

On 12 October the 42nd Division, on the 82nd's right, began to get into position to attack the Kriemhilde Stellung. Once the Rainbow Division began its attack the All-Americans would have to move forward to maintain contact with it. The memory of the 77th's situation with the "Lost Battalion" was fresh; no one wanted a gap or an open flank. Time was not, however, to be wasted. General Rhodes's 157th faced a difficult situation when the 78th Division began to move north, making contact with the rear elements of the 82nd Division. To deal with the arrival of the 78th, Duncan ordered Rhodes to move his command post from Châtel-Chéhéry to a point several miles north. Rhodes's signal troops had just finished laying and repairing telephone wire to the regiments, and all that now had to be disrupted. Rhodes told Duncan that his brigade would not really be ready to support operations until 13 October.[38] That was not good news for Duncan and Wainwright; the situation in the artillery brigade had an impact on division plans for 12 and 13 October.

Regardless of the condition of the troops, certain tasks had to be accomplished. On the night of 11 October Company H, 325th Infantry, under the command of First Lieutenant C. B. McDaniel, Jr., had occupied the town of Sommerance, which the enemy had evacuated. McDaniel, new to command, set up a ring of outposts around the ruined town. By the corps order Sommerance belonged to the 42nd Division, but it had yet to come up and occupy it. At midnight, Company H was told to make contact with the Rainbow division; several attempts to establish contact between the two divisions had failed. But at 2 a.m. Company H finally linked up with Brigadier General Michael J. Lenihan's 83rd Brigade. Once assured that Sommerance would be occupied by the 166th Infantry, McDaniel moved his small company back across the corps boundary.[39]

While the young Lieutenant McDaniel was moving his company to the east, the 82nd Division was making every effort to get all of its troops fed and resupplied. The job was made more difficult by constant shelling by German artillery north of St. Juvin. By 5:30 p.m. the 328th Infantry had been fed a hot meal, but only one battalion of each of the other regiments had been supplied. The division logistics officer was able to report more success establishing ammunition dumps to support infantry and artillery operations on the 13th.[40] The situation had become so severe that the machine gun battalions were gleaning the battlefield for German weapons and ammunition and using them against their former owners.[41]

On 13 October the division continued to resupply and prepare for the next push to the north, toward St. Juvin. There was a realignment of brigades; by late afternoon the 163rd and 164th had the regiments which they had started the Meuse-Argonne attack with.[42] Around 5 p.m. the division began to probe German lines toward the wire that had stopped it on 11 October. The division received an order from I Corps to begin the attack again on the morning of 14 October. The division ordered a maximum effort against the wire of the Kriemhilde Stellung, keeping contact with the 42nd and the 77th divisions, which were also to attack again against strong German defenses.[43]

Late on 13 October the chief of staff of I Corps, (whose code name was "Bonehead 7"—all the corps staff was "Bonehead") informed the 82nd Division that supplies of high-explosive rounds were running low. The 157th Brigade would have to use a higher percentage of shrapnel rounds on 14 October.[44] High-explosive rounds were meant for the destruction of enemy wire and pillboxes; shrapnel rounds had little effect on either. The fight on 14 October was not starting out well for the division.

The operational plan was simple. On the left was the 163rd Brigade, whose 326th was on the left, attacking in a column of battalions (3rd, 2nd, 1st), and on its right the much-reduced 325th. The 325th was attacking with only the 1st Battalion: the brigade reserve was the 3rd Battalion, and the 2nd Battalion was held back as a divisional reserve. To the right, Lindsey's 164th attacked with Richard Wetherill's 328th Infantry in a column of battalions (1st, 2nd, 3rd), with the 327th Infantry as the brigade reserve. Just prior to the start of the fight, Company E, 1st Gas and Flame Regiment, joined the 82nd Division to provide covering smoke for the attack. The attack was scheduled to begin at 8:30 a.m., after the 157th delivered a two-hour preparatory fire.[45]

For a unit in the shape the 82nd was, this plan of attack offered some definite advantages. First, combat power would be concentrated, hitting at a narrow point; second, if one battalion faltered another could be passed through to continue the assault with no break in the momentum of the attack. Also, there was only one company of the 1st Gas and Flame Regiment available, and a narrow front would suit its capabilities. Finally, hitting the wire at a narrow point, supported by smoke, meant that the enemy would have a smaller target to shoot at. Moving quickly through the wire would deprive the Germans of the opportunity to bring all their guns to bear.

At division headquarters Jim Wainwright and his G3 section labored to turn out a field order which could be sent down to the brigades. Field Order No. 24 was issued at 10 p.m., 13 October, and it outlined a simple plan of attack. There were some problems in the order, however. For instance, the artillery was to fire two hours prior to the infantry assault, and its mission was to cut the wire, but the critical shortage of high-explosive shells made success doubtful. On the other hand all woods and ravines would be especially targeted with nonpersistent chemicals.[46]

At 8:30 a.m., when the artillery barrage lifted, the infantry surged forward. Colonel Wetherill's 328th moved north until it encountered troops from the Rainbow division in its sector; it took about two hours for Wetherill to get the 42nd Division's soldiers moved to the east.[47] By noon Cronin had reported that elements of the 326th were actually to the north and east of St. Juvin, with light casualties.[48] But a situation was beginning to develop around St. Juvin. Field Order No. 24 had clearly stated that "the 77th [Division] is charged with taking St. Juvin, attacking from the South and East."[49] As the 82nd's 326th attacked it had lost contact with the 77th, and the Statue of Liberty apparently had not maintained the rate of advance.[50] The question now arose as to what to do with the German defenders in the town of St. Juvin.

The taking of St. Juvin was necessary if the 77th and the 82nd were to continue the advance north. Given the magnitude of the struggle in the Meuse-Argonne, the fight at St. Juvin would normally merit only a footnote, but after the war both division associations would claim credit for taking the pile of rubble; the two division commanders exchanged heated correspondence with the American Battle Monuments Commission. The dispute began late in the day on 14 October, when 82nd soldiers captured two hundred German defenders in St. Juvin, but the 77th claimed them as St. Juvin was in their area of operations.[51] The problem went back to the corps order and the maps laying out for the advance. The town of St. Juvin had been divided between the 77th and the 82nd Divisions, which must have been inadvertent on the part of I Corps G3. (No key terrain feature or objective should be split between two attacking divisions.)

The 77th Division's attack, which began at about 8:30 a.m., the same time as the 82nd crossed its line of departure, had been held up by heavy machine gun fire from German defensive positions near St. Juvin. The 82nd was by that time moving through the wire toward the St. Juvin-Sommerance Road.[52]

Wainwright and the division command post had been well aware of what was going on near St. Juvin. Colonel John McArthur, commanding the 326th Infantry, informed General Cronin that Major David Watkins, commanding 3rd Battalion, and his men were taking heavy small arms and machine gun fire from St. Juvin. The 77th had been nowhere in sight, and Watkins had moved into the east end of the town to silence the German infantry and machine guns.[53] Cronin had approved of the action and ordered Watkins and his troops to go north of St. Juvin. But the remainder of the town still had German defenders. Major John Muldrow, commanding the 320th Machine Gun Battalion, was well aware of the continual fire from St. Juvin and had sent elements of Company A into the town to stop the deadly German machine guns. The troops went into the town and, fighting as infantry, cleared out more Germans,[54] the western part of the ruins, however, yet continued in enemy hands, with the Germans using destroyed houses as infantry strong points and machine gun nests.

Major General Robert Alexander remembered the events at St. Juvin differently. By the late afternoon of 14 October St. Juvin had become a sore point, because 82nd units moving to the north were taking fire from the remaining Germans into their flank. If the 82nd, or for that matter the 77th, was to continue attacking the Kriemhilde Stellung, the St. Juvin boil would have to be lanced. Captain J. O. Oliver in H, 306th Infantry, 77th Division had arrived at St. Juvin some time in the late afternoon. Evidently he had met troops from Company A, 320th Machine Gun Battalion, who warned him about the Germans' strong defensive positions. Oliver (who later was promoted to major and commanded 3rd Battalion, 306th) had moved his small force of fifty infantrymen and one machine gun crew into the town, cleaned out some German machine gun nests, and moved on to occupy Hill 182 about three hundred meters north of St. Juvin.[55]

Who then took St. Juvin? By noon on 15 October the German defenders were all dead, wounded, or prisoners of war, and both American divisions were continuing the attack to the north, where a hot fight had developed that threatened to halt the entire American Meuse-Argonne offensive. It appears from the records that both divisions could claim credit for the reduction of the town. In the fog of war, and due to some bad planning graphics from I Corps, the responsibility for St. Juvin had fallen to both. In any case, the St. Juvin fight was over by the time the overall American attack came to a halt.

One of the tasks which the 82nd had to complete was to maintain contact with the 42nd Division. The Rainbow division on 14 and 15 October slammed into the some of the most difficult and well prepared defenses in the Kriemhilde Stellung. Orders came from I Corps to begin an attack north of St. Juvin at dawn on 15 October. This attack was to be in coordination with Charles P. Summerall's V Corps; its momentum would depend on units like the 77th, 82nd, and 42nd taking their objectives, which would be no mean task. The 82nd Division was nearing the end of its rope as far as combat effectiveness was concerned. On the afternoon of 15 October Lindsey reported that his 164th Brigade was seriously reduced in manpower. Wetherill's 328th had nineteen officers and 406 enlisted men present for duty. Burr's 327th could count seventeen officers and 490 soldiers for the fight, but 3rd Battalion had no officers left.[56] In the 163rd conditions were just as bad: Colonel Walter Whitman had just lost one of his best battalion commanders. Major Thomas L. Pierce, commanding 3rd Battalion, had sustained two wounds on 11 October but had refused to leave his battalion; late on 14 October he had received another severe wound, in the fighting near St. Juvin. Pierce had ordered his medics not to remove him until a new battalion commander was in place. For his bravery under fire, in great pain, Pierce was awarded the Distinguished Service Cross.[57]

The numbers were so small that Lindsey combined the 1st and 2nd battalions into one unit. Tough Lieutenant C. B. McDaniel of Company H, 325th Infantry, reported that almost all his men were sick from the rainy weather and from lack of hot food and drink.[58] The sick and wounded continued to suffer even after they were evacuated. The 307th Ambulance Company reported that their hospitals, aid stations, and triage units were constantly shelled by the Germans with high-explosive and gas rounds.[59] Stalwart Corporal Fred Takes and some of his men found some dry German clothes and put them on. One of his soldiers found some rations at a dump, and they ate cold coffee, beef, and hardtack in a driving rain-storm. Every piece of clothing was wet, and the temperature remained chilly.[60]

Charles Rhodes's brigade, now reinforced with two French artillery regiments, the 320th and 328th, began firing the initial barrage for the 15 October attack at 4 a.m. The 320th and 321st and the French pounded German positions north of St. Juvin along the St. Juvin–St. Georges road. The Germans immediately fired gas shells at the four regiments, inflicting heavy losses in the 321st, which had gun positions near Sommerance.[61] The 319th Regiment moved into locations near Fléville and fired at targets of opportunity for the infantry, which was scheduled to "go over the top" at about 8 a.m.[62]

The attack northward made the best use of the troops available. The area of operations was divided almost in half, with the Lindsey's 164th on the right and Cronin's 163rd on the left. No sooner had the attack begun than the Germans counterattacked all along the line, with an especially determined effort falling on the 163rd Brigade. Cronin was certain that his two undersized regiments could hold if the artillery fired in support.[63] Major David Watkins, now in charge of the combined 2nd and 3rd battalions of the 326th, took heavy damage from German artillery and small arms fire and had to request that fourteen ambulances be sent as quickly as possible to his command post.[64] Conditions were dire indeed for Watkin's command. Captain Grover Whitley, the battalion medical officer, was carried from the field, a gas victim. Captain E. M. Brown of F Company collapsed from shell shock and had to be evacuated. What was left of the 2nd Battalion was consolidated under the command of a first lieutenant.[65]

It was not apparent at the time, but the morning of 15 October was a time of crisis for the 82nd Division. The German counterattack was, as one All-American later described it, "a golden opportunity to strike, while the morale of our men was a little low due to a continuous cold rain since our first day over, and no warm food and very little cold food since October 9, 1918."[66] Major Warren Lott, commanding 1st Battalion in Whitman's 325th, sensed the dangerous situation that morning. His battalion was forced to retire, with heavy losses, in order to reestablish its defenses. Looking back on the fight, he wrote, "Everyone was almost at the point of exhaustion from the lack of rest, insufficient [*sic*] food and water. It rained almost continuously"[67] When the fight was over and the crisis passed, Lott counted seven officers and 125 enlisted men capable of fighting. That was all that was left of the 1st Battalion. In the 3rd Battalion, once commanded by the brave Major Thomas Pierce, losses were so severe that companies were combined and the remnant placed under the command of Captain Oliver Q. Melton, the senior officer left in the unit.

It was a dismal situation report that Wainwright sent to I Corps. Infantry regiments had an authorized strength of 4,000 officers and men each, but by the end of the heavy fighting on 15 October Jim Wainwright told the corps that there were in all only 150 officers and 4,138 combat soldiers, including the machine gun battalions, ready for combat on 16 October. The division's combat power had shrunk to one-third.[68] The 307th Engineers counted thirty-seven officers and 1,404 men available for duty; its casualties had occurred mainly when its troops had been used as wire cutters or infantry. The regiment was at slightly over one-third strength.[69] The medical officers of the division saw the end as far as continued service was concerned. Captain D. W. Goldstein, surgeon of the 164th, told Lindsey,

> I consider the remaining men of the 328th Inf. physically and mentally unfit for further duty, as practically the entire command has diarrhea—have been gassed to a greater or lesser extent and are at present exhausted. The continued rain is also lowering the resistance of these men.[70]

Lindsey had sent a message of his own about the condition of his brigade to division, two hours before Captain Goldstein's report to him.[71]

By late afternoon of 15 October elements of the 78th Division, the Lightning division, were on the scene and helped relieve units of the 82nd. The 82nd

Division had a problem in that the 42nd on its flank had found it almost impossible to move against the German defenses in its own sector. The 83rd Brigade of the Rainbow division, made up of two solid regiments, the 166th from Ohio on the left and the 165th from New York on the right, suffered extremely heavy casualties on 15 October but made no headway. The 82nd had advanced but was now in an exposed position north of the St. Juvin–St. George road. On 15 and 16 October the 78th Division relieved the battered 77th Division to the left of the 82nd and took some pressure off of the All- Americans left flank.[72]

There were periodic attacks by the All-Americans on 16 October, but it was obvious that this division was in no shape to maintain the momentum of the assault into the Meuse-Argonne. By noon it was clear that there was a lack of coordination. Every regiment reported heavy machine gun fire, and attempts to push forward failed.[73] Marcus Cronin's brigade was so heavily gassed that he decided to pull his troops back from what small gains they had made. At division headquarters Colonel Johnston, chief of staff, was becoming frustrated with constant messages from I Corps asking why the division had made no more progress then it had. Finally Johnston had had enough and in the afternoon explained to "Bonehead 3" (G3, I Corps) in no uncertain terms: "The higher up people should know that the enemy is putting in the best they have and the troops themselves appreciate the work they're doing, that they are saving their comrades and are making a good fight of it."[74]

On 17 October there were localized attacks, but by the end of the day the lines of the 82nd had changes little. At noon Cronin had informed division and the 164th Brigade that no progress could be made toward the town of Champigneuelle or the high ground to the east of the town, because of heavy German fire.[75] All in all, it was an unsatisfactory day for the 82nd Division, but given the condition of the troops little else could be done.

During the night of 17 October Wainwright prepared a field order to continue operations toward the town of Champigneulle, two miles due north of St. Juvin and about one mile from the lines of the 82nd Division. The main action of the day of the 18th fell on Cronin's 163rd Brigade. The 326th Infantry was tasked to maintain contact, while trying to move forward, with elements of the 78th Division on the division's left. Corporal Fred Takes, who had survived the fighting without a scratch, was disgusted with the orders. There were thirty-five men left in Company A of 325th; they were wet, cold, and poorly fed. "When we got the orders," Takes wrote, "to go over the top at 5 a.m. we were all disgusted thinking they wanted to kill us all off. . . . The captain said he knew none of us was hardly able for any more scrapping. He said to go as far as we could and then get in a shell hole."[76] As the company moved forward almost every man in the company suffered a wound of some sort. Takes, scratched and bloodied but not seriously wounded, simply fell into a shell hole. By now most of the companies of the four regiments could count perhaps one officer and about thirty men capable of combat action.[77]

The operational planners at I Corps continued to want the division to attack north, and during the afternoon they issued an order to continue operations toward Champigneulle. Wainwright ordered the 163rd to push patrols toward the town during the night of 18–19 October.[78] By 7:30 p.m., however, the G3 at division had rethought his patrol order and rescinded it, telling Cronin not to allow any patrol to get within a kilometer of the town.[79]

One of the problems facing the 82nd was ammunition. The commander of the 307th Engineers was tasked to find out what was happening to the flow of ammunition and other supplies, and to work on the roads to facilitate the logistics flow to the north.[80] One factor was that while men were wearing out from continual combat, horses were casualties as well. In the 307th Engineers and 307th Supply Train it was becoming more and more difficult to accomplish tasks because of the dwindling number of horses available. Animals suffered from wounds, lack of fodder, and especially from gas.

The 78th Division, like any unit new to combat, had difficulty in maintaining the thrust of its attack to the north. Since the 82nd had to maintain contact with and align on the Lightning division, there was little forward movement. On the right of the 82nd were the Rainbows, who had lost heavily in the fighting for the Kriemhilde Stellung; they were not moving either. The 42nd Division was scheduled to be relieved by the 2nd Division, and the 82nd by the 80th Division, but it would take some time for these units to effect the reliefs.

The day of 19 October was marked by patrols and by maintaining contact with the 42nd and the 78th Division. At 10 a.m., I Corps artillery and the 157th Brigade drenched the town of Champigneulle with gas. In fact the barrage was so heavy that all troops were pulled back another five hundred meters; Wainwright issued a warning about the quantity of gas in the town and the danger from shifting winds.[81] Major David Hawkins, still commanding his tiny battalion, 1,500 meters from the town, observed that despite the massive amount of gas the Germans were still there and that their machine gunners were quite capable of making a fight.[82]

It was also time for shifting of regimental commanders. Colonel Frank Ely, who had suffered badly from German gas early in the campaign, returned to the division. Colonel John McArthur, the solid commander of the 326th, collapsed from a combination of physical exhaustion and the effects of gas. Ely went back to his old regiment, the 327th, and Lieutenant Colonel Frank Burr was transferred to take command of McArthur's 326th.[83] It was becoming difficult to keep the command structure of the 82nd Division intact. On 20 October Charles D. Rhodes's promotion to major general was announced by GHQ, AEF, and it was certain that he would be leaving the command of the 157th shortly.[84] Rhodes had a replacement in the person of Colonel Earl D'A. Pearce, who had been with the brigade for a long time and who was serving as commander of the effective 319th Regiment.[85]

Between 20 and 28 October the division conducted patrols and fired periodically on the enemy. It was a time of preparation for another attack against the Germans, but the 82nd would not be involved in the operation. The All-Americans had been bled white in the Argonne Forest and then in the fighting around Cornay and St. Juvin. Sickness continue to reduce the ranks of the division; on 25 October Cronin's brigade reported that it could muster only seventy-two officers and 2,192 men, a far cry from the nearly eight thousand who began the fight in early

October.[86] The 164th was in the same shape, and both brigades reported that almost every soldier suffered from a variety of illnesses.

During the period of preparation the condition of the troops occupied the attention of every officer. Marcus Cronin suggested to Duncan that units be relieved not every night but every other night. This would give the men more rest and allow mess details to get hot food and drink to those in position. Food distribution would not be hindered by a nighttime rotation of troops. This suggestion was approved by General Duncan and became standard operating procedure in the 82nd.[87] Every effort was made to get the men clean clothes and hot baths, and to rid them of cooties and lice.[88] On 31 October the All-Americans were finally relieved by elements of the 80th ("Blue Ridge") Division. The 157th Artillery Brigade was attached to the 80th Division to support its attack to the north. Charles D. Rhodes was not with his gunners, however; he had been transferred to command the 42nd Division, whose commander, Charles Menoher, had just been promoted to corps command.[89]

There was no way for the division to know how many men it had actually lost in the Meuse-Argonne offensive. A preliminary report indicated that 224 officers and 5,154 men had been killed, wounded, or captured in the fighting. Almost four hundred were listed as missing. How many of that number were actually missing or had straggled from their units could not be ascertained.[90] Then there were men like Sergeant Marion C. Tucker, Company L, 328th Infantry, who had been wounded and carried to an aid station unconscious. He had awakened before being processed and left the station to rejoin his squad. He served there until 30 October, sixteen days after he was wounded, despite being severely gassed. Tucker, from Moultrie, Georgia, was awarded the Distinguished Service Cross by General Pershing.[91] How many who served while badly injured can never be known.

On 1 November 1918, a battered 82nd Division began the long march south to a rest area. The men expected a rest and a return to combat at some time when they were capable, but in fact the end of the war was a little over a week away. They had, the division would argue, spent more time in battle than any other AEF unit in the Meuse-Argonne. George Duncan had every reason to be proud of the men he commanded throughout the fight. Pershing had thrown them into the Argonne Forest as shock troops, and the division had done well. What awaited the 82nd Division, after rest and reorganization no one could tell, but it was a combat-experienced division now, and with a good reputation. When the word reached the division on 11 November that the armistice was in effect, there was no cheering or wild celebration. There were too many good friends missing from the ranks of the All-Americans.

NOTES

1. *Official History of the 82nd Division, American Expeditionary Forces, 1917–1919* (Indianapolis, IN: Bobbs-Merrill, 1919), 79–81.

2. Major Warren Lott to American Battle Monuments Commission, 16 June 1926, in Records Group 117, Records of the American Battle Monuments Commission, National

Archives, Washington, DC, carton 249 [hereafter cited as RG 117 with appropriate carton].

3. American Battle Monuments Commission, *82nd Division: Summary of Operations in the World War* (Washington, DC: Government Printing Office, 1944), 29–30.

4. A. C. Slattery to Whitman, 15 January 1919, Walter C. Whitman Papers, Scrapbook No. 2, U.S. Army Military History Institute Archives, Carlisle Barracks, PA [hereafter cited as MHI with appropriate collection].

5. HQ, 163rd Infantry Brigade, After Action Report, 4–31 October, 1918, c. 15 November 1918, in Records Group 120, Records of the AEF, 82nd Division, National Archives, Washington, DC, carton 15 [hereafter cited as RG 120 with appropriate carton].

6. HQ, Company C, 307th Engineers, Report of Engineer Operations and Condition, 10 October 1918, ibid., carton 28.

7. Second Lieutenant Raiford J. Wood to Whitman, 1 February 1919, Whitman Papers, MHI.

8. Diary entry, 11 October 1918, Rhodes Diary, ibid.

9. HQ, 163rd Infantry Brigade, After Action Report, 4–31 October 1918, c. 15 November 1918, RG 120, carton 15.

10. Typed copy, History of the Brigade Headquarters, 157th Field Artillery Brigade, ibid., carton 22.

11. G3, HQ, 82nd Division, Operation Report No. 83, 11 October 1918, ibid., carton 24.

12. Diary entry, 11 October 1918, Fred Takes Diary, MHI.

13. HQ, 164th Infantry Brigade, Preliminary Report on Operations, 11 October 1918, RG 120, carton 16.

14. Pierce to Whitman, c. January 1919, Whitman Papers, MHI.

15. Diary entry, 11 October 1918, Fred Takes Diary, MHI.

16. Duncan to Rockenbach, 18 February 1919, RG 120, carton 86.

17. HQ, 82nd Division, Field Order No. 23, 10 October 1918, ibid., carton 24. For more on the Sommerance and the 1st Infantry Division see The Society of the First Division, *History of the First Division During the World War, 1917–1919* (Philadelphia: John Winston, 1922), 202–12. This work indicates that the 1st Division took Sommerance. The records of the 82nd Division tell a different story.

18. George McIntosh Sparks, *The 327th under Fire* (n.p.: c. 1920), 73–74.

19. Blanchard to the American Battle Monuments Commission, c. 15 August 1930, RG 117, carton 250.

20. Sparks, *The 327th under Fire*, 76–78.

21. HQ, 82nd Division, General Orders No. 1, 13 January 1919, RG 120, carton 83.

22. Ibid.

23. HQ, 164th Infantry Brigade, Message Log, 9:50 a.m., 11 October 1918, ibid., carton 16.

24. Captain James R. Cooke to Whitman, 23 January 1919, Whitman Papers, MHI.

25. HQ, 2nd Battalion, After Action Report, 31 October 1918, RG 120, carton 17.

26. HQ, Company F, 325th Infantry, After Action Report, ibid.

27. Lott to Whitman, c. 1 November 1918, Whitman Papers, MHI.

28. HQ, 164th Infantry Brigade, Message Log, 2 p.m., RG 120, carton 16.

29. HQ, 327th Infantry, After Action Report, 6 November 1918, ibid., carton 17.

30. Sparks, *The 327th under Fire*, 80–81.

31. HQ, 82nd Division, Message Log, 4:35 p.m., 11 October 1918, RG 120, carton 4.

32. HQ, 164th Infantry Brigade, Situation Report, 11 October 1918, ibid., carton 16.

33. Diary entry, 11 October 1918, Rhodes Diary, MHI.

34. Diary entry, 11 October 1918, Fred Takes Diary, ibid.

35. HQ, 163rd Infantry Brigade, After Action Report, 4–31 October 1918, c. 15

November 1918, RG 120, carton 15.

36. John J. Pershing, *My Experiences in the World War*, II (Blue Ridge Summit, PA; Tab Books Reprint, 1989), 333–34.

37. HQ, 82nd Division, Message Log, 8:30 p.m., 11 October 1918, RG 120, carton 4.

38. Diary entry, 12 October 1918, Rhodes Diary, MHI.

39. HQ, Company H, 325th Infantry, After Action Report, 31 October 1918, RG 120, carton 17.

40. HQ, 82nd Division, Message Log, 3:30 p.m., 12 October 1918, ibid., carton 4.

41. HQ, 82nd Division, Message Log, 3:30 p.m., 12 October 1918, ibid.

42. HQ, 163rd Infantry Brigade, After Action Report, 4–31 October 1918, c. 15 November 1918, ibid., carton 15.

43. HQ, 82nd Division, After Action Report (Meuse-Argonne Offensive), c. December, 1918, ibid., carton 7.

44. *Official History of the 82nd Division*, 124. Orders went from brigade to the subordinate regiments to use shrapnel "whenever practical" and where American troops were not in danger. See HQ, 320th Field Artillery Regiment, Operations memorandum B-7, 13 October 1918, RG 120, carton 24. This expedient was, however, far from satisfactory or safe.

45. American Battle Monuments Commission, *82nd Division, Summary*,38–39.

46. HQ, 82nd Division, Field Order No. 24, 13 October 1918, RG 120, carton 24.

47. American Battle Monuments Commission, *82nd Division, Summary*, 39.

48. HQ, 82nd Division, Message Log, 11:04 a.m., 14 October 1918, RG 120, carton 4.

49. HQ, 82nd Division, Field Order No. 24, 13 October 1918, ibid., carton 24.

50. HQ, 82nd Division, Message Log, 12:35 p.m., 14 October 1918, ibid., carton 4.

51. Duncan to American Battle Monuments Commission, 23 February 1927, RG 117, carton 248.

52. American Battle Monuments Commission, *82nd Division, Summary*, 40–41.

53. HQ, 82nd Division, Message Log, 12 Noon, 14 October 1918, RG 120, carton 4.

54. HQ, 320th Machine Gun Battalion, After Action Report, 31 October 1918, ibid., carton 22.

55. Major J. O. Adler, After Action Report, 6 February 1919, RG 117, carton 235.

56. Courier Message from Lindsey to HQ, 2:15 p.m., 15 October 1918, RG 120, carton 23.

57. GHQ, AEF, G1, Decorations Section, 24 February 1919, ibid., carton 83.

58. HQ, Company H, 325th Infantry, After Action Report, 31 October 1918, ibid., carton 17.

59. HQ, 307th Sanitary Train, After Action Report, Ambulance Section, 2 November 1918, ibid., carton 29.

60. Diary Entries, 15 and 16 October 1918, Fred Takes Diary, MHI.

61. Diary Entry, 15 October 1918, Rhodes Diary, MHI.

62. Typed copy, History of the 319th Field Artillery, 21 December 1918, RG 120, carton 25.

63. HQ, 82nd Division, Message Log, 8 a.m., 15 October 1918, ibid., carton 4.

64. HQ, 82nd Division, Message Log, 9:55 a.m., 15 October 1918, ibid.

65. HQ, 2nd Battalion, 326th Infantry, After Action Report, 1 November 1918, ibid., carton 18.

66. HQ, Company C, 1st Battalion, 325th Infantry, After Action Report, 26 December 1918, Whitman Papers, MHI.

67. HQ, 1st Battalion, 325th Infantry, After Action Report, c. November 1918, ibid.

68. HQ, 82nd Division, Operation Report No. 87, 15 October 1918, RG 120, carton 24.

69. HQ, 82nd Division, Message Log, 7 p.m., 16 October 1918, ibid., carton 5.

70. Goldstein to Lindsey, Message Log (164th Brigade), 12:30 p.m., 16 October 1918, ibid.

71. Lindsey to 82nd Division HQ, Message Log (164th Brigade), 10:15 a.m., 16 October 1918, ibid.

72. American Battle Monuments Commission, *Summary, 82nd Division*, 45–47.

73. HQ, 164th Brigade, Message Log, 11:45 a.m., 16 October 1918, RG 120, carton 5.

74. Johnston to Cronin, Message Log (164th Brigade), 2 p.m., 16 October 1918, ibid.

75. HQ, 164th Infantry Brigade, Message Log, 12:20 p.m., 18 October 1918, ibid.

76. Diary entry, 18 October 1918, Fred Takes Diary, MHI.

77. HQ, Company F, 325th Infantry, After Action Report, 31 October 1918, RG 120, carton 17. I have used this AAR as an example. The remainder are in carton 17 and can be individually consulted.

78. HQ, 82nd Division, Message Log, 6:25 p.m., 18 October 1918, ibid., carton 5.

79. HQ, 82nd Division, Message Log, 7:15 p.m., 18 October 1918, ibid.

80. HQ, 307th Engineers, Chronological History—307th Engineers, 28 February 1919, ibid., carton 28.

81. HQ, 82nd Division, Message Log, 10 a.m. and 1:33 p.m., 19 October 1918, ibid., carton 5.

82. HQ, 82nd Division, Message Log, 11:15 a.m., 19 October 1918, ibid.

83. *Official History of the 82nd Division*, 199.

84. Diary entry, 20 October 1918, Rhodes Diary, MHI.

85. Typed copy, History of the Brigade Headquarters, 157th Field Artillery Brigade, c. March 1919, RG 120, carton 22.

86. HQ, 163rd Infantry Brigade, After Action Report, c. November 1918, ibid., carton 15.

87. HQ, 82nd Division, Message Log, 4:55 p.m., 22 October 1918, ibid., carton 5.

88. HQ, 82nd Division, After Action Report (Meuse-Argonne Offensive), c. December 1918, ibid., carton 7.

89. Diary entry, 30 October 1918, Rhodes Diary, MHI.

90. HQ, 82nd Division, Battle Casualties, c. November 1918, RG 120, carton 97.

91. GHQ, AEF, G1, Decorations Section, 24 February 1919, ibid., carton 83.

Chapter 9

Trains to Italy

Corporal Fred Takes, Company A, 325th Infantry, had survived the heavy fighting with only a few deep cuts and scratches, and this Friday, 1 November, he was a happy man. After a good night sleep,

> We left right after breakfast for a bath, it was three miles to the bath house. This was a German bathhouse, but is now used by the Americans. They also had large steam boilers there to sterilize our clothes. Here I got all new clothes but a cap and overcoat. We sure did enjoy a bath and change of clothes. We were as lousy as a coocoo. This was our first bath and a change of clothes for about six weeks.[1]

Like most of the survivors of Company A, 325th Infantry, Takes was content to put up his tent in the rain and just sleep. In the distance the rumble of artillery signaled the last great push of the AEF in the war.

As the division left the St. Juvin area there was no really accurate count of the troops remaining. Major John Paul Tyler, the senior chaplain of the 82nd, reported to General Duncan that chaplains had buried 450 men by 19 October and that he believed that an equal number remained to be given proper burial. Duncan simply could not account for 1,086 soldiers who were missing in action. As he reported to I Corps, the nature of the fighting had been such that some would probably never be found. There were few stragglers; most appeared to be dazed from combat. Duncan added, "It is noted that about 75 percent of the stragglers are foreign-born and with an improper knowledge of English. Every effort is being made to correct the evil of straggling."[2] General Hunter Liggett, commanding First U.S. Army, was livid over the number of troops who straggled—simply wandered away from their units—and he was making his displeasure known to everyone. At some point straggling became desertion under fire, and that carried a very serious penalty.

Once out of combat the division conducted a head count and found that it was short 291 officers and 7,577 men. Also, it was missing a thousand horses and mules, which was one-third of the authorized number. Artillery, supply, and medical units were having difficulty in moving guns, supplies, and men.[3] The G1 of First U.S. Army promised that replacements would reach the division as soon they became available, and on 13 November over eight thousand men came into the division. Many of the new men came from the 39th Division, which had been designated as a depot division.[4]

The AEF had begun designating certain divisions as depots, to supply troops to other units for combat. This process had begun in the fall of 1917, when the 41st was so designated. It was a terrible waste of training and manpower; entire divisions were broken up and parceled out. The 39th ("Delta") Division had been made up of units from the National Guards of Mississippi, Arkansas, and Louisiana and had been trained at Camp Beauregard, Louisiana, before embarking for France. To complicate matters for everyone, Pershing's headquarters required divisions to send officers to the depot divisions to train men for service at the front. According to GHQ, AEF, those trainers were to spend five months.[5] The war ended, however, before the 82nd could send such valuable officers to the 39th.

It would take several weeks before the 82nd Division could be ready for combat operations again, given the condition of the troops, materiel, and animals. The division was moved from the Argonne Forest to a French training area near Vaucouleurs, where the 42nd and other AEF divisions had trained in 1917 and early 1918. The 82nd arrived there on 7 November; on 16 November the unit shifted farther south to a training area near Prauthoy, where the All-Americans would make their winter quarters and continue to train.[6]

When word reached the 82nd that the armistice had been signed, the question arose of when the All-Americans would be going home. They were not leaving France immediately, however. Pershing had agreed to send a combat force into Germany, to the west bank of the Rhine River, so that if the armistice fell apart the allies could renew operations immediately. Five experienced divisions were sent into Germany, and several others went into Belgium and Luxemburg to guard the line of communications between the port of Antwerp and Germany. Other experienced combat units were held in France as a reserve, and the 82nd Division was one of those. The troops of the 82nd watched as new combat divisions arrived in France and literally turned around and headed back to the United States. It was a wise policy to retain the best-trained, battle-tested units, however, because it was not clear that the armistice would last. At any rate, the 82nd Division would spend at least one Christmas in France.

With the 82nd recovering from the Meuse-Argonne campaign, attention turned to promotions, courts-martial, and training. A number of key staff officers were reassigned during the months of November and December. Lieutenant Colonel Jonathan M. Wainwright, the steady G3, was ordered to the general staff of Third U.S. Army at Coblenz, Germany. Jim Wainwright had made a good reputation as a soldier and planner, and assignment to Major General Theodore Dickman's staff was a good indication of a solid future in the Army. Wainwright would remain with Third U.S. Army until 1920. This new post also meant that Jim Wainwright would retain his lieutenant colonel's silver oak leaves until he left the troops on the Rhine.[7] He was replaced by Major George E. Roosevelt, who had served in the G3 section and was a recent graduate of the General Staff School at Langres.

Major General George Duncan recommended a number of other officers for promotion. As soon as the division settled into its new quarters at Prauthoy, Duncan wrote directly to his old friend John J. Pershing requesting promotion to brigadier general for his chief of staff, Gordon Johnston. Johnston had served and commanded the 77th Division's 307th Infantry Regiment in combat and then came to the 82nd to head up the staff, giving it a steadying influence. At the same time he recommended Brigadier General Douglas McArthur of the Rainbow division for major general.[8] Neither officer received promotion, however; the War Department halted all promotions in the National Army once the armistice was in place. Pershing continued to pressure Washington to approve promotions, especially those requested prior to 11 November, but the War Department was adamant. The U.S. Army was demobilizing quickly, and there was no need for such numbers of general officers, or any other senior officers, for that matter.

Marcus Cronin left the 163rd Brigade for a new assignment, and his place was taken by Brigadier General John J. Bradley, a regular infantry officer. The 327th Infantry was taken over by Colonel John F. Preston, who had seen combat with the 303rd Infantry Regiment. General Lindsey remained in command of the 164th Brigade until February 1919, when he was replaced by Colonel John F. Preston. Colonels Richard Wetherill and Walter Whitman retained command of their regiments. While the changes were being made in the command structure, the troops were given a strict training schedule, which came as an unpleasant surprise to most of the men in the ranks.

The All-Americans still did not have the 157th Field Artillery Brigade with them at Prauthoy. Until the armistice of 11 November Rhodes's gunners had still been fighting in the Meuse-Argonne campaign. When Pershing decided to begin the final attack against German positions south of the Meuse River on 1 November it was obvious that the divisions making the assault would have to be supported by more artillery than just the three-regiment field artillery brigade. On 26 October, the G3, 80th Division, issued Field Order No. 26, which placed Rhodes's brigade under the command of the division. The field order assumed command of the 82nd's 307th Ammunition Train as well.[9]

What the AEF had finally realized was that the concept of the rolling barrage did not accomplish much in the way of cutting wire, protecting advancing trips, or reducing German strong points. Major General Adelbert Cronkhite, commanding the 80th Division, wanted an extra battalion of 75mm guns attached to each infantry brigade to engage and reduce German strong points at point-blank range. The divisional artillery brigade would then be able to fire normal missions. Rhodes did not have much to do, as his three regiments were allocated to portions of the line in support of infantry.[10] On 2 November Rhodes left his artillerymen for command of the 42nd Division, and the 157th came under the command of Colonel Earl D'A. Pearce, who continued the fight toward the Meuse River.[11]

From the afternoon of 31 October until 9 November, the 157th followed the infantry of the Blue Ridge division northward. Roads were poor, due to constant rain and enemy shelling, and food, forage, and fresh water became scarce. The

319th Artillery Regiment recorded that everywhere it had to contend with mud over a foot deep.[12] On the afternoon of 6 November the order came from Colonel Pierce to halt in place, service the guns, and rest. Word had reached the 80th Division that the 1st Division, under Brigadier General Frank Parker, would pass through the Blue Ridge men and continue the attack to the Meuse River. On 8 November elements of the Big Red One cleared the sodden roads, and the 157th was given the order to proceed south to rejoin the 82nd Division, wherever that might be.[13] Given the confusion of the armistice and the sending of combat divisions to the Rhine River, the artillery brigade waited on orders and transportation. Finally, on 17 December, the last element of Pearce's gunners arrived at their destination, and the 82nd was finally reunited.[14]

It was a command that was involved in intensive training. When the fighting ended on 11 November 1918 the staff emphasis from GHQ, AEF, down to the lowest level shifted from the G3, operations, to the G5, training. Pershing knew that the armistice might not hold and that combat operations might begin again. The units selected to go to the Third Army and those held in France as a reserve could not allow the sharp edges obtained in combat to dull. They had trained for and engaged in combat, and what they needed now was sustainment training. Also, there was an influx of new men, most with no battle experience, who would have to be brought up to standard if they were to be committed to fighting. Pershing's G5, Brigadier General Harold B. Fiske, understood exactly what Pershing wanted done, and he pressed the divisions to begin a rigorous, eight-hour-a-day training schedule. Fiske became known as "the most hated man in the AEF," because of his insistence on post-combat training, but there were sound military reasons for the program.

On the other hand, Pershing understood that the AEF had been involved in intensive training and operations over a considerable period of time. The 82nd Division had been in contact with of the enemy for over a hundred days, and there was no reason why leave could not be granted to a reasonable number of men, especially those still serving in France. Attention would also have to be paid to the health and the morale of the troops facing a winter that turned from the relentless rains of October and November into the snows of December and January. From late November to mid-January training and rebuilding the division was the main focus of the 82nd.

A typical day for an infantry battalion specified four hours of drill and rifle instruction in the morning, two hours of physical training after lunch, and two hours of maintenance of equipment and inspections. Every day there was at least a half hour devoted to unit singing, as had been done at Camp Gordon. This was to build unit morale and esprit de corps and offer some relief from the continual drill.[15] In all battalions there was an emphasis on physical training as a preparation for combat and as a way to keep soldiers healthy. There were ten different sports that men were required to participate in: 100 and 440-yard dash, 220-yard walk, broad jump, three-legged race, relay race, equipment race, sack race, 12-man tug-of-war, and an assortment of basketball, football, soccer, and boxing. Each battalion was required to take note of promising boxers for division and corps competition.[16] On Saturday the routine varied, in that each battalion held a full guard mount for two hours followed by two hours of personal and billet inspection. After the noon meal a number of men were allowed to go to local towns to restaurants, cafés, and to see the sights. Sunday was considered a day of rest, religious services, and preparation for the following duty day.

General George Duncan could count himself a successful division commander. He had taken command of the 82nd in early October and had found a first-class staff. His intent was to keep the fighting edge of the 82nd Division sharp, and to do this he favored terrain exercises and maneuvers, when the weather allowed. Duncan prescribed that exercise or practical application be preceded by a full explanation of the objective of the day's training. He required that at the end of the training a critique be held to tell the troops what had gone right and what had gone wrong. Woe betide the trainer, officer or NCO, who began the exercise with only a broad title or a general explanation of the day's tactical training. The troops, in Duncan's mind, should be made aware of the specific tasks that they were to practice that day. Company commanders were required to present a "lecture and conference" about a phase of the 82nd's operations in the Meuse-Argonne fight. Duncan himself conducted the first lecture, on 9 December, with the brigade commanders and their staffs in attendance. Once they saw how Duncan wished to proceed, they in turn held their own conferences, with regimental commanders and staffs in attendance.[17]

No unit in the 82nd was neglected as far as training was concerned. The 307th Sanitary Train, which had done good service under trying circumstances, began its day's training with physical exercise and singing. The unit then did close-order drill, followed by such classes as litter drill, first aid, and other medical-related topics. The day ended with more athletic events, such as basketball, races, and football.[18]

The 307th Engineers faced some challenges in training in that units were designated to do actual tasks, such as road improvements, barracks construction, and support for infantry and machine gun training. At the same time the requirements for intensive physical training and infantry-style close-order drill remained in order. The longtime commander of the 307th Engineers, Julian L. Schley, was transferred to Third Army, and on 10 December Colonel Henry A. Finch assumed command of the regiment.[19] Of all of the regiments of the 82nd Division the 307th Engineers faced the most difficult job, doing actual work and fulfilling training requirements for close-order drill, athletics, and other required subjects. Schley had been a good organizer, but he was replaced by an officer with equal abilities.

The machine gun battalions came up with some innovative ideas for training and motivation. All these battalions spent a great deal of time in assembly, disassembly, and maintenance of the weapon, and supporting infantry regiment tactical training. To keep up interest in training, Captain John C. Benjamin, commanding the 319th Machine Gun Battalion, held a competition between squads in assembly and disassembly of the machine gun. The best squad was excused from standing reveille formations at 5 a.m. for two weeks.[20] Major Joseph F. Muldrow, commander of the 320th Machine Gun Battalion, instituted a test on squads' knowledge of the names of the division commander, chief of staff, division machine gun officer, brigade and battalion commanders, and the location of all command posts. The winning squad got time off from training.[21] The battalions faced some of the same problems that the 307th Engineers faced, in that they had to conduct training, submitting to the division their schedules for the week, but also support infantry brigade and regimental tactical exercises. By designating one battalion in turn to support other activities, training integrity in the battalions could be reasonably maintained.

Since this was an infantry division, there was an emphasis on weapons and live firing on the range to maintain competence in marksmanship. The area which the 82nd occupied had been used as a training area, and ranges were already in existence; commanders could take companies and battalions to them at any time. In addition to marksmanship training and firing, the ranges had courses for throwing and detonating grenades and for firing mortars and machine guns.[22] In many ways the 82nd had better training and range facilities than their counterparts on the Rhine River in the Third Army; that area of Germany had not been developed for military training.

Duncan continued to stress military discipline, with particular emphasis on the appearance and behavior of his officers. He warned that John J. Pershing would "personally inspect and review" the 82nd.[23] Every commander in the AEF knew that "Black Jack" demanded continual emphasis on military courtesy and uniforms, and on diligence in training. A visit from the General of the Armies was something that every unit prepared for in detail. When Pershing and his entourage from Chaumont visited the 82nd Division they were pleased with what they saw. Training was going well, and the morale and physical condition of the troops appeared to be at high levels.

While troops trained with an eye on the great discussions taking place at Versailles, the division had to attend to some longstanding personnel problems. There would be investigations into the conduct of a number of officers, and the Judge Advocate General of the 82nd began to prepare for a courts-martial for misconduct during the St. Mihiel and Meuse-Argonne operations. There was also the nagging problem of trying to account for soldiers missing in action. The War Department and the General Headquarters of the AEF at Chaumont were bombarded by parents and spouses frantic to know the fate of their loved ones. Duncan ordered that each case be looked into and that every soldier who had served with the missing men be questioned in detail.

Before the division had disengaged from the fighting in the Meuse-Argonne campaign, Duncan had directed Major G. Edward Buxton, the division's inspector general, to take a long look at the senior medical officers serving in the 82nd. Buxton found that Lieutenant Colonel Robert H. Mills, the chief dental surgeon, was basically worthless to the division; he did little dental work and did not supervise his subordinate dentists. All other medical officers were competent, hardworking officers, especially Major George A. Blakeslee, the division psychiatrist, who had a very difficult task in sorting out shell-shock cases, self-inflicted wounds, and insanity brought on by the stress of combat. Lieutenant Colonel L. H. Reichelderfer, overall commander of the Sanitary Train, was also a problem, in that he seemed to lack initiative and drive.[24] Colonel Conrad E. Koeper, a regular Army officer and the 82nd's division surgeon, wanted Reichelderfer transferred to a base hospital somewhere in the AEF, where he could work as a physician rather then as a doctor-administrator. Luther H. Reichelderfer, a graduate of George Washington University Medical School and a longtime member of the National Guard of the District of Columbia, was too valuable to send home, so he was transferred to Base Hospital No. 2 near Bordeaux.[25] Colonel Mills was simply ordered back to the United States for discharge.

At the same time, Duncan relieved Major Bernard A. Purcell, the division motor officer, after reports reached division headquarters that inspection and maintenance of vehicles was not being done in a satisfactory manner.[26] The trucks, automobiles, and trucks of the 82nd Division had become a sore point for Duncan and the staff. Vehicles were always in short supply, as were spare parts, and any laxity in vehicle maintenance was a matter of serious concern. In November Duncan had relieved Purcell's predecessor, Lieutenant Colonel Manfred Lanza, a regular Army officer, as division motor officer;[27] Purcell was himself relieved one month later. From all accounts and records, the problem was having too few vehicles for the tasks assigned; also, the flow of repair parts was very slow, especially for vehicles manufactured in the United States. At any rate Purcell, a civilian who had volunteered for war service, was returned to the United States upon his request for discharge. Lanza, who had a career at stake, was assigned to an infantry regiment in the 90th Division. The problem with motor vehicles in the 82nd Division was never solved.

Once battle is over—and this is true for any combat division—there is a none-too-subtle shift in emphasis at the staff level. In the heat of conflict the focus must be on the G2 (intelligence) and the G3 (operations) sections, because there are battlefield missions to be accomplished, plans to be made, and orders to be written; there are men dying accomplishing those missions. Out of combat, however, the G1 (personnel) and the G4 (logistics) take on a new importance. For the 82nd Division training of the infantry remained all-important, but in post-combat training, aside from accidents, no one died. Other critical considerations came into play, such as troop morale and recreation, cleanliness of permanent barracks and billets, operation of mess halls, etc. The lion's share of day-to-day tasks fell to the G1 and the G4 once the All-Americans were out of combat and in their reserve-training role.

First U.S. Army was as concerned about these matters as was the division; and Hunter Liggett sent Colonel Leon B. Kromer to inspect the division, particularly in G1 areas. Duncan had known Kromer in the prewar Army. Under the G1 was Major John Paul Tyler, the senior chaplain, the second most important officer involved with morale and welfare issues. Kromer began an in-depth inspection of the 82nd Division, with special emphasis on questions of troop morale and personnel. What he found should have pleased Duncan. Of interest to both Kromer and to Tyler was the YMCA, which had functioned so well in combat, but which had a slow start once the division arrived in the Prauthoy training area. There were twenty-six active Y-workers in the division to serve the 82nd, which had grown to 926 officers and 25,190 enlisted men. Each subordinate unit had either a special "Y-Hut" or the use of a building. Entertainment was held in all areas, with professionals from America and Europe frequently visiting the 82nd. Kromer visited one Y function per day as part of his duties.[28]

Kromer also instituted an inspection, every two weeks, of troop billets and barracks, and he directed the commanding officer of the unit and a medical officer to accompany him or his representative on the inspection. With influenza causing serious health problems and a considerable number of deaths in the AEF, healthy living areas were of great importance to the G1. He also found that incidences of drunkenness, venereal disease, and absence without leave were at a minimum. All in all, this was a disciplined combat unit with few personnel problems.[29] When Kromer returned to First Army, his inspection schedules remained as a part of the division's standing procedures.

The chaplains, under the director of Major Tyler, were hard at work for the division. Looking back on the battles of October, Tyler reported that one chaplain, Daniel Smart of the 328th Infantry, had been killed and two others had been wounded. Of the volunteers from the Knights of Columbus working with the 82nd, John Stewart had been gassed and Joseph Crow had been wounded, his leg having been amputated. Combat had been as hard on the religious organizations as on the soldiers. Burial services were so numerous during Meuse-Argonne that Tyler secured a battalion of the 53rd Pioneer Infantry Regiment to dig the graves for over a thousand bodies. Two problem areas which Chaplain Tyler said needed to be dealt with were the lack of a sales commissary unit for the 82nd Division and the need for the senior chaplain of the division to have some control over the volunteers working for the 82nd.[30]

Throughout the time at Prauthoy the division's chaplains worked to raise morale and care for the welfare of the troops. Tyler was able to report by the end of January that there was full cooperation between his office and the YMCA, the Red Cross, and the Knights of Columbus. January also marked an effort by the chaplains and the volunteers to provide educational opportunities for the troops.[31] More than eight thousand soldiers took advantage of courses offered in everything from English to gardening.[32] In early March, when the division had been alerted to be ready for movement back to the United States, Tyler and his chaplains began to prepare for the move to the ports of embarkation. An effort was made to inform the home church or synagogue of each soldier of his arrival to arrange a welcome and continue the religious work done in the AEF.[33]

Lieutenant Colonel James P. Barney became the G1 when Troupe Miller left the 82nd Division, and it fell to him to supervise a number of activities in the division. None were more serious than trying to account for missing soldiers, and conducting courts-martial. Letters poured into Washington and into all AEF units asking about the missing in action, and every effort was made to find them. The Central Records Office of the AEF did not want to verify that a soldier had been killed unless there was some solid proof, but often that was difficult to find. When asked about missing or presumed dead buddies soldiers usually stated that in the heat of battle it was almost impossible to keep an eye on everybody. Sometimes artillery obliterated a person. Soldiers were required to keep two identity disks ("dog tags"), but often they were lost. A wounded soldier who could not speak and who had lost his disks could not be identified.[34]

Burial reports went to the G1 of the division from each chaplain conducting a service. The name, rank, serial number, and unit was included in the report, if known. The chaplain who accompanied the 82nd's battalion of the 53rd Pioneer Infantry also filed reports with the 82nd's G1, but often the notation read "unknown," due to the condition of the body. By the time Lieutenant Colonel Barney compiled the list it was over seventeen pages long for the known killed in the Meuse-Argonne battle alone.[35] The division was also fairly certain that the 42nd, 77th, and the 78th buried All-American soldiers along with their own dead. There were also constant reports of identifiable bodies found by burial parties in ravines and thickets after the armistice.

Units usually left no stone unturned to ascertain what had happened to the missing. A good case in point was the effort made by Colonel Walter Whitman of the 325th concerning a five-man patrol sent out by the regiment during the St. Mihiel battle. After four months in a German prisoner of war camp, one member, Corporal Frank Slavens, rejoined the regiment. He claimed that he did not see any bodies after they had stumbled into a German ambush. Chaplain Tyler reported that a captured German officer told him that two officers from the patrol were prisoners. Whitman sent a team to the spot and searched for graves for several miles. French villagers were questioned, but no one recalled wounded or dead Americans. Whitman continued his search until the regiment left France, never having learned what had happened on the night of 29 August.[36]

The wounded presented another problem; they were scattered all over France in hospitals. Major Oliver O. Feaster, commanding the Headquarters, 307th Sanitary Train, compiled a list of the wounded who could be accounted for and who were still in hospitals. By mid-January there were well over a hundred men, but not every hospital in the jurisdiction of the AEF responded. Some soldiers from the 1st Division and the 77th Division who had been initially treated by the 82nd's field hospitals and had been evacuated by them were reported to the 82nd, not to their home divisions, which had the responsibility for accounting for them.[37] Of course, some of the 82nd Division soldiers could not respond to questions, because they did not understand English.

To complicate the picture even more there were questions of American prisoners of war. Some PWs, taken in the St. Mihiel battle and early in the Meuse-Argonne, were properly processed by the Germans and reported to the American attaché in Bern, Switzerland. But as conditions for the Germans became more chaotic, reporting and processing ended. Some Americans were sent to temporary holding areas, while others were just released by the units which had captured them. A number of Americans were turned loose in Germany, reporting to the early-arriving units of the Third Army. The Germans cared for American wounded, but many who were unable to speak and who had lost their identification remained in Germany in military hospitals, unaccounted for. The Central Records Office, which obtained lists of names of men who were still held in Germany but had no unit designation, circulated those lists to all combat divisions to see if they could be identified. Then there was a short list of soldiers known to have been taken prisoner but as yet not found in reports from the Germans. Their fate could only be guessed at.[38]

All in all, it was a very unsatisfactory process, but in the fog of heavy combat it was obvious that men would be lost and never accounted for. With the collapse of the German war effort in November, the ensuing chaos and turmoil ensured that there would be grave difficulties in finding everyone who was missing. For decades after the Great War bodies would be found in shallow graves or in the ravines and thickets where they had fallen, unnoticed by their comrades. Nothing, however, could really answer the letter that General Duncan received from a small town in Maine in March, 1919, from a hopeful sister,

> He entered the army over a year ago and last October he was reported killed or rather died after he was shot. I do not for some reason believe he is dead because there is another man by the same name who has often recieved his letters and boxes[.] So you see it is hard to tell which is the dead man. We think that there is a mistake and he is in the hospital and can't write or perhaps he is coming home soon and does not write for that reason.[39]

Private Louis Nadeau, Company F, 327th Infantry, would not go home to Old Towne, Maine. There was no mistake. He had died north of St. Juvin on 15 October 1918, and he was buried in the American cemetery at Verdun, where he still rests.

Courts-martial fell into two distinct categories. The first, the most severe, were for desertion under fire, and there were about three dozen such cases tried during January and February 1919. In every instance the soldier was found guilty, sentenced to dishonorable discharge and penal servitude for ten years.[40] The other cases ranged from public drunkenness to stealing from French civilians. On one occasion soldiers of the 327th had become rowdy after too much strong red wine and had stolen thirty-two chickens and eleven rabbits and had broken two windows, all belonging to a café owner, Jules César Alexandre Houette. Major Charles B. Zimmerman, assigned to the 82nd to take care of claims such as this, paid Monsieur Houette almost a hundred dollars for his loss, and the soldiers were apprehended and punished for their crime.[41] Normally this involved loss of rank and pay, and time in the division guardhouse. More serious was the case of an officer who contracted syphilis from a Mademoiselle Rénant. When the dread disease had been diagnosed, the infected soldier had returned to the café, where he struck the woman and broke a number of windows, glasses, tables, and chairs. Given the seriousness of the infection and the stress caused by it, the 82nd paid a hundred francs to the café owner. Rénant could not be found by French authorities, and the infected officer was not allowed to return to the United States with his unit.[42]

While the division was trying to sort out a myriad of personnel matters, the question of decorations surfaced. A number of soldiers were cited for gallantry, and the paperwork to award the Distinguished Service Cross was initiated. Colonel Richard Wetherill of the 328th Infantry began to investigate the extraordinary deeds of now Sergeant Alvin C. York at Châtel-Chéhéry on 8 October 1918. After interviewing all the surviving enlisted men, Wetherill became convinced that York deserved the Medal of Honor. General Lindsey read the eyewitness accounts and agreed, and on 10 February the recommendation was sent forward to Duncan.[43] Pershing in turn read the endorsement from Duncan and all the testimony, and he agreed that York had indeed gone above and beyond the call of duty and had exceeded the requirements for the Distinguished Service Cross.[44]

But there was a problem: Sergeant York already had his DSC, and the Medal of Honor would supercede it. One could not award two medals for the same action; it was decided that York would have to return the DSC and ribbon to General Duncan. It was explained to York why he had to surrender Distinguished Service Cross number 421, and he agreed. A ceremony would take place with all honors due to the Medal of Honor and the brave soldier who had earned it.[45] On 18 April 1919, in front of the entire division, Major General George Duncan presented York his Medal of Honor, and a legend was born.[46]

The award ceremony came at the end of a very hectic period for the 82nd Division. There were major changes in the division staff in mid-February: Colonel Gordon Johnston, chief of staff, was transferred to a command in the 7th Division, and Major George E. Roosevelt, who had replaced Wainwright as G3, was promoted to Johnston's position; Lieutenant Colonel John Barney, the G1, became seriously ill, and his place was taken by Captain Frederick T. Robson, longtime member of the G1 section during the St. Mihiel and Meuse-Argonne campaigns. Both Roosevelt and Robson were promoted to the next higher grades.[47]

On 20 February GHQ, AEF, informed the 82nd that it was to move by train to the Bordeaux area to make ready for shipment home. The movement was to begin on 26 February, but the division had been expecting the orders for some time. A vast amount of equipment had to be transferred to American authorities. Of special importance were trucks and automobiles, which were in very short supply in Third Army.[48] The G4 had the responsibility of issuing three days' rations to each soldier and maintaining a three days' supply for emergency use. An advance party of billeting officers was ordered to precede the division to make barracks and officer's billets ready to receive the division. Baggage officers were appointed to oversee the loading of what little organizational equipment was on hand and the personal equipment and baggage the troops were to take with them.[49] The division veterinarian and his twenty-man unit began the transfer of all horses and mules to the 6th Division; all harness, bridles, saddles, feed bags, and horse gas masks would go with the animals. Once the 82nd Division got on the trains everyone except the general officers would become walking infantry. The only items of unit equipment to be taken to Bordeaux were lister (water) bags, mess equipment, field ranges, lanterns, medical and dental equipment, and some headquarters items such as typewriters.[50]

Once at the camp at Bordeaux several important things had to happen. All men and equipment were cleaned and disinfected, and the troops underwent complete medical examinations, especially for venereal diseases. If a soldier had contracted a disease of that nature, he would be retained in Europe until medical treatment was complete. The AEF Adjutant General's office sent teams of clerks and personnel officers to process soldiers for eventual discharge. When all of that was completed, which took about a week, the troops had to wait for ships. The 82nd Division estimated that the troops would be in Base Camp Number 2 about one month. Actually, they were still there in late April.

The question of boredom was uppermost on the mind of Roosevelt, Robson, and Chaplain Tyler. When the 82nd moved into its barracks it brought with them its YMCA and Knights of Columbus workers, but there were already permanent workers at Base Camp 2. Tyler had to sort out who would do what; the 82nd thus had a surplus of workers, which helped the troops considerably during the long wait for the ships. A number of chaplains requested further service with the AEF, and several others left the 82nd for service with the AEF, mainly with the Third Army in Germany.[51]

Robson and Roosevelt agreed that soldiers should be granted short leaves to relax and sightsee before returning to the United States. But the 82nd Division had a special problem to deal with: It had over 2,500 soldiers who had come from Italy, and a very large number had requested leave to visit parents and relatives in the land of their birth. The AEF had a policy of granting two men leave every six weeks to visit Italy, and this caused a great deal of complaint from the Italian-Americans. Roosevelt surfaced the problem with Duncan, who requested that the leave policy be waived so that every soldier could go home for at least a week. As Duncan wrote, they had "rendered excellent service" during the war.[52]

After some consideration the AEF agreed to a change in policy, and a leave train with room for 1,200 soldiers was allocated for the 82nd Division. This special policy meant that the G1 had to organize the men, assign train commanders, issue five days' rations for the trains, and prepare them for the trip. There were inspections to ensure that the doughboys returning to Italy maintained the high standards of appearance required by AEF regulations. Lectures were held warning the troops about the dangers and consequences of venereal disease. A warehouse to hold the soldiers' weapons, gas masks, and helmets, items which they could not carry while on leave, was found. The train departed for Italy on 24 March with over 1,200 happy Italian-American combat veterans.[53] To everyone's surprise every soldier returned to the division for the trip back to the United States.

Once the Italian soldiers were assured of their visit home, the G1 secured trains to take five hundred men per day to Bordeaux to see the city and enjoy time away from the camp.[54] A few weeks later Robson got permission to send men on day excursions or short leaves to the Pyrenees, to a camp run by the AEF and the YMCA. Over three hundred soldiers per day visited the mountains.[55] Like the All-Americans visiting Italy, the soldiers who got short leave had to take their own blankets and personal gear; gas masks, helmets, and weapons were stored in the guarded special warehouse. Perhaps because the troops knew that they were close to leaving for the United States, incidents of drunkenness were rare, and very few cases of venereal disease were reported to division authorities. Conditions for the soldiers improved as well, simply because spring was in air; the temperatures were warming, and outside drill and athletic competitions could be held in relative comfort. However, the daily drills, sports events, and frequent visits to the YMCA and Knights of Columbus buildings were wearing thin. The 82nd had been at Base Camp Number 2 for almost six weeks.

During the afternoon of 12 April, newly promoted Lieutenant Colonel Roosevelt met with Colonel Stanley H. Ford, Chief, Bureau of Embarkation, and was told that the first elements of the 82nd Division would depart on 19, 20, and 21 April. There would be no change in the schedule, because the 78th Division was due to occupy the 82nd's barracks on 26 April. Billeting officers from the 78th were already at the base, and the schedule was therefore set.[56] There was no complaint from Roosevelt, who informed Ford that the 82nd would embark 864 officers and 26,600 enlisted men. At dawn on 19 April 1919, one year and nineteen days after William Burnham and the staff left Camp Gordon, the first infantrymen of the 82nd Division, in crisp uniforms sporting the red, white, and double-A patch, boarded the USS *General Goethals* for the trip back home. The 82nd Division had left behind 7,554 men killed and wounded and thirty-eight men still unaccounted for.[57]

There were no parades for the All-Americans. Upon arriving in the United States the division was divided between Camp Mills and Camp Upton and demobilized as quickly as possible. By 1 June the 82nd's divisional and regimental colors had been furled, and the men had received sixty dollars and most a Victory Medal. In many ways the boring days at Bordeaux had worked to the advantage of the troops, whose records were in order and medical examinations complete. The division had even reviewed the records of soldiers who had taken out bonds during the various Liberty Loan drives and ensured that they received full credit for their monetary contribution to the war effort. Some soldiers, like Alvin York, got to visit New York City, but he was anxious to return to Pall Mall, Tennessee.

It had been the experience of a young man's lifetime. From Camp Gordon to the misery of the fighting north of St. Juvin in the Meuse-Argonne, the division had made a commendable record in training and in combat. It lacked the panache of the Rainbow division, and it did not have the iron-hard reputation of the 1st Division, but this melting-pot unit had performed its duty.

Many a doughboy of the 82nd believed that for the All-American division service "over there" was over and that the old flags would find their resting place in some military museum. A quarter-century later, however, the double-A shoulder patch would again be seen on the battlefields of France.

NOTES

1. Diary entry, 1 November 1918, Fred Takes Diary, the United States Army Military History Institute Archives, Carlisle Barracks, PA, carton 23. [hereafter cited as MHI with appropriate collections].

2. HQ, 82nd Division, Report on Stragglers in the 82nd Division, 19 October 1918, in Records Group 120, Records of the AEF, 82nd Division, National Archives, Washington,

DC, carton 1 [hereafter cited as RG 120 with appropriate carton].

3. HQ, 82nd Division, Shortages in 82nd Division, 13 November 1918, ibid.

4. Adjutant General, AEF, to 82nd Division, 21 October 1918, ibid, carton 4.

5. Ibid.

6. *Official History of the 82nd Division, American Expeditionary Forces, 1917–1919* (Indianapolis, IN: Bobbs-Merill, 1919), 214–15.

7. Biographical Files, General Jonathon M. Wainwright, MHI.

8. Duncan to Pershing, 18 November 1918, RG 120, (Records of the Adjutant General, AEF), carton 2264.

9. HQ, 80th Division, Field Order No. 26, 26 October 1918, RG 120, carton 25; HQ, 80th Division, Operational Memorandum for 157th Field Artillery Brigade, 28 October 1918, ibid., carton 24.

10. Diary entries, 1–3 November 1918, Rhodes Diary, Rhodes Papers, MHI.

11. Typed copy, History of the Brigade Headquarters, 157th Field Artillery Brigade, c. March 1919, RG 120, carton 22.

12. HQ, 319th Field Artillery Regiment, After Action Report, 5 January 1919, ibid., carton 25.

13. HQ, 320th Field Artillery Regiment, After Action Report, 31 December 1918, ibid., carton 26.

14. Typed copy, History of the Brigade Headquarters, 157th Field Artillery Brigade, c. March 1919, ibid., carton 22.

15. For a typical schedule see HQ, 326th Infantry, Schedule of Training, 27 January 1919, ibid., carton 10.

16. HQ, 326th Infantry, Schedule of Athletics, 27 January 1919, ibid.

17. HQ, 82nd Division, General Staff Memorandum No. 233, 5 December 1918, ibid.

18. HQ, 307th Sanitary Train, Training Week for January 20th to January 25, 1919, 20 January 1919, ibid., carton 29.

19. HQ, 307th Engineer Regiment, Report of Operations, 4 January 1919, ibid., carton 28.

20. HQ, 319th Machine Gun Battalion, Training Schedule, 24 January 1919, ibid., carton 10.

21. HQ, 320th Machine Gun Battalion, Training Schedule for January 27th–February 1st 1919, 26 January 1919, ibid.

22. For example see HQ, 325th Infantry Regiment, Drill Schedule for Week Beginning 27 January 1919, 26 January 1919, ibid.

23. HQ, 82nd Division, General Staff Memorandum No. 233, 5 December 1918, ibid.

24. Buxton to Duncan, 26 October 1918, ibid., carton 85.

25. Brief History in the Case of Lieut. Col. Luther H. Reichelderfer, MC, c. November 1918, RG 120 (Adjutant General, AEF, Records), carton 2271.

26. Brief History in the Case of Major Bernard R. Purcell, QMC, c. January 1919, ibid.

27. Brief History in the Case of Lieutenant Colonel Manfred Lanza, QMC, c. January 1919, in Records Group 200, the John J. Pershing Papers, National Archives, Washington, DC, carton 10.

28. HQ, First U.S. Army, Report of Inspection of 82nd Division, 23 December 1918, RG 120, carton 85.

29. Ibid.

30. Senior Chaplains Report, 1 November 1918, RG 120 (G1, AEF, Office of the Chaplain), carton 3822.

31. Senior Chaplains Report, 1 February 1919, ibid.

32. *Official History of the 82nd Division*, 220.

33. Senior Chaplains Report, 11 March 1919, RG 120 (G1, AEF, Office of the Chaplain), carton 3822.

34. These lengthy reports and investigations are found in cartons 98 through 101 in the 82nd Division's records in RG 120.

35. These burial reports appear in carton 101.

36. Whitman to Duncan, 22 January 1919, RG 120, carton 92.

37. Feaster to Duncan, 15 January 1919, ibid., carton 101.

38. Central Records Office to G1, 82nd Division, 25 January 1918, ibid.

39. Mrs. Joseph Violette to Duncan, Great Works, Maine, 6 March 1919, ibid.

40. The courts-martial records, usually one sheet with charges, specification, plea, and findings, are found in carton 117.

41. Zimmerman to Adjutant, 82nd Division, 14 December 1918, RG 120, carton 63.

42. Colonel E. D. Pearce to Duncan, 16 April 1919, ibid.

43. Lindsey to Duncan, 10 February 1919, ibid., carton 84.

44. Adjutant General, AEF to Duncan, 1 April 1919, ibid.

45. Duncan to Adjutant General, AEF, 18 April 1919, ibid.

46. Duncan to Adjutant General, AEF, 18 April 1919, ibid.

47. Duncan to Adjutant General, AEF, 26 February 1919, ibid., carton 66.

48. HQ, 82nd Division, General Staff Memorandum No. V, 21 February 1919, ibid., carton 1.

49. HQ, First U.S. Army, Special Orders No. 37, 22 February 1919, ibid., carton 91.

50. HQ, 82nd Division, General Orders No. 1, 22 February 1919, ibid., carton 1.

51. Senior Chaplain's Report, 30 March 1919, RG 120 (G1, AEF, Office of the Chaplain), carton 3822.

52. Memorandum by Duncan, 6 March 1919, RG 120, carton 74.

53. HQ, 82nd Division, General Staff Memorandum No. 54, 19 March 1919, ibid., carton 118.

54. HQ, 82nd Division, General Staff Memorandum No. 51, 15 March 1919, ibid.

55. HQ, 82nd Division, General Staff Memorandum No. 64, 3 April 1919, ibid.

56. HQ, Base Section No. 2, Memorandum to Chief of Staff, 82nd Division, 12 April 1919, ibid., carton 91.

57. G1, HQ, 82nd Division, Casualties of the Division, 1 April 1919, ibid., carton 97.

Chapter 10

Conclusions

Memories of combat faded, and veterans looked back on their service with their buddies, on battles, on drinking too much wine. The real miseries of war were eclipsed. The 82nd Division was no different than any other AEF division in that regard. The division association, founded in 1918, called for yearly meetings, the publication of a newsletter known as *The All-American*, and for continued comradeship between those who wore the double-A patch. In 1919 an official history of the division was published, but little else was done. In the 1920s and 1930s Sergeant Alvin York did not appear on the membership roles. General Duncan attended meetings only periodically. Unlike the 1st, 26th, or 42nd Division associations, the 82nd veterans group seemed small in size. This was due to the basic makeup of the division, with draftees from many states and a large number of immigrants. The 82nd had a good record in the AEF. It had spent a hundred days in the presence of the enemy suffering a casualty rate over seven thousand, the equal of the 78th, 79th, and 89th divisions. That was a good performance for a unit from which so little had been expected because it contained so many foreign-born soldiers who had such problems with the English language.

While at Camp Gordon and during training with the British and French, the division had been suspect in the eyes of AEF planners. Once it was committed to the St. Mihiel fight, the picture changed; the 82nd became known as a steady, if unspectacular, combat unit. It fought well and accomplished difficult missions in the Meuse-Argonne until it became too weak to fight—which happened to the 1st and 42nd divisions as well, at the same time. What brought the 82nd Division up in the estimation of the AEF was leadership and training. The division was blessed with solid commanders at all levels, and the reservoir of potential battalion commanders in the ranks of the captains was strong. Toward the end of the Meuse-Argonne campaign a number of captains commanded the depleted battalions, with good results.

The All-American division had two good commanders in Burnham and Duncan, but of the two it was George Duncan who made the unit function in October 1918.

Burnham was steady, but he had little influence over the course of combat; the 82nd never had the imprint of Burnham's personality. John J. Pershing never hesitated to remove a weak commander, but Burnham, especially when Hunter Liggett heaped praise upon the 82nd Division after St. Mihiel, could not be simply cast aside. Burnham got an important post in Greece, and in 1929 he retired with the rank of brigadier general. Had he really run afoul of "Black Jack" Pershing that probably would never have happened. Duncan, on the other hand, never had to contend with the constant drain of manpower and shifting of personnel that occurred at Camp Gordon. George Duncan was a firm, knowledgeable commander but not a martinet. It never hurt that he was very close to Pershing. Duncan, while commanding 1st Brigade in the 1st Division, was the first American officer to be awarded the French Croix de Guerre; Pershing was delighted and sent him hearty congratulations.[1] Pleasing to Pershing was the fact that Duncan chose not to make much of the decoration preferring to cite his French counterpart for gallantry in the fight.[2] In August, when Duncan was relieved from command of the 77th Division for medical reasons, Pershing stood by his friend, and eventually Duncan was assigned to the 82nd Division. Duncan never forgot Pershing's belief in him, and Pershing, who prized personal loyalty, had reciprocated.[3] Duncan was a staunch disciple of the Pershing orthodoxy of open, or maneuver, warfare, and that stood him in good stead as well.

Duncan had an exceptionally good staff, especially with Jonathon M. Wainwright as the G3 and Gordon Johnston as the chief of staff. When Lieutenant General Robert Lee Bullard evaluated Duncan in late 1918 he wrote that his knowledge of staff work "was not up to line work. He is really an outdoor commander of men."[4] At the same time Duncan was evaluated by Major General Charles P. Summerall; Summerall, a future Chief of Staff of the Army, also commented on the great deal of time he spent with his troops. Summerall, who never minced words when it came to a weak general officer, wrote, "He is superior as a brigade or division commander in peace or in war."[5] In 1920 Duncan was promoted to brigadier general by the War Department, a rapid rise in the peacetime army, where ex-general officers were numerous. Sitting on the War Department General Officers Board was Robert Lee Bullard, Hunter Liggett, Joseph Theodore Dickman, James Guthrie Harbord, and Charles P. Summerall, all men who owed their rank, position, and fame to John J. Pershing.[6]

Duncan had two steady brigade commanders in Julian Lindsey and Marcus Cronin. In turn they both had reliable regimental commanders in Colonels Ely, Wetherill, McArthur, and Whitman. They were constant in the St. Mihiel battle and the Meuse-Argonne operation. It appears that they were good organizers in training and in combat, and all four did well, if not well enough to rise to general rank after the war. In Charles Rhodes, the cavalryman turned artillery brigade commander, Duncan had his best brigadier general. The 157th Field Artillery Brigade flourished under Rhodes and became a fine combat outfit. After his service with the 82nd he briefly commanded the 42nd Division. Appointed to the Inter-Allied Armistice Commission at Spa, Belgium, Rhodes was badly injured in an airplane crash flying from Spa to Paris in late 1918. In 1920 he attended the Army

War College, and then served from 1921 to 1922 as chief of staff of the Philippine Department. In 1925 Rhodes was promoted to regular one-star rank. Three years later he got his second star, and retired from the Army in 1929. With Rhodes in command of the 157th Duncan had very little to worry about with respect to artillery.

To fight and win, a general needs good troops who are motivated, trained, and competently led. Frankly, Burnham had not trusted his troops, because of their lack of facility with the English language. In battle there is not much talking, however, and commands are often communicated with arm and hand signals; Burnham underestimated his soldiers—once in battle they did well. However, there were problems at times with men who could not properly respond to questions in English. This was especially vexing when the 82nd was in the trenches at Lagney and was new to deadly combat. The learning process was difficult, and some troops were wounded by friendly fire. Eventually squad leaders, platoon sergeants, and lieutenants worked out their problems within their units. There can be no question that Burnham's constant complaints about his non–English speakers hurt his standing with GHQ, AEF. Duncan never seemed to have that problem, or least he never troubled Chaumont with his doubts. Duncan did what Burnham did not: as a good commander he relied on a solid staff and concentrated on his three competent brigade commanders. Those brigade commanders oversaw their regimental and battalion commanders. Personnel problems belonged to the G1, and Duncan had a good one in Lieutenant Colonel Troupe Miller. Duncan allowed Gordon Johnston to do his job, to make the staff function, and he went out of the command post to see what his soldiers were actually doing in training or in combat.

In the area of logistics the 82nd did as well as any other AEF combat division. Every unit was short of motor vehicles, and horses were in short supply. Despite heroic efforts of the Service of Supply, food, equipment, and ammunition were not always delivered, because of shortages in transportation and a poor road system, which was made worse by the constant heavy rains in the fall of 1918. A look at the 1st and 42nd divisions in combat in the Meuse-Argonne, on the right flank of the 82nd Division, reveals that those "old divisions" of the AEF had the same problems. Very few doughboys of any division ever got enough hot food; that was due to the nature of combat and the necessity of feeding troops at night. Medical and chaplain support was the equal of any AEF division. What emerged was fairly efficient G1 and G4 sections, and Duncan was wise enough to let those two staff officers do their jobs.

Johnston had a star in Jim Wainwright, who had been trained at the AEF's Staff College at Langres. That course was three months long, and graduates were sent to divisional staffs. Wainwright knew how to transmit the commander's intent in the orders to the combat brigades. Orders were short, direct, to the point, and, of importance, they were issued in time for the subordinate commands to dissect them, write their own orders, and instruct their subordinate commands. Johnston and Wainwright also maintained a viable message system under trying circumstances. From the records it appears that the division was never "in the dark" as to the progress of the battle. It was, and is, vitally important that brigade and division headquarters be kept informed as to what was happens during a fight. Those head-quarters, while not actually firing rifles or throwing grenades, can influence a bat-tle, but only if they know what to respond to. Wireless and telephone communica-tions, a new addition to battlefield, were maintained by the division's communica-tion section, and field message logs appear to have been complete. Both the divi-sion and the brigades were able to respond to changing circumstances.

The 82nd Division had had a rocky start at Camp Gordon. General Eben Swift did a creditable job in getting the unit organized, but the constant drain on man-power to fill up other divisions hurt training and unit cohesion. Pershing thought highly of Swift's ability, and when Swift was ordered as chief of the U.S. military mission to Italy Pershing believed that he would eventually be assigned to the AEF in France. This was not to be, as General Peyton March, Chief of Staff of the Ar-my, turned down Pershing's request for Swift's services. (Swift retired on 1 Sep-tember 1918.)[7] By the time Duncan took command of the 82nd the division had been stabilized and trained and had seen action at St. Mihiel.

The history of the All-American division is illuminating in that it tells what can be done with a diverse group of draftees. The 82nd Division was a mirror of the United States at the turn of the century. There were sturdy Southern men, immi-grants from the great eastern cities, and soldiers from small Midwestern towns. With strong leadership and meaningful training the division became a unified body despite obvious cultural, linguistic, and ethnic differences. The many frustrations inherent in such diversity were eventually overcome by the necessities of mortal combat against a well-trained and well-commanded German army. The division never lost, however, its variegated flavor. The number of soldiers who visited fam-ilies in Italy, Ireland, and elsewhere after hostilities attests to the many voices and accents heard in the 82nd Division. The fact that all the men returned from their sojourns to make the Atlantic crossing to the United States indicates the discipline instilled in the unit. Discipline came from good leadership, solid training, and shared combat experiences. The 82nd Division, the melting-pot division, had in-deed become real All-Americans.

NOTES

1. Pershing to Duncan, 27 September 1917, John J. Pershing Papers, Library of Con-gress, Washington, DC [hereafter cited as LOC with appropriate collection].

2. Duncan to Pershing, 15 September 1917, ibid.

3. Duncan to Pershing, 1 May 1919, ibid.

4. HQ, Second U.S. Army, Report by Lieutenant General Robert Lee Bullard, 13 Decem-ber 1918, in Records Group 120, Records of the AEF, Records of the Adjutant General, AEF, National Archives, Washington, DC, carton 2263.

5. HQ, V Corps, Report by Major General Charles P. Summerall, 13 December 1918, in the Charles P. Summerall Papers, LOC.

6. War Department, Special Orders 134-0, 8 June 1920, in Records Group 200, John J. Pershing Papers, National Archives, Washington, DC.

7. The Eben Swift Papers are not especially informative in regard to the 82nd Division at Camp Gordon. They are kept at the U.S. Army Military History Institute Archives, Carlisle Barracks, Pennsylvania.

Epilogue

The vibration of the aircraft kept the men awake. Some smoked, some talked, some seemed deep in thought. Outside, as a man could see through the windows, it was dark. Below lay the English Channel, a body of water everyone had thought about crossing since 1942. At the end of the channel were the beaches and then the countryside. As the aircraft neared the coast there was activity. Officers and senior NCOs were up, standing near the door. One sergeant pulled on the steel cable which ran the length of the plane as if to see if it was still firmly in place. Below could be seen flashes of light, perhaps from a farm house.

The soldiers were in khaki battle dress, double-A patches on their left shoulders. Weighed down with equipment, weapons, and steel helmets, they watched the officers and sergeants, took a few more puffs on their cigarettes. There was silence until the beaches were behind them. One man joked then about how many beautiful young girls they could find on the sand on that warm June day. One soldier took a knife from his boot and inspected the blade. Was it sharp enough for the work ahead? He slipped it back into the book scabbard, satisfied that it would do the bloody work it would have to do. England was a lifetime ago.

Twenty-six years had been a long time. No one knew who Duncan, Lindsey, Blanchard, or Johnston had been. Lights came on. "Stand-up, hook-up," the sergeant commanded by arm signals. The door was open, and it was not warm anymore; the cold night air shot into the plane. "Stand in the door!" Green lights, move forward, step into the dark of the night—what was down below? Each felt the shoulder-wrenching snap as his parachute opened. There were no lights on the ground, which was rushing up to meet them. Every man relaxed, waiting to meet Mother Earth, and they did: butts, shoulders, roll over, stand up, and then grab the lines of the parachute, which wanted to pull the soldiers with the breeze. Soldiers in khaki jump smocks were landing all around. Some now stood, free of the independent-thinking parachute, weapon in hand, listening for the guttural German voices that Pike, York, Takes, and Wetherill had heard twenty-six years ago. The 82nd Division, the All-Americans, had returned to France after a long absence.

Selected Bibliography

ARCHIVAL SOURCES

Library of Congress. Washington, DC. James G. Harbord Papers, John J. Pershing Papers, and Charles P. Summerall Papers.

National Archives. Washington, DC. Records Group 117. Records of the American Battle Monuments Commission. Records Group 120. Records of the AEF, 82nd Division and Records of the Adjutant General. Records Group 165. Records of the War Department, General and Special Staff. Records Group 200. Harold B. Fiske Papers, John J. Pershing Papers.

United States Army Military History Institute Archives. Manuscipt Division. World War One Survey and Questionnaires. Charles D. Rhodes Papers, Hugh Drum Papers, Eben Swift Papers, Jonathon Wainwright Papers, and Walter Whitman Papers. Carlisle Barracks, PA.

OFFICIAL AND UNIT HISTORIES

The All American (Publication of the 82nd Division Association).

American Battle Monuments Commission. *1st Division, Summary of Operations in the World War*. Washington, DC: Government Printing Office, 1944.

―――. *28th Division, Summary of Operations in the World War*. Washington: Government Printing Office, 1944.

―――. *35th Division, Summary of Operations in the World War*. Washington: Government Printing Office, 1944.

―――. *42nd Division, Summary of Operations in the World War*. Washington: Government Printing Office, 1944.

―――. *77th Division, Summary of Operations in the World War*. Washington: Government Printing Office, 1944.

―――. *78th Division, Summary of Operations in the World War*. Washington: Government Printing Office, 1944.

―――. *82nd Division, Summary of Operations in the World War*. Washington: Government Printing Office, 1944.

―――. *90th Division, Summary of Operations in the World War*. Washington: Government Printing Office, 1944.

History of the Seventy-Seventh Division. New York: Wynkoop, Hallenbeck, Crawford, 1919.

Masseck, C. J., *Official Brief History of the 89th Division*, U.S.A. N.p.: War Society of the 89th Division, c. 1919.

Meehan, Thomas F. *History of the Seventy-Seventh Division in the War, 1917–1919.* New York: Dodd, Meade, 1921.

Milham, Charles G. *"Ata Boy!" The Story of New York's 77th Division.* New York: Brooklyn Daily Eagle, 1919.

Official History of the 82nd Division, American Expeditionary Forces, 1917–1919. Indianapolis: Bobbs-Merrill, 1919.

Reilly, Henry J. *Americans All: The Rainbow at War.* Columbus: H. J. Heer, 1936.

Society of the First Division. *History of the First Division during the World War, 1917–1919.* Philadelphia: John C. Winston, 1922.

Sparks, George McIntosh, *The 327th under Fire.* N.p.: c. 1920.

U.S. Army, Center of Military History. *The United States Army in the World War.* 17 vols. Washington: Government Printing Office, Reprint, 1989.

U.S. Army War College, Historical Section. *The Genesis of the American First Army.* Washington: Government Printing Office, 1938.

U.S. War Department. *Battle Participation of the American Expeditionary Forces in France, Belgium, and Italy, 1917–1919.* Washington: Government Printing Office, 1920.

———. *The Official Record of the Great War.* New York: Parke, Austin and Lipscomb, 1923.

Wallace, E. S., ed. *The Twenty-Eighth Division: Pennsylvania's Guard in the War.* Pittsburgh: 28th Division Society, 1924.

White, Lonnie J. *The 90th Division in World War I.* Manhattan, KS: Sunflower University Press, 1996.

Wythe, George, *A History of the 90th Division.* N.p.: 90th Division Association, 1920.

MEMOIRS

Alexander, Robert. *Memories of the World War, 1917–1918.* New York: Macmillan, 1931.

Baker, Newton. *Frontiers of Freedom.* New York: Doubleday, Doran, 1931.

Broun, Heywood H. *The AEF: With General Pershing and the American Forces.* New York: Appleton, 1918.

Bullard, Robert Lee. *Personalities and Reminiscences of the War.* Garden City: Doubleday, Page, 1925.

Dickman, Joseph T. *The Great Crusade.* New York: Appleton, 1927.

Harbord, James G. *The American Army in France.* Boston: Little, Brown, 1936.

———. *Leaves from a War Diary.* New York: Dodd, Meade, 1925.

Johnson, Thomas M. *Without Censor.* Indianapolis, IN: Bobbs-Merrill, 1928.

Liggett, Hunter. *AEF: Ten Years Ago in France.* New York: Dodd, Meade, 1928.

———. *Commanding an American Army: Recollections of the World War.* Boston: Houghton-Mifflin, 1925.

MacArthur, Douglas. *Reminiscences.* New York: McGraw-Hill, 1964.

March, Peyton C. *The Nation at War.* Garden City, NY: Doubleday, Doran, 1932.

Marshall, George C. *Memoirs of My Service in the World War, 1917–1918.* Boston: Houghton-Mifflin, 1976.

Palmer, Frederick. *America in France.* New York: Dodd, Meade, 1919.

———. *Our Greatest Battle*. New York: Dodd, Meade, 1919.

Pershing, John J. *Final Report of General John J. Pershing*. Washington: Government Printing Office, 1920.

———. *My Experiences in the Great War*, 2 vols. Blue Ridge Summitt: Tab Books Reprint, 1989.

Pershing, John J. and Hunter Liggett. *Report of the First Army, American Expeditionary Forces*. Fort Leveanworth, KS: General Service Schools Press, 1923.

SECONDARY SOURCES

Adams, R.J.Q. *The Great War, 1914–1918*. College Station: Texas A&M Press, 1990.

Army Times Publishing. *The Yanks Are Coming: The Story of John J. Pershing*. New York: G. P. Putnam, 1960.

Braim, Paul. *The Test of Battle: The American Expeditionary Force in the Meuse-Argonne Campaign*. Newark: University of Delaware Press, 1987.

Branham, Charles N., ed. *Cullum's Biographical Register of the Officers and Graduates of the U.S. Military Academy*. West Point, NY: Association of Graduates, USMA, Vol. VIII 1930–1940, Vol. IX, 1940–1950.

Bullard, Robert L. *Fighting Generals*. Ann Arbor, MI: J. W. Edwards, 1944.

Cecil, Hugh, and Peter H. Liddle, eds. *Facing Armageddon: The First World War Experienced*. Barnsley, UK: Pen and Sword, 1996.

Chase, Joseph C. *Soldiers All: Portraits and Sketches of the Men of the AEF*. New York: Scribners, 1920.

Coffman, Edward M. *The War to End All Wars: The American Military Experience in World War I*. Madison: University of Wisconsin Press, 1986.

Cooke, James J. *Pershing and His Generals: Command and Staff in the AEF*. Westport, CT: Praeger, 1997.

———. *The Rainbow Division in the Great War, 1917–1919*. Westport, CT: Praeger, 1994.

———. *The U.S. Air Service in the Great War, 1917–1919*. Westport, CT: Praeger, 1996.

Crowder, Enoch H. *The Spirit of Selective Service*. New York: Scribners, 1920.

Douglas, Lawrence J. *Fighting Soldier: The AEF in 1918*. Boulder: University of Colorado Press, 1986.

Every, Dale van. *The AEF in Battle*. New York: Appleton, 1928.

Freidel, Frank. *Over There: The Story of America's Great Overseas Crusade*. New York: McGraw-Hill, 1990.

Gavin, Lotti. *American Women in World War I: They Also Served*. Boulder: University of Colorado Press, 1997.

Goldhurt, Richard. *Pipe Clay and Drill: John J. Pershing*. New York: Crowell, 1977.

Hallas, James H. *Squandered Victory: The American First Army at St. Mihiel*. Westport, CT: Praeger, 1995.

Harris, Frederick, ed. *Service with the Fighting Men*. 2 vols. New York: YMCA, 1922.

House, Jonathan M. *Toward Combined Arms Warfare*. Fort Leavenworth, KS: Combat Studies Institute, 1984.

James, D. Clayton and Anne Sharp Wells. *America and the Great War, 1914–1920*. Wheeling: Harlan Davidson, 1997.

Johnson, Ellis J. *The Military Experiences of General Hugh A. Drum, 1898–1918*. Madison: University of Wisconsin Press, 1975.

Kaspi, André. *Le Temps des Américains à la France en 1917–1918*. Paris: Publications de la Sorbonne, 1976.

Kennedy, David M. *Over Here: The First World War and American Society*. New York: Oxford University Press, 1980.

Lonergan, Thomas C. *It Might Have Been Lost*. New York: Putnam's, 1929.

Mayo, Virginia. *That Damned Y*. New York: Houghton-Mifflin, 1920.

Nenninger, Timothy K. *The Leavenworth Schools and the Old Army: Education, Professionalism and the Officer Corps of the United States Army, 1881–1918*. Westport, CT: Greenwood, 1978.

Palmer, Frederick. *John J. Pershing: A Biography*. Westport, CT: Greenwood, 1948.

Risch, Erna. *Quartermaster Support of the Army*. Washington: Center of Military History, 1962.

Smythe, Donald. *Pershing: General of the Armies*. Bloomington: Indiana University Press, 1986.

Stallings, Lawrence. *The Doughboys: The Story of the AEF*. New York: Harper and Row, 1963.

Toland, John. *No Man's Land 1918; The Last Year of the Great War*. New York: Doubleday, 1980.

Trask, David F. *The AEF and Coalition Warmaking, 1917–1918*. Lawrence: University of Kansas Press, 1993.

Vandiver, Frank. *Black Jack: The Life and Times of John J. Pershing*. 2 vols. College Station: Texas A&M Press, 1977.

Wilson, Dale E. *Treat 'Em Rough: The Birth of American Armor*. Novato, CA: Persidio Press, 1989.

Index

About the Author

JAMES J. COOKE, a Professor of History at the University of Mississippi, researches and publishes on World War I topics. He is author of four books: *100 Miles from Baghdad* (Praeger, 1993), *The Rainbow Division in the Great War* (Praeger, 1994), *The U.S. Air Service in the Great War* (Praeger, 1996), and *Pershing and His Generals: Command and Staff in the AEF* (Praeger, 1997).

ISBN 0-275-95740-3

EAN

90000>

9 780275 957407

HARDCOVER BAR CODE